FAMILY HISTORY
MADE EASY

KATHY CHATER

FAMILY HISTORY MADE EASY

HOW TO TRACE YOUR FAMILY TREE
AND FIND RELATIVES IN ENGLAND,
IRELAND, SCOTLAND AND WALES

southwater

This edition is published by Southwater

Southwater is an imprint of Anness Publishing Ltd
Hermes House, 88–89 Blackfriars Road, London SE1 8HA
tel. 020 7401 2077; fax 020 7633 9499
www.southwaterbooks.com; info@anness.com

© Anness Publishing Ltd 2004

UK agent: The Manning Partnership Ltd, 6 The Old Dairy, Melcombe Road, Bath
BA2 3LR; tel. 01225 478444; fax 01225 478440; sales@manning-partnership.co.uk

UK distributor: Grantham Book Services Ltd, Isaac Newton Way, Alma Park Industrial
Estate, Grantham, Lincs NG31 9SD; tel. 01476 541080; fax 01476 541061;
orders@gbs.tbs-ltd.co.uk

North American agent/distributor: National Book Network, 4501 Forbes Boulevard, Suite
200, Lanham, MD 20706; tel. 301 459 3366; fax 301 429 5746; www.nbnbooks.com

Australian agent/distributor: Pan Macmillan Australia, Level 18, St Martins Tower, 31
Market St, Sydney, NSW 2000; tel. 1300 135 113; fax 1300 135 103;
customer.service@macmillan.com.au

New Zealand agent/distributor: David Bateman Ltd, 30 Tarndale Grove, Off Bush Road,
Albany, Auckland; tel. (09) 415 7664; fax (09) 415 8892

Publisher: Joanna Lorenz
Editorial Director: Helen Sudell
Executive Editor: Joanne Rippin
Jacket Design: Adelle Morris
Book design: Michael Morey

Previously published as part of a larger volume, *Tracing Your Family Tree*
1 3 5 7 9 10 8 6 4 2

Contents

Introduction

In today's increasingly globalized world, there is a desire to know more about ourselves as individuals and where we came from. As a result of this, family history is one of the fastest-growing hobbies.

This book is aimed at those who have British ancestry. There may be many other nations from which our forebears sprang, but, because British people (the English, the Welsh, the Scots, the Irish and the inhabitants of the many offshore islands that make up the United Kingdom) went to all the countries of the world, many of the world's billions of inhabitants have at least a drop of British blood in their veins.

Thirty years of tracing my own family history and working professionally as a television researcher have taught me a great deal about how to find and use information. One of the most important things I have learned is that you don't have to be an expert at everything; instead, you need to be able to find an expert in the relevant field and then tap into his or her expertise. Luckily, the world of genealogy is full of knowledgeable and enthusiastic people who are generous with their help and experience. The current enthusiasm for the subject has also led to the appearance of a large number of magazines and publications, which provide further help for everyone from the total beginner to the highly experienced.

No single publication can hope to cover everything a family historian might need to

British people have always been great travellers for work, exploration or to settle.

Before the 20th century, this girl would have been lucky to see her second birthday.

The nursing profession has come a long way since it became a job for respectable women.

The children around this table in the early 1950s may have grown up to live and work all over the world.

Members of the armed forces may have brought brides from overseas back home to Britain.

know. The researcher needs to be aware of what the law was at a particular time and how legal changes would be reflected in records produced by the government and private organizations, which is what I have concentrated on here. This will help genealogists find out in the most interesting way how their ancestors contributed to their community and the wider world.

Abbreviations

Genealogy has a host of abbreviations and acronyms. The main ones used in the text are:

BMD = births, marriages and deaths
CMB = christenings, marriages and burials
CRO = County Record Office
DRO = Diocesan Record Office
FFHS = Federation of Family History Societies
FRC = Family Record Centre
GRO = General Register Office
IGI = International Genealogical Index
IHGS = Institute of Heraldic and Genealogical Studies
LDS = Church of Jesus Christ of Latter-day Saints (Mormons)
LMA = London Metropolitan Archives
PCC = Prerogative Court of Canterbury
PCY = Prerogative Court of York
PRO = Public Record Office, now known as The National Archives
PRONI = Public Record Office of Northern Ireland
SRO = Scottish Record Office
SoG = Society of Genealogists
TNA = The National Archives, previously known as the PRO

Many people, like this Italian ice-cream seller, settled in Britain because of political or economic factors.

First steps

Whatever sparks an interest in your family history, whether it is a photograph, a cache of family documents or a chance remark by a relative, you are starting out on one of the most fascinating journeys there is. It is a voyage into the past that ends in the present and may yet continue into the future. We all wonder sometimes about the chain of events that led to us being alive here and now, and which characters and actions made us the people we are. Let us now take the first steps to finding out who we are and where we came from.

How to begin

There are several things that can spark off an interest in tracing a family's history. Sorting out possessions after a death, or when selling a family home usually reveals certificates, photographs and other mementos that give tantalizing clues to past joys and sorrows. Often these will be the starting point for a journey back in time.

A great deal of information can be gained from these items, and this, in turn, will give clues to further avenues of research. The first thing to do, therefore, is to sift through what you have found, concentrate on one particular individual, and use this information to create an outline of his or her life. Study these possessions to see if you can glean when and where the person was born, went to school, worked, married, etc. Dates and other information may come from what was

Interpreting the evidence

Among the treasured possessions found in an ancestor's home, you might find some of the following items:
- certificates (birth, marriage, death, adoption, baptism, confirmation)
- photographs and drawings
- home movies
- correspondence (letters and postcards)
- scrapbooks
- diaries
- household and/or business accounts books
- insurance policies
- newspaper cuttings
- family bibles and prayer books
- apprenticeship indentures
- books presented as prizes or inscribed to commemorate a special event
- examination or school-leaving certificates
- identity cards
- ration books (rationing in Britain started in World War II and continued until 1955)
- medals, badges and other objects connected with service in the armed forces
- membership of clubs or organizations such as friendly societies or the Freemasons
- passports
- holiday or travel souvenirs
- retirement presents
- memorial cards
- wills and other legal documents

written or inscribed on the items, but sometimes, especially with pictures (either photographs or movies), this can only be inferred from the content.

RECORDING YOUR FINDINGS
Write down all the information you have found in chronological order. It is a good idea to use a piece of paper divided into two columns. The first column, which should occupy about two-thirds of the page, is where you write the information gained; the other is for a note of its source. On another piece of paper, write down all the questions that are raised.

LEFT Florence Nightingale's birth certificate shows that she was born in the Italian city after which she was named.

LEFT This early photo was taken c.1840. The dress and hairstyle give clues to the date.

RIGHT A passport issued in 1921. Were the couple going abroad for a holiday or to work?

BELOW A couple sign the wedding register in 1947.

You may find that you recall being told stories relating to him or her. Write these down too (but bear in mind that they may not be accurate).

INVESTIGATING FAMILY MYTHS

Many families have myths and legends about their origins. These usually contain a nugget of truth, but it has probably been distorted over the centuries.

"We came over with William the Conqueror" is a common family myth. Although you will probably find out that your ancestor did not arrive in England from France in 1066 with William the Conqueror, you may discover that you do indeed have French ancestry: perhaps a Huguenot fleeing religious persecution in the 16th or 17th century, or someone escaping from the Reign of Terror that followed the French Revolution in the 18th century. More prosaically, perhaps, your ancestor may prove to be a French sailor who deserted his ship, perhaps smitten by the charms of a British girl.

Other stories, on further research, may prove to be not quite so romantic. Those with Irish ancestry, for example, may be told that their ancestors were heroes transported for political activity. Further research may indicate, however, that the Irish person was in fact transported for a squalid murder or theft, with no glamorous or political circumstances at all.

Another common family myth is illegitimate descent from a noble family. There are very few families who do not have an illegitimate child in their history, but often the story about aristocratic connections is just that – a tale concocted to make a child feel better about his or her fatherless state.

Family history is frequently full of surprises, some pleasant but others less agreeable. When doing research, you have to be prepared for both types.

BELOW This family shot was taken in 1947. Where are all the children now and do they have any useful documents or information?

CHOOSING A NAME TO RESEARCH

It is worth giving some thought to the branch of your family with which you decide to begin your research. Most people begin with their own family surname, but as your first steps into research should be regarded as practising, you should try to make your task as easy as possible. Therefore there are two major factors to consider before deciding which name and which family branch to research: the name and the location.

Name If you have a very common name, such as Smith, Jones or Brown,

you may be setting yourself too hard a task to begin with. An unusual name is far easier to extract from records.

Location London is the location of the major repositories, such as the Family Record Centre (FRC), The National Archives (TNA), the Society of Genealogists' (SoG) library and a number of County Record Offices (CROs) and other archives, so you might think that a London ancestor would be a good starting point. The problem with London, however, is that there are so many places where records relating to your ancestor might be located. Londoners

BELOW If one of your parents had a more unusual name than the other, it will be easier to track down their relatives.

ABOVE A London-dwelling ancestor may well be harder to locate than a town- or village-dwelling relative.

BELOW The exotic background of this picture is a photographer's set, not a clue that the girl was born abroad.

were highly mobile, and a house move of only a few hundred metres (yards) might mean that you have to shuttle between one record office and another. Moving from north to south of the river before 1888 also means changing the CROs and Diocesan Record Offices (DROs) that you will be using (there are at least seven covering different parts of the Greater London area).

If you do not live in London yourself, you will probably spend as much time travelling as you will researching. In addition, you will often find that records in London give much less detail than those elsewhere in Britain. Clerks in the capital were busy and did not know as much about the people who appeared before them as they did in a small neighbourhood.

Tracing ancestors in a smaller city, town or village can be easier. Each county usually has one main record office for all the places in it (although there may be small, local archives). This means that, even if your ancestor moved 32 km (20 miles), as long as he did not cross a county boundary, you will usually find the records in the same place. There are also less voluminous records to search in a small place. Going through the registers of some London parishes can occupy a whole wearisome day, while those in a rural town or village may take only a couple

ABOVE Malvina Brandeis's unusual name will make finding references to her easy, but, as she was born abroad, tracing her ancestors is too hard at this stage.

BELOW Postcards sent home from the front will show where a fiancée was living before marriage.

ABOVE This guard's pocket watch and the railway guide will give clues to an ancestor's job.

of hours. Even names that would be common in a town or city, such as Wood or King, may be rare in a small place, which means that you can be fairly sure that all those of the same name are potentially related.

If you are not doing the research yourself and are planning to hire someone to do it for you, consider how much time all this record searching will take and whether you are prepared to pay for it.

FURTHER HELP

Getting Started in Family History (TNA)
Swinnerton, Iain *Basic Facts about Sources for Family History in the Home* (FFHS)

Family photographs

Photographs of family members not only allow us to debate just who has inherited Great-grandmother's eyes or Uncle Charlie's nose, they also allow us to put faces to the names on official and unofficial documents. There may also be clues in the photographs which will suggest further avenues of research.

COLLECTING PHOTOGRAPHS

Get copies of as many family photographs as you can. Needless to say, if any of them are borrowed, make sure that you return them in good condition. If you need to send them, package them safely and use a secure, insured form of delivery. Ideally, though, they should be returned in person. This has the additional benefit

> ## Interpreting photographs
>
> It is, unfortunately, rare to find that your ancestors have written the date of the photograph, where it was taken and the names of all the people in it on the back (Note that this is a lesson for you to learn about your own snapshots.) Even if you can identify the people, it may be difficult to estimate the date, though clues include:
> - the clothes or uniforms the people were wearing
> - the approximate ages of any children in the picture (children's ages are easier to guess than adults')
> - cars or other methods of transport, such as bicycles or trains
> - shops or other buildings
> - the name of the photographer stamped on the back
> - the type of photographic process used

BELOW This photograph was taken in Northamptonshire around 1900. The grandfather's jacket suggests a countryman.

of giving time in which both you and the owner of the photograph may have thought of other things to discuss.

There are commercial companies that will copy photographs for you. They usually advertise in family history magazines, or you can look for them in local telephone directories. If a member of your family is a good photographer, you can get them photographed directly. They easiest way to do it today, however, is to scan them into your computer.

CLOTHES

People usually dressed up in their best to have their photograph taken. The clothes will therefore be their newest and most fashionable. A book on the history of costume should help you to identify roughly when the photograph was taken. Poor people, however, would not necessarily dress in the height of fashion. Employers often passed on their clothes to their servants, and many people could afford to dress only in second-hand garments.

People dressed in the uniforms of the armed services were often either just joining up or about to go away to war, which might give a clue to the year. As well as estimating the date, you can get a lot of information from the uniform itself. From the style of the uniform, the cap, badges, medals and other insignia you get clues to identify which service they served in, their rank and their regiment, ship or squadron, if you don't already know this from other sources.

Other uniforms can help you to find out what members of your family did. Policemen, postmen, lifeboatmen, bus conductors, hospital nurses and a host of other people all had different uniforms depending on where they worked. Lawyers and judges still wear different styles of wig. You may also find an ancestor wearing the regalia of a Freemason.

Even if your ancestors did not wear the formal uniform of a particular organization, you may get clues about their job from what they wore. It was far easier in the past to tell occupations from clothes than it is today. Many people wore aprons: parlour maids

LEFT A group of nurses pictured where they worked. Unfortunately, the photo is too small to offer any clues about where this might be.

BELOW LEFT Three Air Force pilots in Canada in 1941. The shot's informality shows they were on leave rather than on duty.

usually wore decorative ones, while maids-of-all-work wore much rougher coveralls; butchers' aprons were striped; carpenters' aprons had pockets to hold tools, and woodworkers wore a special side apron with a breastpad to protect their chests. The smocks of farm workers had different motifs and styles depending on what kind of work they did and the area they came from. Fishermen's sweaters also had different motifs, often unique to them, so that bodies washed up after accidents at sea could be identified. All these can be researched through books.

BUILDINGS
If you have a photograph taken outside a shop and the name is visible, you can find out how long it was in business by using street directories. The same applies to pictures taken outside a nursing home, perhaps of a group of nurses that includes your ancestor. If you know in which town it would have been, a street directory will help you to identify the place, and by looking through different years you can find out how long it was in existence there, which will give you dates between which the photograph might have

been taken. Books on transport will also help you to date cars or other vehicles in the photograph.

PHOTOGRAPHERS AND THEIR PHOTOGRAPHS
Street directories will also enable you to locate the photographer who took the picture, if the name is stamped on it. By looking through a succession of years, you can narrow down how long the photographer was in business. The photographic method used can also give clues, but you will need to consult an expert about this.

FURTHER HELP

Pols, Robert *Photography for Family Historians* (FFHS)
Pols, Robert *Looking at Old Photographs* (FFHS)
Pols, Robert *Dating Old Photographs* (FFHS)
Pols, Robert *Family Photographs 1860–1945* (TNA)
Pols, Robert *Understanding Old Photographs* (FFHS)
Swinnerton, I. *Identifying Your World War I Soldier from Badges and Photographs* (FFHS)

A basic family tree

From the very earliest stages of your research, you should find information that, combined with your own family knowledge, can be used to draw up a basic family tree. There are a number of ways in which you can record what is called a pedigree, which is the technical term for an outline showing descent from an ancestor. You will be doing more than simply charting the people from whom you descend – you will be finding out events in their lives to create a family history – but you still need a pedigree as a basis to work from and to refer to.

PREPARING A DROP-LINE CHART

The most common way of drawing up a basic family tree, and the method with which most people are familiar, is the drop-line chart.

Notes

- Keep each generation on the same level.
- Put men/husbands on the left and women/wives on the right.

- Put children in the order of their birth, oldest on the left, not (as was sometimes done in the past) all the boys first and then all the girls.
- Show children descending from the marriage or relationship of two people, not from the father or mother. Legitimate children are

ABOVE A pedigree of King James I, prepared c.1605, shows his descent from various Scottish kings and also the god Wodan. Accuracy cannot be relied on.

BELOW A drop-line chart shows descent from a single couple and contains only one family line.

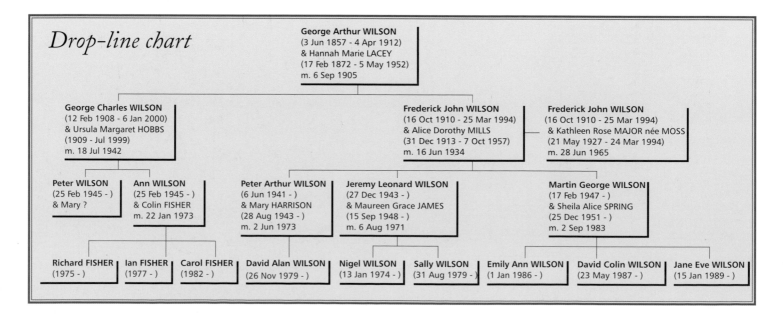

Drop-line chart

George Arthur WILSON
(3 Jun 1857 - 4 Apr 1912)
& Hannah Marie LACEY
(17 Feb 1872 - 5 May 1952)
m. 6 Sep 1905

George Charles WILSON
(12 Feb 1908 - 6 Jan 2000)
& Ursula Margaret HOBBS
(1909 - Jul 1999)
m. 18 Jul 1942

Frederick John WILSON
(16 Oct 1910 - 25 Mar 1994)
& Alice Dorothy MILLS
(31 Dec 1913 - 7 Oct 1957)
m. 16 Jun 1934

Frederick John WILSON
(16 Oct 1910 - 25 Mar 1994)
& Kathleen Rose MAJOR née MOSS
(21 May 1927 - 24 Mar 1994)
m. 28 Jun 1965

Peter WILSON
(25 Feb 1945 -)
& Mary ?

Ann WILSON
(25 Feb 1945 -)
& Colin FISHER
m. 22 Jan 1973

Peter Arthur WILSON
(6 Jun 1941 -)
& Mary HARRISON
(28 Aug 1943 -)
m. 2 Jun 1973

Jeremy Leonard WILSON
(27 Dec 1943 -)
& Maureen Grace JAMES
(15 Sep 1948 -)
m. 6 Aug 1971

Martin George WILSON
(17 Feb 1947 -)
& Sheila Alice SPRING
(25 Dec 1951 -)
m. 2 Sep 1983

Richard FISHER
(1975 -)

Ian FISHER
(1977 -)

Carol FISHER
(1982 -)

David Alan WILSON
(26 Nov 1979 -)

Nigel WILSON
(13 Jan 1974 -)

Sally WILSON
(31 Aug 1979 -)

Emily Ann WILSON
(1 Jan 1986 -)

David Colin WILSON
(23 May 1987 -)

Jane Eve WILSON
(15 Jan 1989 -)

shown by a solid line, illegitimate ones by a broken line.

- Put multiple marriages in order, left to right, and write the number against each one.
- Write the details of the marriage under the mother's name.
- Try not to cross lines of descent. This can be difficult if cousins marry and their descendants also marry, but with careful planning it should be possible.
- Do not include more than one branch of the family in the chart or it will soon become too big and unwieldy to use easily.
- Draw up a different chart for each branch, though this may be impossible where you find that different branches are descended from the same people through relatives marrying each other. When this happens, you may have to break some of these rules to fit it all in, especially if the people who marry are from different generations.

Uncles, aunts and cousins

The drop-line chart method is particularly useful for working out family relationships.

The types of relationship that sometimes give people trouble include great-aunts and great-uncles. In the diagram shown on the right:

- A and B are siblings.
- A is D's aunt/uncle; D is A's niece/nephew.
- A is F's great-aunt/uncle; F is A's great-niece/nephew.
- A is H's great-great-aunt/uncle; H is A's great-great-niece/nephew.

Cousinship is something else that gives people problems, especially when getting into the realm of second/third/fourth, etc., and trying to sort out who is a first/second cousin "removed". The rules, in fact, are very simple:

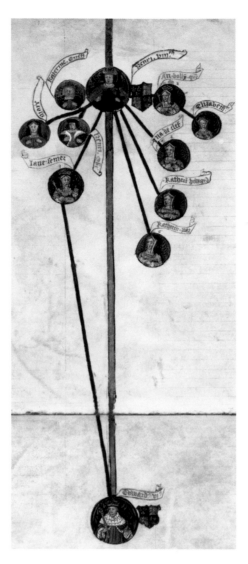

ABOVE A pedigree of Henry VIII, his six wives and their offspring. His son, the future Edward VI, is joined by a thick line.

BELOW Sorting out relationships can be complicated, but this chart should help.

- First cousins have the same set of grandparents.
- Second cousins have the same great-grandparents.
- Third cousins have the same great-great grandparents.

(The quick method is to count the number of "greats" and then add one to get the degree of cousinship.) Cousins are of the same generation, but not necessarily of similar age. When you want to work out the relationship between cousins who are "removed", i.e. who are not of the same generation, you need to go to the generation line on the family tree of the person from the younger generation, and then to move up to the generation of cousinship. In the diagram below, E is the first cousin once removed of D, because E's parent C is D's cousin. E's child G is the first cousin twice removed of D, because G is of the second generation below. G is the second cousin once removed of F, because E is F's second cousin and G is one generation below. Note that cousinship can be removed only upwards, i.e. F is not G's second cousin once removed.

This level of information can seem confusing, but in diagram form can become quite easily discernable.

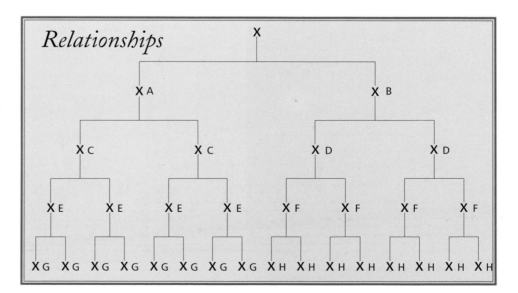

CHOOSING ANOTHER METHOD

Alternative formats for beginning to build up a visual representation of your family tree to the drop-line chart include the birth brief, the narrative indented tree and the concentric tree.

Once you have gathered a substantial amount of information about your ancestors, you might want to construct a more elaborate chart for display; there are many decorative charts available, both as printed copy and on CD-rom. The computerized versions are obviously more flexible as you can add or change information as you go.

The birth brief

This is a simple chart that is useful when you are first starting out. The birth brief is a representation of only the direct ancestors of one individual and it usually includes only the last four generations. Brothers, sisters and any second or third marriages are omitted. The format of a birth brief is similar to a drop-line chart, it simply holds less information.

The narrative indented tree

This is the method used for publications such as *Burke's Peerage* or *Debrett's*. It does allow lots of children to be included, but it can be a bit confusing to find your way around. Each generation is assigned a number or letter, and the children of a couple are listed with details of their marriages and, indented, their children. It is important to make sure that every person has a unique number that applies only to him/her, so the tree requires very careful drafting. A lot of information can be packed into less space, so it is worth considering this style when you have done a great deal of research. You also need to be familiar with this type of tree in case the pedigree of any of your relations appears in such books.

RIGHT When you see "of whom presently" (last line) this means that the descent of that person has been written out elsewhere and a new line of descent started for him/her.

BELOW The birth brief shows direct descent and does not include siblings.

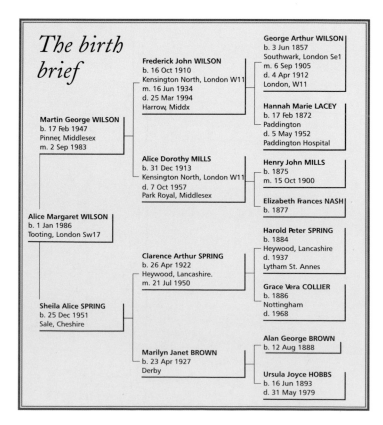

The birth brief

Martin George WILSON
b. 17 Feb 1947
Pinner, Middlesex
m. 2 Sep 1983

Frederick John WILSON
b. 16 Oct 1910
Kensington North, London W11
m. 16 Jun 1934
d. 25 Mar 1994
Harrow, Middx

George Arthur WILSON
b. 3 Jun 1857
Southwark, London Se1
m. 6 Sep 1905
d. 4 Apr 1912
London, W11

Hannah Marie LACEY
b. 17 Feb 1872
Paddington
d. 5 May 1952
Paddington Hospital

Alice Dorothy MILLS
b. 31 Dec 1913
Kensington North, London W11
d. 7 Oct 1957
Park Royal, Middlesex

Henry John MILLS
b. 1875
m. 15 Oct 1900

Elizabeth Frances NASH
b. 1877

Alice Margaret WILSON
b. 1 Jan 1986
Tooting, London Sw17

Clarence Arthur SPRING
b. 26 Apr 1922
Heywood, Lancashire.
m. 21 Jul 1950

Harold Peter SPRING
b. 1884
Heywood, Lancashire
d. 1937
Lytham St. Annes

Grace Vera COLLIER
b. 1886
Nottingham
d. 1968

Sheila Alice SPRING
b. 25 Dec 1951
Sale, Cheshire

Marilyn Janet BROWN
b. 23 Apr 1927
Derby

Alan George BROWN
b. 12 Aug 1888

Ursula Joyce HOBBS
b. 16 Jun 1893
d. 31 May 1979

The narrative indented tree

William Williamson b 1840, Rector of Chawleigh Regis, Somerset, m 1868 Harriet Peel (2nd dau of James and Elizabeth Peel of Edinburgh), d 1903 and had issue:

1 William b & d 1869
2 Harriet b 1870 d 1880
3 Thomas b 1871, took holy orders, m 1891 Sophia Ann Bristow, d 1950 and had issue
   a Thomas William b 1891 Fellow of St Chad's College, Cambridge, m 1922 Olive Johnson, d 1949 and had issue
      i Julia Mary b 1923
      ii Ann Elizabeth b 1925 m 1950 Christopher St John Lucas, Esq.
      iii Christine Ann b 1929 m 1949 Percy Arthur Black
   b George Frederick b 1893 m 1918 Ivy Kavanagh and had issue
      i Percival Thomas William b 1925 m 1952 Joyce Lewis
   c Cyril Edward b 1895, sub-lieutenant on HMS Dragon, d 1916
4 George b & d 1872
5 Charles b & d 1872
6 James b 1875, headmaster of Bellingham School, Somerset m 1900 Mary Ann Weston (elder dau of the Hon. Roderick and Lavinia Gascoigne-Hunter), d 1962 and had issue
   a Sarah Catherine b 1902
   b John James b 1904 d 1915
   c Leonard Thomas b 1906 m 1930 Elizabeth Mary James (only dau of Alexander and Aileen McKellan), d 1990 and had issue
      i Marian Mary b 1931
      ii Kenneth Thomas b 1935
   d Ronald Albert b 1909, m 1928 Jessica McDonald and had issue
      i Roderick James b 1928 m. 1955
   e Ethel Rosamund b 1913 m 1933 Professor William Goldblatt
7 John b 1877 <u>of whom presently</u>

The concentric tree

This is useful to show, at a glance, your direct descent from all the different branches of your family. Your details (or those of your children) are placed in the centre. In the next circle appear the father and mother: father at the top and mother at the bottom. The one after is used for the central individual's grandparents, and so on.

The problem with this method is that, because the most distant ancestors appear in the outer sections, where there is more space, annoying gaps can soon open up. However, this kind of chart makes a decorative picture and a good instant reference that

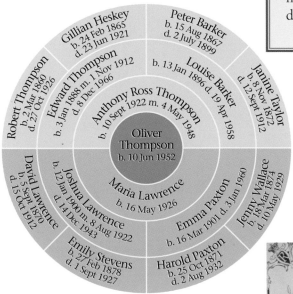

ABOVE The concentric tree puts the most recent generation at the centre. It does not include siblings.

you can hang in your home or give to relatives as a present, but it is best prepared when you have done a good deal of research.

Decorative charts

The other kinds of pictorial and decorative charts that are available to record your family tree are ideal for the culmination of your research, and make perfect special gifts for relatives.

Abbreviations

Whatever form of chart you use, you will find the following abbreviations vital both to record your own information in a concise manner and to understand the information you find in existing charts.

b.   born
bp   baptized
m.   married
=   shows a marriage. There are different ways to show illegitimacy: some people use ≠ to show that the couple were not married but either cohabited or had children.
mar.   marriage
diss.   dissolved (i.e. divorce)

▼ a downward arrow shows that the couple had a child or children but that they are not included

d.   died
d. yng died young
bur.   buried
dsp   died without issue (English/ Latin died *sine prole*)
c.   about (Latin *circa*) in front of an approximate date
fl.   flourishing (i.e. was alive) before a date
MI   Memorial Inscription (used to show there is a gravestone or a memorial in a church/chapel/ temple, etc.)
Will   Will proved
prov.

FURTHER HELP

McLaughlin, Eve *Laying Out a Pedigree* (McLaughlin Guides)
Palgrave-Moore, Patrick *How to Record Your Family Tree* (Elvery Dowers Publications)

BELOW Not everyone has quite so flourishing a family tree as Queen Victoria. This kind of chart is decorative but not much use in sorting out relationships.

Names

Researching names can tell us a great deal about our families and their histories. Surnames may reveal where a family originated or what an ancestor did for a living, or it may be a patronymic or nickname. First names, too, can suggest regional links.

UNDERSTANDING NAMING PATTERNS

As you draw up your first family tree, you may notice naming patterns emerging. In the past it was common to call the first child after a parent or grandparent. Second or subsequent names might also be given in honour of a member of the family or to preserve the mother's maiden name. This is how many double-barrelled surnames originated.

Naming children after relatives means that a family might share a small pool of names. For men the most common names were John, William, Henry and Thomas, for women Elizabeth, Mary, Ann/e and Sarah. In the 17th century, biblical names were common, the 18th century brought a fashion for classical names, and in the 19th century Old English names were revived. The name of the current monarch was always a popular choice.

There were also names that had only local popularity. A daughter called Frideswide (sometimes Frideswith), for example, suggests that the family had connections with Oxford, since the cathedral there is built over the remains of an early English saint of that name who founded a convent. Used in the 19th or 20th century, it may suggest that the family were Catholics. Loveday, given originally to

Until the 20th century, it was common to call subsequent children by the same name as a deceased child in order to make sure that the name continued in the family.

both boys and girls but later to girls only, suggests Cornish links, while Marmaduke, which was popular in the north, particularly Yorkshire, was rare in the rest of Britain.

THE HISTORY OF SURNAMES

Before the Middle Ages, people had only one name; it was only in the 13th century that surnames began to be used in England. These names seem to have been developed from four different sources: places, occupations, nicknames and patronymics.

Place names

These can be a large town such as Chester, or a village such as Oulton, which is the name given to four different places in Cumbria, Norfolk, Suffolk and Yorkshire. They may also come from a local landmark, such as Ditchfield, Atwell, or Wood. It is

worth looking up your surname in an atlas or dictionary of place names to see if it comes from a small village.

Occupations

Names such as Smith, Baker, Glover (glove maker) or Fletcher (arrow maker) show that your ancestor played an important part in the economy of his community. A skilled woman among your forebears will have left a surname ending in "-ster", such as Brewster (a female brewer) or Collister (a female collier – a charcoal burner or seller). We call unmarried women "spinsters" because they earned their living by spinning wool – a major source of England's wealth in the Middle Ages. Some of these surnames, such as Faber, meaning a smith, have French or Latin origins. When surnames were introduced, Norman French and Latin were both used by officials.

Nicknames

In these politically correct times it would be unthinkable to call someone Cruikshank (crooked legs), but our ancestors had a much rougher sense of humour. Other names record personal eccentricities, such as Pennyf(e)ather, meaning a miser.

Patronymics

This means a name derived from the name of the person's ancestor or father, such as the son of John being called Johnson, and that of William being called Williamson. Robinson and Wilson preserve pet names for men named Robert or William. Some women are also commemorated in names such as Allison (Alice's son) or Widowson, which may show that an ancestor was illegitimate or posthumous (born after the father died).

Celtic surnames

The Celtic countries (Wales, Scotland and Ireland) adopted surnames much later than England, and they generally

Younger children often received more fashionable names than their older siblings.

used patronymics. In Welsh, "ap" means "son of", but the first vowel disappeared, producing names such as Price (ap Rhys), Pritchard (ap Richard) or Prothero, a variant of Prydderch (ap Rydderch). Such names therefore indicate Welsh origins. A fixed surname here was not common until the 18th century. As an alternative to putting "ap" at the beginning or "son" at the end of the father's name, the Welsh often simply added "s", so names such as Edwards (son of Edward) and Jones (son of John) are common there.

Cornwall, another major Celtic area in England, also tended to use the father's name, though with no prefixes or suffixes. The Cornish also started using a fixed surname much later than the rest of the country. George, for example, did not become a common name until the Hanoverian kings, who started in 1714, long after the majority of surnames in England were formed, so someone with the surname George or John or Thomas should suspect Cornish or Welsh origins.

"Mac" or "Mc" means "son of", so the Macdonalds, the McCraes and the Macmillans have Scottish ancestry, but some of the Mcs, such as McNulty or McMullan, are of Irish origin. (Both the Scots and Irish spoke Gaelic.)

The purely Irish equivalent of the patronymic is "O", as in O'Casey and O'Neill. Sometimes the "O" was dropped, giving just "Casey" or "Neill".

Although patronymics were the most common method of surname formation in the Celtic countries, place names and nicknames were also used.

Uncommon surnames

Although the majority of surnames were, in England at least, fixed by the mid-13th century, and so preserve what was normal in the medieval

period, family historians will find many other names in their ancestry that don't appear in the standard reference books. Some may be indications of immigrant ancestry. Others perhaps preserve some long-forgotten incident. The answer may lie in a document somewhere, waiting to be discovered, or it may remain a puzzle for ever.

Until very recently, women automatically took their husband's surname on marriage.

Research skills

Try to get into good research habits right from the start of your work. The first rule in genealogy is that you must always work backwards from the known to the unknown; this means starting with yourself. The second rule is that you should never presume that what you have always been told is the truth. There are many stories in the family history world of people who have industriously traced their ancestry back several generations only to find, after getting a birth certificate for some other purpose, that they were in fact adopted but were never told this by their parents. You may also find that it is not only what has been passed down orally that may be wrong. The information given in official records is not always totally accurate, though you should be prepared to take what is written at face value until there is strong evidence against it.

COPING WITH ANY INFORMATION GAPS

The first 100–150 years are often among the hardest to research. Many official records are closed for 100 years in order to protect the privacy of people who could be still alive; gaining access to these records can be difficult or impossible. Most indexes and easily accessible genealogical information date from the mid-19th century. When there is a gap between two pieces of information, beware of making assumptions. For example, you may find a published family tree for someone with the same name as your ancestor in a place where you know your family were living fifty years later. It would be tempting to assume that

someone in the last generation on the published tree is the father or grandfather of your ancestor, but a lot can happen in fifty years – perhaps your forebear moved into a town where a distant relative was already living, or it may just be a coincidence that the two families have the same name.

RECORDING INFORMATION ACCURATELY

When you are copying information, it is vital to distinguish between what is actually there and what you can infer from it. If you cannot read a word or a number, but think that you can guess what it is, record this as a guess, not as a fact. The same applies to abbreviations: don't assume that W. Smith is William Smith – it might be Wilfred or Walter or even Winifred. If you make the firm assumption that it is William, and record this name in your copy of the document, there is a danger that when you come back to this information at a later stage, you will

Following the best research methods will make recording your information easier.

have forgotten that the name was only a guess. As a result of this, your researches may take you up a blind alley, which may not be apparent for a while, wasting your time and effort. The standard way of indicating that this is a supposition is to write the disputed words in square brackets or with a question mark, e.g. W[illiam] Smith of [illegible 5 or 8?] Nelson R[oa]d.

FINDING ANSWERS TO QUESTIONS

In drawing up a family tree, you will probably find that a number of questions are raised. Write them down as they occur to you, or you are likely to forget them. If you have been inspired to compile your family tree by clearing out the contents of a house because elderly people (your parents or other relatives) are moving into a smaller house, you will be able to put your questions to them. If, however, the inspiration was the death of a parent or other relative, then the very person who could have answered your questions is no longer here, and you will have to see if other family members can help you. Get in touch with as many relations as you can, explaining what you are doing.

As you list the questions your research raises, ask yourself where you are likely to find the answers. The rest of this book is concerned with the various different sources, how to contact them, and what information you can expect to find there, but it is worth noting here the various types of sources. Knowing which is the most appropriate one will save you much in the way of time and money.

Telephone directories

If you have a very unusual name, it might be worth writing to everyone with that name in the telephone directory. Directories for the whole country should be available in main libraries. Alternatively, they are obtainable on the Internet, though that is a more complicated procedure.

It is better to write to the contact rather than ring them. How would you feel if a complete stranger suddenly phoned out of the blue and started asking detailed questions about you and your family? Always enclose a stamped, addressed envelope. This is not just a courteous gesture: it also, in an odd way, puts an obligation on the recipient to answer.

Note where the people with your name are living and how many there are in each district. If you plot these on a map, you may see a pattern emerging. The biggest concentration of these people today is likely to be where they were living a few hundred years ago.

The government

Every area of life is regulated in some way by the law. Money and land were, and still are, major concerns of government, and all but the very poorest families will be found in records covering them. Which aspects of your ancestors' lives were covered by legislation, such as paying taxes or rates, that might have generated documentary evidence? Would it have been administered at national or local level?

The Church

Until fairly recently, religion played a major role in everyday life. In Britain, the Church is established, which means that it is part of the government, and it was only during the 20th century that religious belief and attending places of worship stopped

Government records, such as this census, show where individuals were born and give other information, such as ages and occupations, that might help in finding other records.

being part of the majority of people's lives. The Church also had a prominent role in education.

Associations and clubs

Many people belong or belonged to associations connected with their occupation, or to clubs where they shared a hobby or interest with other people. In some cases, membership of a professional association gives the right to work in a particular area, such as freemen of a town or city, or to practise a profession, such as the law.

Charities

Charitable institutions play a large role in some people's lives. Some were run by professional associations, especially for people who had retired from an occupation. Others were set up to help a particular section of society, and distributed sums of money to assist in times of hardship or for specified purposes, such as education.

Was your ancestor eligible for some kind of charitable support, and if so, why would he or she have qualified for

this? Alternatively, your ancestor may have helped with the administration of a charity, in which case, he or she might have been involved in distributing money or other benefits.

Newspapers and periodicals

Britain has had a thriving print industry since the 17th century. Are there events in your ancestors' lives that might have been of public interest? If so where would they be reported?

Some events might be documented in many of the above sources. If your ancestor committed a crime, for example, he or she would have been tried in court, an account of which will appear in government records. If the crime was connected with their profession, they might have been struck off or expelled from an association's membership. A report of the proceedings will probably appear in a newspaper. Other events which might be recorded in print are marriages and births, awards and prizes, even bankruptcy. Obituaries and accounts of funerals can often give an entire life history.

Keeping records

Although you may not have much paper to file yet, a lot will soon accumulate, so setting up an efficient filing system is essential. Most people already have or develop individual methods that best suit them and the records they collect.

STARTING A FILING SYSTEM

A good way to start is to get two large ring binders. The first one will include information you are certain of; the second will include notes you have taken that may be relevant but that you cannot yet link to your family. Divide both into one section per family name you are researching. As your research progresses and the paperwork increases, you may need to give a separate ring binder to each name.

You will also need a master copy of your descent. You could draw your own, but they are available by mail order or in the bookshops of record offices and libraries such as the Society of Genealogists. These are daunting but exciting – the one produced by the Church of Jesus Christ of Latter-day Saints (LDS) has space for 12 generations, which potentially includes over 3,000 ancestors.

CHOOSING A SYSTEM OF IDENTIFICATION

Each ancestor must have a unique number. This can be a single figure (usually already printed on the chart) or you might want to assign each generation a number, usually a Roman numeral, starting with yourself as I1, your parents as II1 (your father) and II2 (your mother), and so on. This will tell you straightaway which generation

When you copy any information from documents, ensure you note where it came from and the archive's reference number.

you are dealing with, but will present problems for your descendants. You also run into difficulties with marriages between cousins, especially those from different generations, which could make a great-grandparent also a great-great-grandparent.

Some professional genealogists use letters instead of numerals. One system, devised by the Surname Index in Sussex, gives each 30-year period from 1380 onwards a letter of the alphabet, starting with A (1380–1409) and finishing with Z (2130–59), which future generations will use. The period of 30 years was chosen because that is the average length of a generation. This system has the advantage of letting you know which period of time you're dealing with, but it presents problems if one of your ancestors had children in two different time periods,

perhaps because he or she married twice. You will have a different problem if an ancestor was born at the beginning of one of these periods and married and had children young. His or her children would then share the same generation letter and possibly even the same name, since it was very common for the eldest child to be named after a parent.

As you file material related to a particular ancestor, you should annotate it with the ancestor's number (or letter) to prevent confusion between family members with the same name. You might also want to give all the children of an ancestor a reference number. To prevent numbers getting out of hand, you could assign the siblings of an ancestor the same number plus a, b, c, d and so on. Your father's brother (your paternal uncle) would become 2a or II1a.

Alternatively, you might prefer to write "William Smith brother of John Smith 2/II 1" on any notes relating to him.

KEEPING FURTHER RECORDS

In addition to the files containing your research results, you will need a notebook. A hardback book is a good idea because it is sturdier and more difficult to lose than single sheets of paper, but you will have to copy the information in order to file it in the right section of your master research file. A more sensible alternative is a block of paper with ring binder holes punched in it: sheets with errors on can just be torn out and disposed of, and once a sheet is completed it can be filed in a ring binder. You should use a separate sheet of paper for each document or source.

Whether you choose to have a separate book in which you list all the sources you have searched, or whether you record this information at the back of your main notebook, is up to you. Making lists of everything you look at is essential to prevent reading the same document more than once. It is also a good idea to have a small copy

Computers are a convenient way to store and manipulate your findings.

of each separate family tree on an A5 index card in a small ring binder or display book. It needs to give just the dates and places of birth/baptism, marriage and death/burial of each family member (including siblings). It is surprising how often you will be researching one branch of the family when you unexpectedly come across something that could relate to another branch. If you have a basic chart with you, you can refer to it on the spot and open up a whole new avenue of research.

When you get in touch with other people who share your research interests, you will need to decide whether to have a separate file for their correspondence or whether to file their letters with the relevant branch of the family.

USING A COMPUTER

There are a number of software packages for family historians. They are excellent for drawing up charts and so on, but are not a complete substitute for paper-based files. This is mainly because, even if you make backup copies (and you must), you still run the risk of losing all your research through computer or disk failure. Print out your work regularly so that if there is a problem you will lose comparatively little information. Anything you do

lose should be able to be easily reconstructed from your most recent notes.

You can buy or produce on your computer standard forms to help with your record-keeping. They include:

1. Family sheets, which give details of a marriage and all the children of it, including where they were born/baptized, whom they married and when, and the date of their death/burial. Each sheet is numbered, and at the bottom of the entry for each child there is a space in which to write the number of any further sheets relating to them.

2. Individual sheets, which contain details of an individual's life. As well as birth, baptism and parentage; marriage(s); children; death and burial; there is space for where they were living at particular dates, what they were doing, the dates the will (if any) was written and proved and where this information came from, e.g. census returns, street directories or electoral registers.

FURTHER HELP

TNA Family History Starter Pack This contains an introductory booklet, a bibliography and pro forma sheets on which to enter research information.
Swinnerton, Iain *Basic Approach to Keeping Family Records* (FFHS)

Interviewing people

Whether you are asking the owners of some mementos about them or trying to find out more from other family members or friends, there are ways of putting questions that will help you to obtain what you need.

GROUP AND INDIVIDUAL INTERVIEWS

Talking to people in a group can be a very good way of getting information, because what one person says may spark off the memories of others. You will need to choose the members of the group carefully, however. One very dominant speaker might not give the others the chance to say much. Alternatively, one shy person in a group of three extroverts may feel too overwhelmed to contribute at all. Group interviews will almost certainly have to be supplemented with individual conversations, since there are frequently pieces of information that people are unwilling to divulge in front of others.

Photographs can help to trigger family memories and may help to fill in some of the gaps in your family tree.

USING OPEN QUESTIONS

Open questions start with the words "Who", "What", "Why", "When", "Where" and "How", and they tend to receive fuller answers than closed questions, which can often be answered with just one word. For example, the closed question "Was your father born in 1920 or 1921?" will probably get one of these dates as the reply. But if you rephrase that as an open question, such as "When was your father born?", you may get a lot more detail: "My father was born in 1920, after the family moved from Nightingale Street. My grandparents already had two kids and they didn't have enough room for a baby as well. Grandad had just been promoted, so they could afford a bigger house." This gives you much more information and prompts other avenues of research that you might otherwise have missed. "Tell me about..." will also get a more detailed reply. You can use closed questions to clarify answers, e.g. "Didn't they have three children then?" "The second one died when he was a baby."

People, especially those from the older generation, may be reluctant to talk about illegitimacy, insanity, suicide or criminal records. They themselves may not have been told the full truth. All this means that you may have to think carefully about how to word the more sensitive questions. When you visit people to interview them, take photographs and other mementos that might prompt memories.

RECORDING THE INTERVIEW

You will need a record of the interview so that you can remember everything that was said. There are three options: a written record, a cassette or a video.

A written record involves making notes as the person talks, but this inevitably breaks your contact with the

Within family groups there are always things that one person will not want the others to know. Such personal secrets must be respected when researching the past.

Asking the right questions

Subjects about which you might want to ask questions include:

- Name: full name and whether the person was known by a different name to the one he or she was officially given.
- Names of other members of the family: father, mother, siblings, as well as more distant relatives with whom they had a particularly close association.
- What the person looked like: height; colouring; size (fat or thin); any physical peculiarities, such as a limp, which might be the result of an accident or illness; dress style; characteristic smell, such as a favourite perfume or aftershave.

- Jobs, including apprenticeship if applicable: what they did and where they did it.
- Hobbies or membership of clubs and associations. These might also reveal special talents.
- Marriage(s) and children, with approximate dates of the end of the marriage, whether by divorce or death. This is where it can get tricky because an ancestor's marriage might never have ended – he or she might simply have gone to live with, and had children by, another person.
- Where the person lived, with approximate dates.
- Holidays and outings: where they went and with whom.

- Religious affiliation, if any, and where they attended church/chapel/temple etc.
- Details of any periods spent in the armed forces: dates; the branch they served with (Army, Navy or Air Force); the regiment, ship or squadron; their service number; whether they volunteered or were called up, either in wartime or for National Service.
- You should also ask if the person you are talking to has any photographs or family papers. If you are allowed to take any documents away with you, you can take copies; alternatively, you will have to ask them to make copies for you.

---

person, as well as slowing down the interview. The seeming formality of the process – which could be seen as rather like giving a police statement – may also make the interviewee feel inhibited and uncomfortable.

If you decide to tape-record the conversation, take a small recorder, such as the type used for dictation, but don't be tempted to record a conversation without gaining permission first. People can be very self-conscious when what they are saying is being recorded, so make allowances for this.

If you have a camcorder, you might want to use it, but it can make the person too self-conscious to speak or it can encourage them to exaggerate stories and give false information to make a good performance. Camcorders are best used in places connected with the family history. Getting the informant to talk about their memories where they took place is not only a good record to have but it may also help to bring back the past to them.

ASKING THE RIGHT QUESTIONS

The box above has a list of suggested questions to which you might want to add other questions based on family documents or objects. You can design or buy forms to make sure you don't forget anything. Remember to note who gave you the information, their relationship to the person you are inquiring about and when you conducted the interview.

STRUCTURING AN INTERVIEW

Once you have decided on the questions, you need to think about the order in which to ask them. You may also need to gain the interviewee's trust before you start, in case they are worried that you will use their information in a way that might embarrass them or upset other members of the family. Reassure them that you are concerned only with recording the family history accurately and that you will honour any requests for confidentiality.

Begin with simple, factual questions to which they will know the answers. This will give them confidence. Then, when they are more relaxed and start to give more personal information, move on to other matters that might perhaps be more difficult for them to talk about. Go carefully on such issues: just because something happened a long time ago it doesn't mean that it isn't still painful to recall. You can also ask about any of the more uncomfortable subjects mentioned above, but don't force the discussion if the person isn't willing. There may be other people who can tell you this or official records where you can find it out.

FURTHER HELP

Amsden, Peter C. *Basic Approach to Making Contact with Relatives* (FFHS)

McLaughlin, E. *Interviewing Elderly Relatives* (McLaughlin Guide)

Back to the early 1800s

By now you should have a basic family tree and some clues that will help you to move back in time. Most of the information you need at this stage is located in the Family Record Centre in London. It holds birth, marriage, adoption and death certificates from 1837 onwards, and records of some of these events overseas. It also holds copies of census returns, held every year from 1841, and wills proved in the Prerogative Court of Canterbury before 1858. There are also lists of Nonconformist registers deposited in The National Archives.

Certificates after 1837

In 1836 an Act of Parliament was passed to set up the General Register Office (GRO) to record the births, marriages and deaths (BMD) of everyone in England and Wales from 1 July 1837. Before that date, there was no requirement to notify anyone of births and deaths (although churches and other places of worship carried out baptisms and burials). Legal marriages could take place only in Anglican parish churches or be carried out by Jews or the Religious Society of Friends (the Quakers). After 1837, other religious denominations, such as Nonconformists or Roman Catholics, could have their buildings registered to perform marriages.

FINDING BMD CERTIFICATES

Unless you are very lucky and find a complete set of certificates among your family papers, you will need to obtain copies of birth, marriage and (sometimes) death certificates in order to reconstruct your ancestry back to 1837. The GRO compiled quarterly indexes from the returns sent to them from all over the country. Each quarter contains the following months:

March quarter: January, February and March

June quarter: April, May and June

September quarter: July, August and September

December quarter: October, November and December

The indexes list all the births together, all the marriages together and all the deaths. These indexes are now on open shelves in the Family Record Centre (FRC) in London, but there are copies on microfiche in local offices and libraries, and on the Internet.

The entries relate to the date of the actual registration, not of the event itself, so that people who were born,

Not all babies would have been baptized but, after 1837, they should all have a birth certificate.

married or died near the end of one quarter may appear in the index of the next. The registers are stored in Southport, Lancashire, where entries are copied on to blank certificate forms. The researcher has to locate the relevant entry in the index and use the reference number there to place an order. Each certificate must be paid for.

Birth certificates

When researching your ancestry, you must start from the known and work back to the unknown. In certificate terms, this means getting the birth certificate of a child in order to find out the parents' names, especially if you do not know the mother's maiden name, and then using this information to look for the parents' marriage certificate, which will give their fathers' names and occupations. You can then order the birth certificate of each parent, and so find out the mothers' names as well.

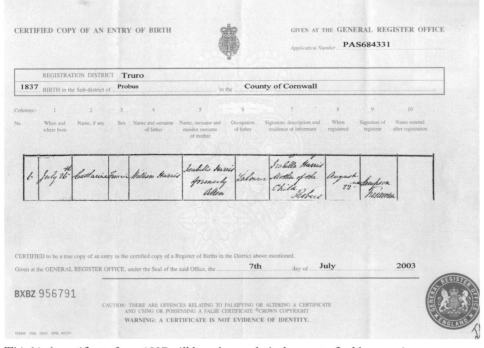

This birth certificate from 1837 will have been relatively easy to find because it was compiled after the setting up of the General Register Office in 1836.

In reality, unfortunately, it never goes as smoothly as this suggests. In the first ten years or so following the introduction of national registration, parents were not obliged to notify the registrar of a child's birth, and if a child was not registered within six months, it could not be included in the records. There seems also to have been some confusion about whether it was necessary to register a child if it had also been baptized. In 1874, fines were introduced for non-notification by the parents, which improved the situation.

This lack of registration, combined with the bureaucracy involved in copying entries as they were passed from level to level in the system, means that a number of events are missing from the indexes, especially in the earlier period. There may be as many as 15 per cent of the births missing for 1837–47, and as many as 1 in 40 marriages missing for 1837–99. There are also the difficulties caused by copying errors and by dealing with illiterate people who did not know how their names were written, and who probably had strong regional accents. Registrars had, in many cases, to guess at the name and how it was spelled.

Marriage certificates

In the days when divorce was practically impossible for poor people, many just left their spouse and set up another family with someone else, claiming to be married to them. Some did marry after the first spouse's death, but others did not, and their children never knew that they were illegitimate.

If either of the parties had connections with Scotland, Ireland or another country, the marriage may have taken place outside England or Wales. There is a link to the Scottish and Irish records at the FRC, which you must pay to access. It is also worth checking

the miscellaneous indexes that cover events at sea and all over the world. A reason for marrying abroad was that the parties were related in a way that made their marriage illegal in Britain.

All these factors may account for people not appearing in registers where they are expected to be.

Death certificates

It's comparatively easy to find birth and marriage certificates, since most people had children soon after the marriage, but, since people can die at any time, finding a death certificate can be a much longer job.

SEARCHING THE INDEXES

Researching information calls for patience, diligence, concentration and also imagination.

Be meticulous

Be careful not to miss the reference. It is easy to overlook a name, especially if you have been searching for a long time and are tired. If you are using the books at the FRC, run a sheet of paper

down the names to keep your eyes focused on the right place. This also ensures that you do not miss the last one lurking at the bottom of the page. This task is more difficult if you're using microfiche. Take regular breaks.

Leave no gaps

As you work, list all the quarters you have checked, both year and month. It is all too easy, if someone is using the next book that you want to consult, to work on another, planning to go back and then either not do so or forget which one you were going to look at. This can lead to you looking at the same one twice and missing the one that you need.

Try alternative spellings

Ask yourself what the surname in question might have sounded like to the registrar, especially if the informant had a heavy cold or a mild speech impediment, for example Searle/Thurle. Names beginning with an H cause particular problems, because dropping the H is common in many

After 1837 marriages could take place in a register office rather than a church, but most people still preferred a traditional church wedding.

Significant dates in the history of BMD records

1837 1 July Civil registration began in England and Wales.

1866 Death indexes recorded age at death.

1907 Deceased Wife's Sister Marriage Act permitted a man to marry his deceased wife's sister.

1911 September Birth indexes contained mother's maiden name.

1912 Marriage indexes showed name of the second party.

1921 Deceased Brother's Widow Marriage Act permitted a woman to marry her deceased husband's brother.

1926 Adoption of Children Act provided for adoption of children, with the creation of an Adopted Children's Register.

1926 Legitimacy Act allowed for illegitimate children to be re-registered on the subsequent marriage of the parents.

1927 Registration of stillbirths made compulsory (but the register was not put on open access).

1929 It became illegal for anyone under 16 to marry. Previously girls could marry at 12 and boys at 14, although they needed their parents' consent until they were 21.

1931 Marriage between uncle and niece/aunt and nephew allowed.

1947 Short birth certificate introduced. (This does not contain parents' names and so is of no use to the genealogist.)

1949 Register of Births and Deaths in Aircraft listed any births or deaths that took place in aircraft registered in Great Britain or Northern Ireland, wherever they occurred in the world.

1959 Legitimacy Act allowed the children born when one of their parents was married to somebody else to be legitimized when their parents married. The child could be re-registered if it had been previously entered under the woman's husband's name.

1969 Death indexes showed date of birth.

1969 Age of majority reduced from 21 to 18. Parental consent to marriage now needed for people under 18.

1975 Children Act 1975 allowed adopted children to obtain the original information on their birth certificate.

1986 People permitted to marry a stepchild or stepgrandchild, but both parties had to be over 18 and the child must not have been treated as a child of the person's family.

---

local accents, so for Horton try Orton. When handwritten indexes were copied, confusion between M and W could occur, such as Mardell/Wardell. If you look at samples of copperplate handwriting, you will see that confusion between F, J and T was also possible.

Consider alternative first names

Consider whether the person was actually given the name by which he or she was generally known. Children named after a parent might have been known by their second or another name to prevent confusion. Others, for reasons long forgotten, might have been called something completely unrelated to their original name. Alternatively, the parents may not have decided on the child's name until after it was registered.

There was, and still is, no obligation to give a first name, so you need to check at the top of the list of surnames to see if there is a likely registration in the area where the family lived.

Consider illegitimacy

Illegitimate children were given their mother's surname until 1926, when they could be re-registered with the father's name if the parents married after the birth. Also, a couple might not have married until after some, or all, of their children were born.

Broaden your time span

Ages are often inaccurately recorded, so check up to five years on either side of the likely date. If you are relying on the ages given on a marriage certificate to find the person's birth certificate, consider that the ages have been falsified.

Ages at death are especially suspect because the informant may not have known the age and just made a guess.

Consider other districts

The event would have been registered where it took place, not where the family lived. Women might have gone to stay with their mothers or other family members for the birth of a child, and so the birth would have been registered there. Even a hospital just a short distance from home might have been in another registration district.

Narrow the field

If you are researching a fairly common surname, you may find a number of entries, any of which might be the person you are seeking. The staff at both the FRC and the local record office will do some (paid) cross-checking for you. You can ask them to check entries until they find a particular piece of information that matches something you know already, such as the father's first name. Alternatively, you could:

1. Order all the possible certificates; but this can be expensive and may not necessarily help you to decide which one is your ancestor.

2. Look for the birth certificate of a brother or sister about whom you know more (such as exact date or place of birth) or who has a rarer first name.

3. Note the quarters and reference details, then seek out other, more distant, family members in the hope that one of them will know something or have a document that will help.

If none of this works, it can mean going back to the original entry and paying for a search to be made in a local register office.

RESEARCHING BMD CERTIFICATES

Consider carefully whether you need your ancestor's birth certificate. You may find that getting a sibling's would be more useful: you will still get the parents' names from it and you might also get the family's address at the time of a census. These took place every ten years from 1841, so if your ancestor was born in 1846 and had brothers or sisters born in 1841 and 1851, get the older child's certificate (see Censuses for the reason why).

In England and Wales, a time given on a birth certificate means delivery of twins or a multiple birth, so you need to look for another child or children with the same surname and reference number to find out their names. If you want to find out in what order they were born, you will have to order the certificates.

Where you know the surnames of both parties to a marriage, look up the less common one in the index. Note the reference number against the one you think is your ancestor, and then look up the other party's name in the same quarter's index. If the reference

number is the same, you can be fairly sure that you have the right marriage.

Death certificates are not especially useful in constructing family trees. After 1866 the ages at death are given in the indexes. Since this information will give you a starting point to look for a birth certificate, you may not need to obtain the death certificate. If you know that the widow or widower remarried, you can look for their marriage certificate after that date.

Levels of registration

GRO in Somerset House, London

A quarterly index, covering the whole of England and Wales, was drawn up from copies of the certificates sent by the local register offices to Superintendent Registrars.

Superintendent Registrars

In 1834, Poor Law Unions (groups of parishes that banded together to care for those who could not support themselves) were set up, and they became the basis for the new registration system. Each union had a Superintendent

Registrar, who was responsible for a number of local registrars. After checking the entries from the registrars in his district, each Superintendent Registrar sent copies to the General Register office (GRO).

Registrars

At the lowest, local level, the 2,193 registrars recorded births and deaths. Four times a year they sent a copy of these certificates to the district Superintendent Registrar's office.

FURTHER HELP

Collins, Audrey *Basic Facts about Using the Family Record Centre* (FFHS)

District Register Offices in England and Wales (Yorkshire FHS)

freebmd.rootsweb.com on the Rootsweb Internet site has the indexes at the FRC

Wiggins, Ray *Registration Districts* (SoG)

Wood, Tom *An Introduction to Civil Registration* (FFHS)

Using Birth Marriage and Death Records (TNA)

It is interesting to know when, where and how someone died, but the actual information on a death certificate will rarely help you move back in time.

Other indexes at the Family Record Centre

In addition to the indexes to BMD certificates, the Family Record Centre also has a number of indexes to other events, such as divorce, adoption and some BMD overseas.

DIVORCES

Divorce files for 1858–1958 have been indexed (except for the period 1945–50). The original papers are in The National Archives (TNA), where, unlike the Family Record Centre you will need to get a ticket to carry out research. Before 1858, divorces could be made only through an Act of Parliament. Formal separations and annulments were obtained through the Church courts.

ADOPTIONS

Before 1926, adoptions were arranged informally. After that date, a register of adopted children was set up. The indexes are arranged by the adoptive name, and the certificates do not contain information about birth parents. Adopted people wishing to obtain their original birth certificate should contact the Adoption Section at the FRC to inquire about the procedures.

EVENTS OVERSEAS

In addition to events in England and Wales, the FRC contains copies of a number of records relating to overseas. These came mainly from maritime, military or consular sources. Most are from the 19th century, but some date back to 1627 and some continue until the late 1950s. The originals are in TNA, but there are microfilm copies at the FRC. They are divided between statutory returns (those that had to be made by law) and non-statutory returns (those that were made voluntarily). Researchers must pay the standard certificate fee to get copies of the information from the statutory returns.

From 1627 onwards, miscellaneous notifications of BMD overseas were returned to Britain. These were largely to ensure that, should any dispute arise, the people concerned could prove that they were married, that their children were legitimate, or that someone was dead. Many are BMD of embassy or other government staff or those notified to the local consulate by British people either visiting the country or resident there. These are not limited to British territories, though some of these are included, but cover places in Europe where there were sizeable British communities,

The Family Records Centre, Clerkenwell, London, contains indexes to some BMD overseas as well as in England and Wales.

and countries elsewhere. From 1849, consuls were allowed to carry out marriages and had to make a return of the ceremonies to the GRO in London.

There is a microfilm of a number of certificates (not indexed) to military deaths that took place during and just after World War I (1914–21). They are mainly of soldiers who died not in action but off the battlefield, plus a few civilians.

ARMY BMD

Regimental registers were kept from 1761 and are most likely to contain births in depots in Great Britain. In addition, Army regiments each had their own chaplain, who generally kept a register of the christenings, marriages and burials (CMB) he carried out. Chaplains' returns from 1796 are most likely to contain births overseas.

BMD AT SEA

From 1837, BMD at sea on British ships had to be notified to the GRO. By an Act of 1874, which did not affect the Royal Navy, certificates of births and deaths on Merchant Navy ships and passenger ships travelling to and from British ports had to be sent to the Register General of Shipping and Seamen. From here, they were distributed to the Register Offices in London, Edinburgh and Dublin, depending on the nationality of the people involved (though this wasn't always strictly observed). Certificates concerning foreigners went to the London office. The English Marine Register indexes, covering the Royal Navy, the Merchant Navy and passenger ships from 1837, are at the FRC.

They contain only births and deaths. There are indexes to deaths in the armed forces during and just after the Boer War (1899–1902), World War I (1914–21) and World War II (1939–48). Deaths at sea during the two World Wars were sometimes sent to the GRO but were mainly passed to the Admiralty, which maintained a separate War Deaths register, so consult both.

THE MISCELLANEOUS INDEXES

If you have to visit the FRC and you know that members of your family spent some time abroad, it may be worthwhile checking out the various miscellaneous indexes.

The information in the miscellaneous returns may be found elsewhere, such as the records of the Bishop of London, which are in the Guildhall Library, or the Oriental and India Office Library, which is at the British Library. If you find that the information you want is recorded on a certificate for which a fee is payable, you will have to decide whether you want to save the money by exploring these alternative sources. This is definitely worth considering if you know you will be doing other research in that particular archive.

Copies of the Marine Registers made for merchant ships are accessible, without a fee, at TNA, where there are also indexes. Seamen who died in the course of a voyage had their wages and effects given to the next of

FURTHER HELP

Stafford, Georgina *Where to Find Adoption Records: A Guide for Counsellors* (British Agencies for Adoption and Fostering)
Tracing the Birth Parents of Adopted Persons (FFHS)

kin or someone nominated in their wills. Records relating to this are at TNA, so if you already know that your ancestor was a merchant seaman, you might prefer to go to TNA rather than the FRC.

Children born at sea were sometimes given the name of the ship on which they were born, so if you trace an ancestor with an odd name that appears to have no family connections, this may be a clue to their birthplace.

ABOVE Deaths of Army personnel who died overseas in wartime are indexed at the FRC but sailors' deaths are more likely to be in Admiralty records at TNA.

LEFT As a resident in France at the time of his death in 1900, Oscar Wilde's death certificate is in the Miscellaneous Foreign Deaths returns.

Censuses

The triggering factor for the first national census in Britain was the need to know whether the population was increasing or decreasing and whether the number of the poor was growing beyond the ability of the country to support them.

A HISTORY OF THE CENSUS

Following some local head counts held at irregular intervals, the nationwide censuses held from 1841 give the family historian a snapshot of the life of their ancestors at ten-yearly intervals.

The first censuses

Although they were not official censuses, there have been head counts of people since the Domesday survey in 1086. Various towns and parishes, such as Poole, Dorset, in 1575 and Ealing in 1522, listed everyone living there, and since those dates many other censuses have been made. Some of them named only the head of the household and added how many people there were in it.

National censuses were first proposed in 1753, but it wasn't until 1800 that legislation to enumerate the entire population of England and Wales was passed. The first census was held on Monday, 10 March 1801, and was carried out by parish officials in England and Wales and schoolmasters in Scotland. Thereafter, a national census was taken every ten years. The next three – in 1811, 1821 and 1831 – were also taken by the same people, but in 1841 the government took over. Only some copies of the first four censuses survive in parish records, but from 1841 there is full coverage of the whole country.

ABOVE Until the last century, a whole family might live in one room, so several, unrelated households may be found in the same house.

BELOW These gypsies have had their census papers brought to them by the police, but many gypsies and other travellers, as well as the homeless sleeping rough, were not recorded in the earlier census returns.

The 1841 census

From 1841, it was decided to seek information about everyone in each house on a particular night (in this case, 6–7 June). The information gathered was broadly similar to previous ones, with the significant addition of the age of each person. Exact ages were required only for children under 16; adults' ages were rounded down to the nearest five years. Thus a person stated to be 30 could have been any age between 30 and 34. People were also required to say whether or not each person had been born in the same county in which they now lived and whether any member of the household was foreign-born. There are, however, omissions from this census: miners on shift were not included, for example, and nor were people on board ships that were in harbour.

The 1851 census

There were several changes in the questions that were asked for this census, which was held on the night of

30–1 March. Instead of asking how many actual houses there were, the government now wanted to know the number of households. More than one household might live in a house, particularly in poor areas, where whole families might live in one room. A line was drawn across the page under each household.

People were also required to state the parish in which they were born. This is what makes this census so useful to the family historian. Those born overseas, however, were required to put only the country, although some did include the place within it. Others put "British citizen", which suggests one of three options: that they were naturalized, had denization or were born in a British colony. For this census, sailors on ships in harbour were included but not, it appears, people on canal barges.

A question about whether a person was deaf, dumb, blind or lunatic was also asked, and researchers are often surprised (and horrified) to find that everyone in their ancestor's family seems to have been disabled in some way, because there is a tick against every option here. Be cautious about this: the column relating to this question was the last on the form, and the ticks are usually just marks made when the numbers were being added up.

Censuses for 1861 and 1871

Held on the nights of 7–8 April and 2–3 April respectively, these asked the same questions as the 1851 census.

The 1881 census

This census, which was held on the night of 3–4 April, is particularly useful to family historians because the entire census for the whole country has been indexed in a project carried out by the Federation of Family History Societies (FFHS) and the Church of Jesus Christ of Latter-day Saints (LDS). This index exists on both

ABOVE Neath Place, London (c.1900), no longer exists. Maps from the 19th century will be needed to find out where it was.

RIGHT A 19th-century census map showing the districts of Epping, Chigwell and Harlow, in Essex.

microfiche and CD-ROM. A separate record was made of those who were lunatic, imbecile or idiot; this replaced the "lunatic" option in the earlier censuses.

The 1891 census

There is no nationwide index for this census, which was held on the night of 5–6 April, so finding ancestors on it depends on knowing where they lived.

The 1901 census

This census, which was held on the night of 31 March–1 April, has been digitized and put on to the Internet at www.census.pro.gov.uk. It can be searched by name to find individuals or by address. A fee is charged for access to the image of the original

From these you can get what is called the piece number and the folio number. The class mark is the reference number used by the government. The following class marks are used: 1841: class mark HO 107; 1851: class mark HO 107; 1861: class mark RG 9; 1871: class mark RG 10; 1881: class mark RG 11; 1891: class mark RG 12; 1901: class mark RG 13.

The piece number is the individual bundle of documents containing an area's census returns, and the folio number refers to a particular street or, in rural places, locality. Once you have the microfilm or microfiche you need, you can use page numbers given in the FRC reference books to find your ancestor's street, or use an index (if one has been made) to find your ancestor's

census page. Microfiche copies are also available in local record offices, but there is no index with them. Individual family history societies may compile indexes for their area, but if this has not been done you can only search the microfiche copies by address.

RESEARCHING THE CENSUSES

Censuses for the whole country for 1841–1901 are on microfiche or microfilm at the FRC. Microfiche are small sheets of plastic, the size of index cards, and microfilm are rolls of film on to which records have been copied. They both need a special machine on which to view them, and copies can usually be made from them. Some censuses also exist on CD-ROMs, which have to be read on a computer. Sometimes you can print out the information. Some County Record Offices (CROs) and other local offices and libraries have copies for their area too. Many have been indexed by Family History Societies. Check whether this has been done for the area you are interested in. If it has, you can use these indexes and so save yourself a lot of work.

You need to find out where your ancestor was living at the time of a particular census. This information can come from various sources, such as

BMD certificates, trade directories, such as Kelly's, and correspondence. At the FRC there are lists of every place in the country; individual towns and cities with more than 40,000 inhabitants should also have a street index.

ABOVE Tracking down people from a census can be a long task if you do not know the address, as often very few districts were indexed.

RIGHT Trade directories, such as Kelly's, can help you find the address of an individual's workplace, which may help you trace them in the relevant census.

Page 20] The undermentioned Houses are situate within the Boundaries of the

Civil Parish (or Township) of	City or Municipal Borough of	Municipal Ward of	Parliamentary Borough of	Town of	Village or Hamlet, &c., of	Local Board, or [Improvement Commissioners] District of	Ecclesiastical District of
Sheffield	Sheffield	St Georges	Sheffield	Sheffield		Sheffield	St Georges

No. of Schedule	ROAD, STREET, &c., and No. or NAME of HOUSE	HOUSES Inhabited	HOUSES Uninhabited (U.) or (Building) (B.)	NAME and Surname of each Person	RELATION to Head of Family	CONDITION	AGE Males	AGE Females	Rank, Profession, or OCCUPATION	WHERE BORN	Whether 1. Deaf-and-Dumb 2. Blind 3. Imbecile or Idiot 4. Lunatic
				Ernest B. Boyd	Son		3			Yorkshire Sheffield	
				Alice M. Do	Dau			1		Do Do	
113	43 Victoria St	1		Ann Moody	Head	Unm		58	Accountant	Do Hurley	Blind Cataract
				Ruth Moody	Sister	Unm		44	Seamstress	Do Sheffield	
114	45 " "			George F. Hodson	Head	Mar	66		Wine Merchant	York	
				Margaret Willshaw	Sis	Unm		22	General Servant	Do Ecclesall	
115	47 " "	1		Joseph Clarke	Head	Mar	57		Commercial Agent	Wilts Chippenham	
				Eleanor Do	Wife	Mar		48		Yorkshire Sheffield	
				Edmund P. Do	Son	Unm	20		Clerk	Do Do	
				William P. Do	Son		17		Student of Chemistry	Do Do	
				Elizabeth I. Do	Daught			13	Scholar	Do Do	
				Lydia J. Do	Dau			10	Scholar	Do Do	
				Beatrice M. Do	Dau			5		Do Do	
				Elizabeth Schofield	Serv	Unm		18	General Servant	Do North Anston	
116	49 " "	1		Edward Lepp	Head	Mar	43		Tobacco Manufacturer	Liverpool	
				Sarah Lepp	Wife	Mar		42			
				Mary E. Do	Dau			11	Scholar	Yorkshire Sheffield	
				Bridget Bambrick	Serv	Unm		40	General Servant	Abby Ireland	
117	50 Victoria St	1		Robert Forbet	Head	Mar	27		Draper	Scotland	
				Jane Forbet	Wife	Mar		26		Scotland	
				John H. Do	Son		5		Scholar	Yorkshire Sheffield	
				Adam Do	Son		3			Do Do	
				Elizabeth J. Do	Dau			2		Do Do	
				Edmund Do	Son		5/12			Do Do	
				Priscilla Platts	Serv	Unm		16	General Servant	Do Do	

| 5 | Total of Houses.. | 4 | | | | Total of Males and Females.. | 10 | 15? | | | |

* Draw the pen through such of the words as are inappropriate.

PUBLIC RECORD OFFICE

Reference:- RG 10/ 4677 f 75 v

A page from the 1871 census.   class mark   piece number   folio number   page number

actual household. If you know only the town, village or area of a city, it's a matter of working your way through the entire piece.

As the capital city, London is a special case. Local and family historians working on it have created a number of indexes and lists of inhabitants.

To find out where your family was living in a census year, it is sometimes better to get the birth certificate of a sibling born in the year of the census rather than the ancestor. This is where death certificates can also be useful. A death certificate might also give the address at which a family was living in which case you can then locate them in a census. You won't, however, know whether the person died at home or in hospital until you've paid for the certificate.

Although marriage certificates give addresses for both bride and groom, you should not rely on this. For a small fee, couples would leave a suitcase somewhere, usually a lodging house in the parish where they planned to marry, and claim to be resident there, thus saving money by having the banns called in one place rather than in two.

If you can't find your ancestor where you expect him or her to be, consider whether they could have been in the workhouse, in hospital or even in prison. Check these places too. If they were simply paying a visit to friends, and so were away from their house on the night of the census, you are unlucky. Check the streets around your ancestor's residence. Most people had relatives nearby and they may have been spending the night with them.

Once you have found out where those ancestors who lived before the advent of civil registration in 1837 were born, go to the parish records to find out more about them.

FURTHER HELP

Gibson, Jeremy and Creaton, Heather *Lists of Londoners* (FFHS)

Gibson, Jeremy and Medlycott, Mervyn *Local Census Listings 1522–1930: Holdings in the British Isles* (FFHS)

Using Census Returns (TNA)

The International Genealogical Index and other indexes

At this stage, you may have enough information to start linking you and your family to information that is already available and to other people researching the same names. Even if you haven't, this is a section to revisit regularly as your research advances – there's no point in laboriously repeating work that someone else has already done. The growth of interest in genealogy has led to the gathering and dissemination of a huge amount of data. It may not be much use to you at this stage in your research, but the sources are described here to encourage you and to reassure you that soon they can be used to reduce the time-consuming record-searching.

One of the granite vaults in Utah where the Church of Jesus Christ of Latter-day Saints stores records and copies of archive material from around the world.

THE INTERNATIONAL GENEALOGICAL INDEX

The International Genealogical Index (IGI) was set up by the LDS. The Mormons believe that, in order to be reunited with their ancestors in the next world, forebears must be retrospectively baptized into their Church. They have a massive programme of entering data on baptisms and marriages. The majority of entries for the United Kingdom are pre-1837 and come from parish and other Church registers. This enormous database has been placed on the Internet but is also available on CD-ROM, and on microfiche held in record offices and libraries. The IGI is most helpful once you get back before the mid-19th century and civil registration.

Names are arranged by county, with all spelling variants listed together. Within each surname, the entries are put in alphabetical order of first and

then subsequent names. Baptisms and marriages are itemized; there are very few burials included.

In some ways the microfiche version of the records is the most useful for the genealogist, since it is easy to get a photocopy from which information can be quickly extracted. You can highlight all the entries before or after a particular date, in a particular place, or all the

children of a particular marriage. This is possible, but more laborious, on printouts from the CD-ROM and Internet versions, and the results are less easy to take in since they do not form a coherent visual pattern.

When using the IGI, there are a number of points to bear in mind. First, its purpose is not primarily for family history: it has been compiled

Records can be sent from Utah to local Family History Centers around the world.

The entrance to the LDS vaults, which are housed within a granite mountain.

for religious reasons, so it does not contain all the information a family historian needs.

Second, there are, inevitably, errors in the data (though this is true of almost all indexes). You must always check the original record, where you may also find additional information. The IGI does not, for example, say whether people getting married were single or widow(er)s of the parish they came from, as opposed to the one where they married. This sort of information will, however, be included in the original record.

Third, although you can, in many cases, compile a rough family tree from the entries on the IGI, not all registers and all dates have been entered. You cannot therefore assume that the John and Mary Smith in a certain village in 1800 are necessarily the ancestors of a John Smith in the same village in 1900. You will need to use other documents before you are able to prove a link.

Finally, the IGI does not include burials, though the word "child" indicates that the person died before the age of eight. This has not been recorded consistently, however, so you cannot always be sure to which entries an early death applies.

The IGI is a finding aid, not a comprehensive record that can be used by itself. With all these reservations, however, it must be said that the IGI is one of the most useful tools a family historian has, so it is worth spending time learning how to use it.

THE ANCESTRAL FILE AND VITAL RECORDS INDEX

In addition to the IGI, the LDS produces the Ancestral File and the Vital Records Index. The Ancestral File contains details of information on CMB from parish and Nonconformist

Using a microfiche reader to search the IGI for family history data.

registers (much of which is also on the IGI) as well as names and addresses of the people who provided the information, generally members of their Church. The Vital Records Index is a database on CD-ROM. It contains lists from records that have been microfilmed.

OTHER INDEXES

There are many other, smaller indexes compiled by Family History Societies and individuals. Some relate to occupations, some are of marriages in a particular area, of criminal records, of inquests, of apprenticeships and so on. They can be recorded on paper, microfiche, microfilm or CD-ROM. Many CROs have copies relating to their areas, and the Society of Genealogists (SoG) library has copies of most of them.

RIGHT GOONS has a website and also publishes material.

FURTHER HELP

Gibson, Jeremy and Hampson, Elizabeth *Specialist Indexes for Family Historians* (FFHS)

THE GUILD OF ONE-NAME STUDIES

An umbrella group of individual societies, the Guild of One-Name Studies (GOONS) consists of members who have an interest in a particular surname. The names vary from the relatively common to the extremely rare.

If you have an unusual name in your ancestry, it is worth getting their directory or logging on to their website (www.one-name.org) to see if one of their members has the same interest as you. Some genealogists also advertise the names they are researching in family history magazines. By getting in touch with them you might save yourself some time-consuming research.

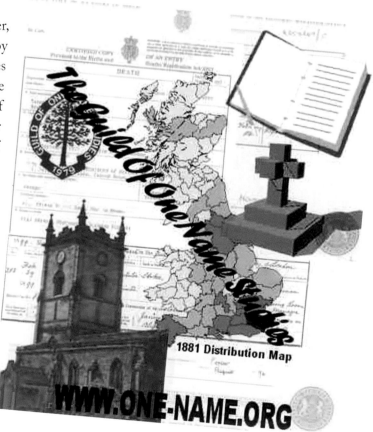

1881 Distribution Map

WWW.ONE-NAME.ORG

Published material

Over the last two decades, a great amount of reference material has been published. The following organizations produce books and booklets on aspects of genealogical records that will help you to find answers to your questions and suggest ways to research information. In addition, there are publishers specializing in books of interest to the family and local historian. Their catalogues are well worth reading for books that may save you doing some research of your own.

THE NATIONAL ARCHIVES

The National Archives (TNA), previously the Public Records Office (PRO), is the repository for govern-

The National Archives is based at Kew, Surrey. TNA, formerly the Public Records Office, produces many useful books and leaflets about the vast number of records it holds.

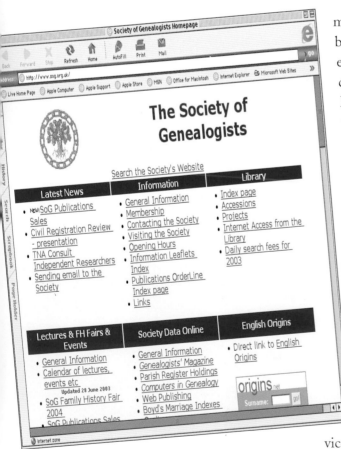

The SoG's website contains details of its holdings, activities and publications.

ment-produced records. It publishes books and research guides on a variety of subjects, concentrating on the different types of records it holds. Its series on the various branches of the armed services are particularly useful. It also publishes *Ancestors*, a magazine for the family historian. Its website contains both the catalogue of its records and leaflets on topics of genealogical research, including its holdings in that area.

THE SOCIETY OF GENEALOGISTS

The SoG has an extensive library of rare books, transcripts of parish registers and documents, archives of family papers and original research, a series of indexes, a book-ordering service and other facilities for the family historian. It also produces a magazine, the *Genealogist's Magazine*, and book-

lets on topics of interest to the family historian. Its series *My Ancestor Was...* is particularly useful. The library catalogue is included on its website, which also has leaflets about aspects of genealogical research. Non-members of the society can use the library on payment of a fee.

THE INSTITUTE OF HERALDIC AND GENEALOGICAL STUDIES

The IHGS concentrates on courses for family historians and genealogists. It has an extensive library, including a heraldic collection.

THE FEDERATION OF FAMILY HISTORY SOCIETIES

The FFHS has an introductory series of booklets on aspects of genealogical research, including the Basic Facts series. It is worth joining your local FFHS because they hold monthly meetings, usually with a lecture on a specialist topic, and most have a computer section where you can get and swap advice. Members may carry out projects to index or reproduce records. Local history societies also host lectures on aspects of local history, which might contain information of use to a family historian with local ancestors.

THE GIBSON GUIDES

Jeremy Gibson has produced a number of booklets, sometimes with a co-editor, published by the FFHS. They detail, county by county, the holdings of record offices on specific subjects, such as coroners' records, poll books and probate. These are known as Gibson Guides. They enable researchers to plan their work in advance by checking whether a record office holds the documents they need to consult. The introductions also give an overview of the records and the kind of information they contain.

PUBLICATIONS

There are many books and booklets available that not only give information about how to do research, and help to track down surviving records, but also suggest further avenues of research.

Magazines

It is worth subscribing to one or more of the magazines aimed at genealogists. They usually consist of articles on how to research a particular aspect of family history, personal accounts of how a genealogical problem was solved, plus topics of general interest, which build up into a useful body of knowledge. They are especially useful for information on aspects of research that might be too rarely encountered to be included in any of the standard books on genealogy, but which are just what you need to solve a problem.

Specialist publishers

Many companies produce books on genealogy and family history, and one of the larger ones is Phillimore.

Since the 19th century the Harleian Society has been publishing transcripts of registers and pedigrees produced as the result of visitations. Although many of the entries in these transcripts have been entered on the IGI, not all are there, and burials have been excluded from it.

The British Record Society also publishes original records. When an interest in genealogy first began in the 19th century, a number of local societies produced transcripts of registers in their area; most County Record Offices have copies of the ones in their counties, and the SoG has a large collection.

Published books and records

Before going to original records, check if what you plan to look at has been published. In many cases the records are simply transcripts, though in some cases they may have been translated from Latin, but it will save you having

to decipher difficult handwriting. The majority of published registers and records have been indexed, making them simpler to search than the original documents.

Do not buy books (including the ones listed in the "Further help" sections in this book), unless it is the only way you can obtain them. It is always preferable to consult them in a library (or borrow them if you can) before deciding how often you will need to use them.

The same is true of indexes: if you only need to look up one person on a CD-ROM, weigh the cost of purchase against that of travel to a CRO or specialist library. Also, check if the information is on the internet.

FURTHER HELP

British Record Society
   www.britishrecordsociety.org.uk
Harleian Society, c/o College of
   Arms, Queen Victoria Street,
   London EC4V 4BT
Phillimore & Co Ltd, Shopwycke
   Hall, Chichester, Sussex PO20
   6BQ www.phillimore.co.uk

If the document you want to see has been published, you may be able to save time and money by getting it through a library, rather than going to a CRO.

Using the internet

Although, in some ways, the internet has made researching family history much easier, the hype around it has raised expectations to an unreasonable level. Although original records are increasingly being digitized and made accessible on it, the majority remain on paper in record offices or have been microfilmed and need to be viewed in an archive or library. What the internet can do, however, is help researchers to locate original documents quickly and conveniently. Most CROs and libraries have a website, and the catalogue of their holdings may be on it. This helps in planning research.

WEBSITES

The websites of organizations of all kinds usually provide a brief history, which will help family historians understand what may be available from its archives and where these are now located. They also give background information that will further your understanding of your ancestors' lives. Many record offices, libraries and museums have on-line fact sheets that you can copy to study at home.

SEARCH ENGINES

A search engine is a way of finding every website that contains the word or words that you enter. They are particularly useful for finding websites on a specific subject, but if you enter just a personal name you will get every site on the web containing that name. If you are researching an individual or a family name, you need to use advanced search techniques. Putting in a common name, such as Johnson, or an ancestor who shares a name with

The internet opens a whole new world of information and allows easy communication with family historians around the globe.

someone famous, such as Elizabeth Taylor, will produce too many irrelevant results. Try adding "family history" – and give dates, places and occupations, and specify the exclusion of certain words, such as "film star".

It is generally agreed that Google is the best search engine, because it arranges the results in order of how frequently they are consulted, but there are many others. If you do not find what you need immediately, it is worth trying searches using two or three search engines. Sometimes, however, you have to accept that the information you need has simply not been researched or put on the web.

In addition to extracting information from the websites of various organizations and individuals (which can contain family histories), there are

also ways of communicating with other researchers. Search engines, such as Google and Yahoo, and genealogical · sites, such as RootsWeb, host groups where people sharing the same interests can exchange information.

E-MAIL

This is the most obvious way of writing to someone who shares the same interests as you. Most individuals who have a website on which, for example, they have placed information about their family history will list an e-mail address, which can be used to communicate directly with that person.

MAILING LISTS

All subscribers receive a copy of every communication sent via e-mail. For some of the larger and more general lists, this can be as many as fifty a day, so consider carefully which mailing list or lists you will find most useful. They have specialist interests: a geographical area; an occupation or group of occupations; ancestors from overseas, etc. The lists are managed by a server, but subscription is generally free.

NEWSGROUPS AND MESSAGE BOARDS

These are the electronic equivalent of a notice board and are also dedicated to particular topics. People can simply post messages, asking for information, recommending (or warning against) professional researchers or websites, or writing about a topic they believe to be of interest. Messages on them are not automatically sent to subscribers, so they need to be checked regularly to make sure something of interest is not

Using the internet wisely

- You may need specific software to access certain types of information on the internet. This can often be downloaded from an internet site, but you should get advice about what is necessary if you are not a confident computer user.
- Be focused: it is very easy to spend a long (and potentially expensive) time going through a lot of unrelated records. Formulate questions and strategies for answering them before you start.
- Regard the internet as a giant index. Like all other indexes, it is basically a guide to original documents.
- Treat information on it with caution: anyone can set up their own internet site and put whatever they like on it. A great deal of supposition might be presented as fact. Ask

yourself: how authoritative is this source?
- Be wary about handing over money on the internet. The reputable genealogical sites, which charge for access to their databases and archives, are reliable and generally safe, but buying objects, such as coats of arms, from sites based overseas can be problematic. You have little redress if the goods are not delivered, and giving credit card details on the internet can present problems of security.
- You will find sites offering books that claim to list all of the people with the same surname as you. These are not researched genealogical publications, but are simply lists of usually unrelated people compiled from readily available sources, such as telephone directories. Ignore them.

FURTHER HELP

Christian, Peter *The Genealogist's Internet* (TNA)
Christian, Peter *Web Publishing for Genealogy* (David Hawgood)
Wilson, Richard S. *Publishing Your Family Tree on the Internet* (Writers Digest Books)

PUBLISHING ON THE INTERNET

As well as using the internet to find and communicate with people with the same research interests, you should consider putting your own family tree and history on the web, so that you can be contacted by others.

Unless you are well versed in this area, you will need help with creating your own website. Investigate some existing sites to get an idea of how best to do it. Look at the sites you find easiest to use and let them guide you in organizing your own genealogical information.

missed. Newsgroups have archives of material that has previously appeared, and it is a good idea to check these out.

NETIQUETTE AND FREQUENTLY ASKED QUESTIONS (FAQS)

There are conventions about communicating on the internet, and if you break the rules you may be excluded from group communication sites. Most will, however, have a list of procedures they expect their members to observe. In particular, people get irritated by beginners posing the same basic questions. To avoid this happening, most sites have a list of Frequently Asked Questions (FAQs) that you should consult to see whether your query has already been answered before you ask it yourself.

The IGI is easily accessible to family historians through the LDS website.

Genealogical sites

The following sites contain information and links for family historians. They all have free information, but some charge for access to certain pages. There is far too much on each site to list the complete contents here, so only the special or most generally useful features are mentioned. The information on these sites is constantly being supplemented, so they are worth checking out at intervals to see what is new. The commercial sites often offer some material free for a limited time.

Cyndi's List *www.cyndislist.com*

This is an American-based site with links to some 140,000 sites worldwide. It is particularly strong on advice about tracing American ancestry. It also contains advice about publishing on the internet.

Family search
www.familysearch.com

This is the on-line database of the LDS. It contains the IGI, which is also available on microfiche or CD-ROM. The microfiche form is often the best format for the genealogist, because it is the easiest to use.

This is a good site for a one-off check or to look at overseas records of events in parts of the UK that may not be available in other formats at a local record office or library. The library catalogue can identify which copies of records it holds, and you can request film copies to be sent to your local Family History Center, where you can view them. You can find the address of your nearest LDS Family History Center on this site.

RootsWeb www.rootsweb.com

An American-based site with links to other sites, this also hosts message boards, mailing lists and newsgroups. There are a number of volunteer projects providing indexes to various types of documents and records. Two of these projects have particular importance to genealogists with UK interests. The first is freebmd, which contains the indexes to BMD

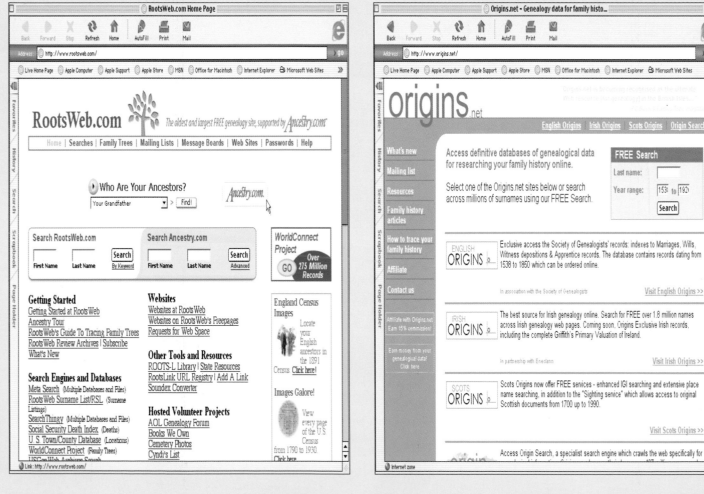

RootsWeb was one of the earliest sites set up for family historians and hosts some volunteer projects to put information on the web.

The Origins site is devoted to British genealogical material from England, Scotland and Ireland.

certificates at the FRC that are more than 100 years old. The second is freereg, which is an index of CMBs in both parish and Nonconformists registers.

Origins www.origins.net

This is a site containing on-line British databases, divided into three sections: English, Scottish and Irish. Fees are charged for access.

English Origins www.englishorigins.com

This website contains indexes from the SoG, including marriage licences, apprenticeship records and PCC wills for the period 1750–1800.

Scottish Origins www.scotsorigins.com

This contains many documents, including parish registers, census returns and wills. It also hosts a discussion group.

Irish Origins www.irishorigins.com

This has census data, Griffith's Valuations, ships' passenger lists and church records. It also hosts a discussion group.

Genuki www.genuki.org.uk

This site contains links to all the CROs in the UK, Family History Societies and one-name groups. It also hosts mailing lists for individual counties.

Familia www.earl.org.uk/familia

This is part of the public library network devoted to genealogical sources in Britain and Ireland. It also has links to a variety of related organizations, including museums and professional researchers.

Ancestry www.ancestry.com

This is a commercial site, so it charges fees for access to most of its records. It contains mainly American data, such as the censuses there, but has information from a number of British sources, which are largely taken from publications not easily accessible outside major libraries. It also has Pallot's Marriage and Baptism Indexes (1780–1837).

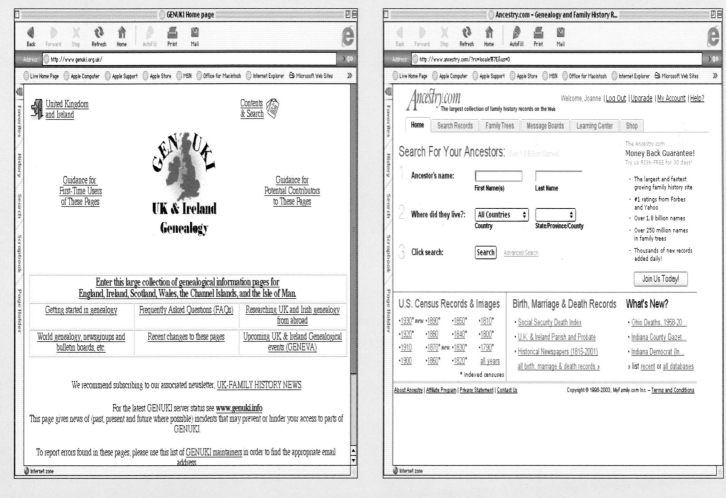

Genuki has links to many genealogical organizations and record offices in the United Kingdom and Ireland.

Ancestry has copies of material from around the world that might not be easily accessible locally.

Wills, administrations and death duties

I t is often said that you can't take it with you, and wills were made to ensure that a person's possessions went to particular individuals after death. If anybody died intestate (without leaving a will), someone had to be appointed to administer the estate. These administrations (or admons) contain much less information than a will and were usually granted to the next of kin.

WILLS

Most people are familiar with the phrase "last will and testament", which shows the distinction made between land, which cannot be moved, and other goods, which can. The will covers the disposal of estates and property; the testament deals with movable goods, chattels and money.

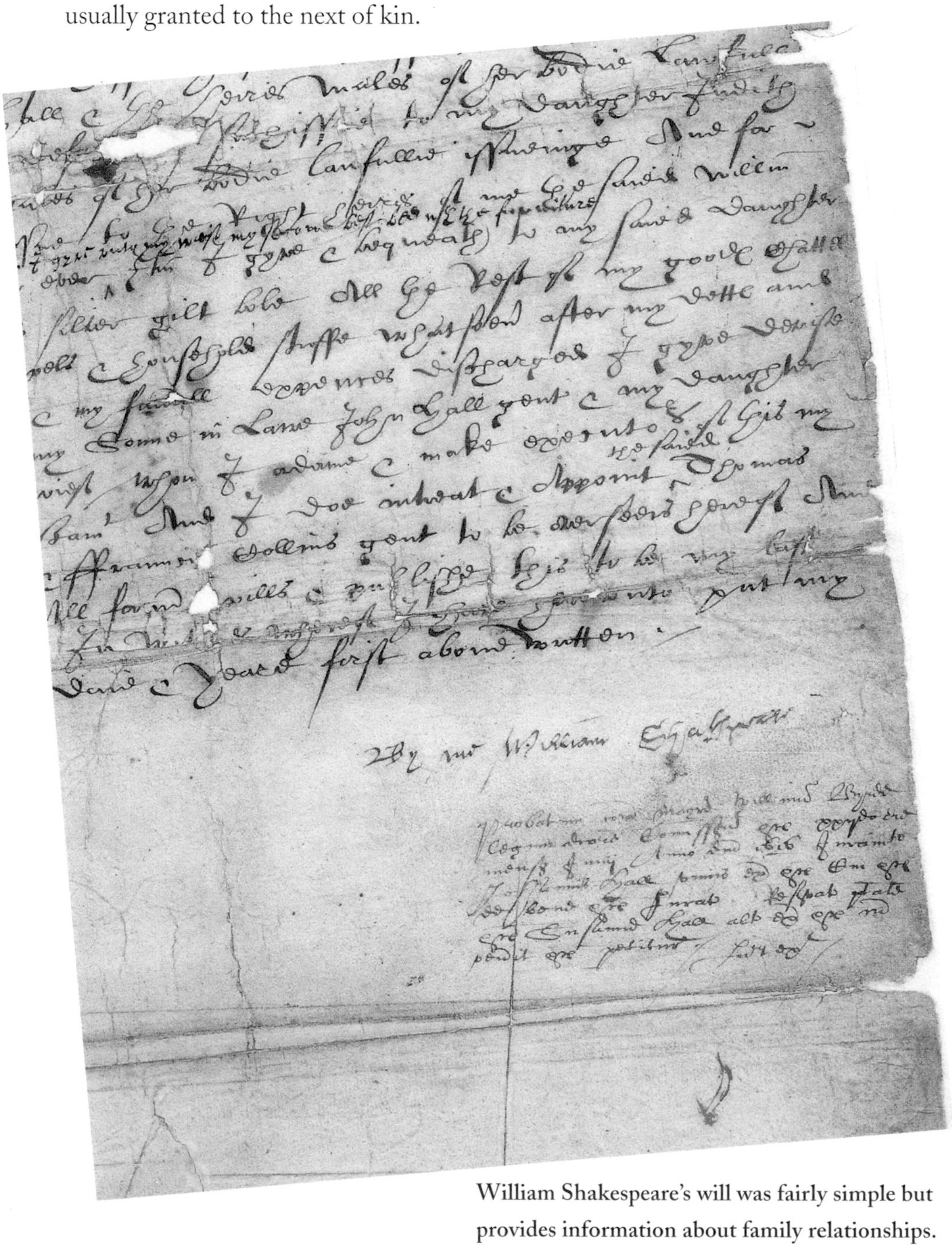

A history of wills

Until 1858, when a national system was introduced, probate was mainly administered by church courts, but "peculiars" and some manors also had the right to prove wills. During the Commonwealth period (1653–60) a government court handled them.

Nuncupative wills

Before 1838, when nuncupative wills became illegal, a statement of how a person wanted to dispose of his or her possessions could be accepted. They were usually dictated when the person was dying and there wasn't enough time to call in a lawyer or someone experienced in writing a proper will. Although it was witnessed, it was not signed. Such wills usually start with "Memorandum", rather than stating that this is a last will and testament, and are found with the other wills of the court in which they were proved.

Wills before 1858

Before 1858 the proving of wills was done by church courts, which all charged for this service. It has been estimated that in the 19th century only 5 per cent of people's estates went through probate, so the family historian must be prepared not to find a will. When they do exist, however, they can supply a great deal of information.

Wills after 1858

After 1858 the authenticity and validity of wills were proved by the state system on a national basis. The will was taken to the local probate office, which made its own copy and then sent another to the Principal Probate Registry in London, now called the Probate Service of the Principal Registry Family Division. In addition to being the

William Shakespeare's will was fairly simple but provides information about family relationships.

probate office for the south-east of Britain, it also deals with wills that present problems from everywhere in the country, and so is a national centre too. The original will was given back to the executor(s) after a note that probate had been granted was added to it. This conferred on the executor(s) the power to administer the estate.

Locating wills

When trying to find a will before 1858, decide how much property was likely to be left, as this should suggest which level of court to start with, but don't assume that a poor person's will would not have been proved in the Prerogative Court of Canterbury (PCC). Check all the courts (see below).

For 1796–1858 the death duty indexes may be a faster way of finding a will than working your way through the various probate courts. These indexes cover all courts before 1811, and after that date each court has its own index. They are especially time-saving if you don't know the exact date on which a will was proved.

Some East India Company (EIC) wills are kept in the Oriental and India Office Library, so those with ancestors living in India, the Far East and other places under the EIC's authority before 1858 might find their wills here.

Indexes to wills for the period 1858–1943 are in the FRC, although the wills themselves are held by the Probate Service. Copies can be obtained by post or a personal search.

If you don't find a will in the area you expect, ask yourself if your ancestor might have died in a "peculiar" (a parish that, for historic reasons, came under the authority of another bishopric or body from the one in which it was geographically located).

Probate could take many years to prove, especially if there were any

The reading of a will might cause dissatisfied family members to challenge its contents through one of the courts that dealt with probate.

difficulties with the will, if it was challenged by the family or if the person lived overseas. In the days before air travel, it could take many months, even years, before the executor(s) might be able to travel to England to prove the will.

If your ancestor was a soldier or sailor, check TNA first. Soldiers and sailors were encouraged to make wills before going overseas, especially in times of war.

Find as many wills as you can for all members of your family, not just your direct ancestors. Married men usually left simple wills, dividing their property between their wives and children. More information may come from the wills of unmarried or childless relations, since they tend to distribute their possessions among a greater number of relatives, and they state the relationship. Maiden aunts are a particularly good source of genealogical information. They may not necessarily have been very rich, but they did like to specify just who would receive a particular piece of jewellery or small sum of money.

If a will isn't listed, see if there is a separate list of administrations. (Sometimes the two are given together; sometimes they are in separate registers.)

The courts you will need to check for wills are listed below.

The archdeaconry courts
These courts were the lowest in the hierarchy and were used by people with property in one archdeaconry. These wills are usually in the CRO but may be in a Diocesan Record Office (DRO).

The diocesan courts
Also called consistory or commissary courts, these came under the jurisdiction of a bishop and were used by people who had property in more than one archdeaconry. These wills are usually in the CRO but may be in a DRO.

The Prerogative Court of York (PCY)
The PCY had jurisdiction north of the River Trent. It covered the dioceses of York, Carlisle, Chester, Durham and the Isle of Man, and wills of people who had property in more than one of these dioceses would have been proved here. These wills are in the Borthwick Institute in York.

The funeral of the Marquis of Bath in 1869. How many of the hundreds of people gathered here were remembered in his will?

The Prerogative Court of Canterbury (PCC)
The PCC was the highest court to prove wills in England and Wales. It was used by those who had property in more than one diocese south of the Trent, or with property in both the PCY and PCC jurisdictions. There was a misapprehension that money invested in the Bank of England counted as property. The bank was sited in the diocese of London, so people who lived elsewhere and had money invested in the bank had their wills proved in the PCC, because they believed that they had property in two dioceses.

The PCC also covered British subjects living abroad in the colonies (including America before the War of Independence, which finished in 1783). During the Commonwealth period (1642–60), all wills were proved in the PCC. Copies of these wills are in the FRC on microfilm, but the originals are stored off site.

All the courts were subject to inhibition from the senior courts. This means that if a bishop were making a visitation to an archdeaconry, the archdeaconry courts would not be able to carry out their functions, including proving wills. So during the time of the visitation (which usually lasted for a few months), wills would be proved by the diocesan courts.

In addition to these courts, there were "peculiars" (see previous page), which came under the jurisdiction of someone or some entity other than a court. This might be a manor, a university, the dean and chapter of a cathedral, or the bishop or archdeacon of another diocese.

A sailor's will might be proved in the court connected to the place where he lived in England or Wales; in the archdeaconry or diocesan court of the port in which his ship docked after his death; in the PCC if he died at sea, or in the High Court of the Admiralty.

Of course, wills sometimes created strife in the family, and might have been contested. Any action of this kind will be found in the courts attached to the jurisdiction where they were proved.

Researching wills

To be legal, a will must include one or more executors or executrices (the feminine form of executors). It must also be dated and the signature witnessed by two or more people who must not benefit from the will. If someone dies intestate (without leaving a will), the next of kin can ask for Letters of Administration to be granted so that they can deal with the deceased person's property. These are

---

Digest of will of Sarah Deschamps

PRO PROB 11/995/87
Sarah Deschamps of Maiden Lane, St Paul Covent Garden, widow of Peter Deschamps

To be buried with late husband at Marylebone

To John Deschamps eldest son of my late husband £10

To Francis Deschamps younger son of my late husband £10

To Mrs Susanna Montelln wife of Mr Joseph Montelln

and the daughter of my late husband £10 and my wearing apparel

Remainder to my worthy and most esteemed friend and executrix Mrs Mary Bonouvrier of Maiden Lane

(signed) 15 July 1767

wit: Sam Coates

Mary Hawkes

Proved PCC 12 March 1774

abbreviated to "admon" in records. Also, if the will has not been properly drawn up, for example it was not dated, the next of kin can apply to administer it.

It was, and is still, not necessary to rewrite an entire will in order to vary slightly the bequests within it. The addition of one or more codicils to the will of a member of your family is an interesting source of information about who came into, or fell out of, favour over time.

An inventory – a list of the movable goods of a person – is sometimes attached to a will. This gives clues as to how rich he or she was and also, in the case of men, what their occupation was, since it usually includes his tools.

Be aware that the word "cousin" was used in a much wider sense in the past than it is today. "My cousin Elizabeth" was not necessarily the daughter of an uncle or aunt: she might have been a much more distant relative. All you can tell without further research is that a cousin was a relation of some kind.

If you see that one person, often the eldest son, has been given only a token sum, usually a shilling, don't assume that this is evidence of trouble in the family. He might have already been given a sum of money on marriage or have taken over the family business. Mentioning the person in the will simply showed that he (or occasionally she) had not been forgotten, and so the will could not be challenged on those grounds.

Making a digest of a will

Wills tend to be long and are couched in complicated legal terms, and it is time-consuming and confusing to keep re-reading them to find information. You do need a complete copy of the document for your records, but a digest (a brief summary, in note form, of the contents) is ideal and convenient for everyday use.

Put where the will comes from, with any reference number given to it by the repository. Enter the person's name, occupation and residence, as given in the document. You can omit the standard opening, but note down any special instructions about funeral arrangements, and so on. Then list all the legatees, their relationship to the testator, what they received and any special conditions attached to the bequest. Also note the name(s) of the executor(s) and whether the testator actually signed the will or simply made a mark (which shows how literate he or she was). Write the date the will was written and the witnesses' names. Add the details of when and where it was proved.

ADMINISTRATION

When a will was found to be valid and proved in court, the executor(s) had to sign a bond for a sum of money that would be forfeited if they did not carry out their duties of administering the estate according to the testator's final wishes, as expressed in the will.

If the deceased person had children who were under the age of majority, it was also the executor(s) job to arrange for their ongoing and future education and welfare by entering into tuition and curation bonds, which were pledges to pay a sum of money if these arrangements were not satisfactory. How this was to be done, including the name of any guardian, may have been stipulated in the will. The bonds that were associated with these various duties should be with the other probate records.

Incomplete or non-existent wills required Letters of Administration to be issued before the estate could be administered.

Some places, such as London, had the right to administer the goods of the orphans of freemen through special courts. These records are separate from the probate courts.

DEATH DUTIES

From 1796, various taxes, called collectively "death duties", were payable on estates worth over a certain amount. Initially this was set quite high, but during the 19th century it was progressively lowered, so that a larger proportion of people's estates had to pay duties. The records relating to these and associated matters are held in TNA, with indexes held at the FRC. They are particularly useful in giving the exact amount that an estate was worth. The death duty registers also contain further information, added for many years after the will was proved, such as the dates of death of beneficiaries, which will also help the family historian with research.

Inquests

If a person died in a way that gave rise to suspicions that the death might not have occurred naturally, then an inquest was held. In addition, inquests on all deaths in prison had to be held, even if it was obvious that the person had died from natural causes.

Even if your ancestor was very law-abiding he might have found himself, (or, more rarely, she might have found herself) imprisoned for debt. If he became ill and died while still in prison, an inquest would have been held and the results recorded in the prison inquest records, which makes such records always worth consulting.

ROLE OF THE CORONER

The office of coroner is first mentioned in 1174, though the post itself seems to be much older than that. The coroner had many legal and political responsibilities, but his main function was to look after the Crown's interests, especially in the event of a death. If a person was murdered, the murderer's property was forfeited to the Crown, so the death had to be investigated to see if any property or money could be confiscated. In medieval times the coroner had many duties, but over the centuries his responsibilities were gradually reduced.

OTHER INQUEST ROLES

There are a number of ways in which an ancestor might have been involved in an inquest, and so appear in the records, apart from being either the coroner or the deceased person.

Member of the jury

Once notified of a death that needed investigation, the coroner drew up a list of potential jurors. The parish beadle then visited all the people on the list to call them to serve. Most of the jurymen were respectable tradesmen. Any compensation they received came out of public money, and they were not

A coroner's inquest held at Charing Cross Hospital, London, in 1861. Inquests might also be held at inns, workhouses or prisons.

usually paid for their attendance before the first quarter of the 19th century. Even after this, individual counties had different practices (London did not pay until the end of the century). It was not, therefore, a popular duty, because they would lose business. Sometimes they paid substitutes to attend in their stead or simply pretended not to be at home when the beadle called.

Publican

Until the middle of the 19th century, the majority of inquests were held at a local inn, so, if you have publicans among your ancestors, it is possible that an inquest was held on their premises. Inquests were also held in hospitals and workhouses, which might have involved members of your family in some way.

Doctor

A doctor had to confirm the death and give an opinion about its cause.

Witness

People who had witnessed the death were called to give evidence. These could include members of the dead person's family, neighbours, friends, medical staff at hospitals, workhouse officials, prison workers and even passers-by.

EVIDENCE OF TREASURE-TROVE

The only other major example of the coroner's role in looking after the Crown's financial interests that survives to the present day is the investigation of treasure-trove. If a hoard of gold, silver or bullion is discovered and the owner cannot be identified, then a coroner must hold an inquest to determine whether it was accidentally lost, in which case it becomes the property of the finder, or if it was deliberately hidden, in which case it becomes the property of the Crown. An ancestor's sudden increase in wealth might be due to hard work, an inheritance or gift, criminal activity or the discovery of treasure-trove. The latter is rare but still worth considering. There are papers relating to treasure-trove for 1825–1925 in TNA. Others should be with surviving inquest papers in CROs.

RESEARCHING INQUEST RECORDS

Whenever you go to a record office, check whether it has any surviving inquest papers. If a death took place in the parish where your ancestors were living at a particular time, it is worth checking to see whether a member of your family was involved as a juryman or, if any of them was an innkeeper, as the proprietor of the place where the inquest was held. They might also have given evidence.

When a verdict that resulted in a trial was passed, always follow this up in criminal records. Although the same evidence as was given at the inquest will be repeated, more evidence might have been discovered by the time the trial took place, so the criminal records will give you more information about what happened. You may also find that the trial jury passed a different verdict from that given at the inquest. There were a number of possible verdicts:

- "Visitation of God" (short for "Visitation of God by natural causes") was used for sudden deaths, such as from a heart attack or stroke.
- "Natural causes/natural death" was used to refer to long-standing illnesses such as tuberculosis, or diseases such as smallpox or cholera.
- "Mishap", "casual" or "misfortune" included in a verdict meant that the death was accidental.

- "Murder" and "manslaughter" are self-explanatory.
- "Justifiable homicide" was used when a person, such as a soldier, had grounds to believe that his life was in danger and so killed in self-defence.
- "Want of the necessities of life", which means starvation, shows how hard life could be for the poor.
- "Inclemency of the weather" (what we would call "exposure") might have been the verdict passed on a beggar who died outside on some frosty night or on someone who fell from his horse on his way home and died from the effects of cold.
- "Suicide". If the jury decided that the person had committed suicide, they had to decide whether he or she was sane at the time. People who were "lunatic" (as it was generally called) could be buried with full rites in a churchyard or burial ground. If, however, they were found to be in full possession of their faculties, a verdict of *felo de se* (literally, self-murderer) was passed. Until 1823, a *felo de se* suicide was buried at a crossroads, often with a stake through the body. After 1823, although the person could be buried in a churchyard, the burial had to take place between 9pm and midnight and was without a burial service. Until 1871 the suicide's property was forfeit to the Crown.

Where jurors could not decide why the death occurred, they passed an open verdict, such as "Found dead", or a narrative verdict, such as "Died from a fall".

FURTHER HELP

Gibson, Jeremy and Rogers, Colin *Coroners' Records* (FFHS)

Newspapers and periodicals

Early newspapers were primarily concerned with politics and did not necessarily appear on a regular basis. When something noteworthy happened, enterprising writers and printers would produce a sheet of paper or a small pamphlet describing events and adding editorial comment. The English Civil War, which began in 1641, produced a number of them, some supporting the King, others the Roundheads. Other newspapers, called broadsheets from the size of the paper used, reported sensational events, such as murders. The British Library has a large collection of them, and they are also available on microfilm.

USING NEWSPAPERS FOR RESEARCH

Newspapers, especially local ones, may contain information about ancestors or be used to find out about life in the past.

The *Weekly Telegraph* was one of the many publications aimed at a mass readership.

Early newspapers mainly covered political and commercial matters.

The London Gazette

The *London Gazette* is the Crown's official newspaper, produced by the government since 1665. It lists government appointments and promotions; bankrupts (which other papers, especially *The Times,* reprinted); promotions, medals and other awards made to members of the armed forces, and other miscellaneous notices.

County newspapers

In 1702 the first daily newspaper, the *Daily Courant,* appeared. Other national papers were also founded about this time, and in the mid-18th century county newspapers, usually published weekly, began to appear. These regional publications were aimed at the ruling classes, and much of what they reported concerned the political events in Westminster, and other London news. They also reprinted stories from other counties.

They had, however, some stories of local interest, such as proceedings in criminal courts (for example the quarter sessions or assizes) and inquests. Counties that had a significant sea trade also reported the comings and goings of ships, which might be of interest to those with sea-faring ancestors. Newspapers with an agricultural readership reported farming prices.

Many local newspapers have been at least partially indexed. The standard way to give references is title, date, page, column (*The Times* 27 Feb 1891 4f).

The Times

The Times has been published since 1785 (when it was called the *Universal Daily Register*) and is indexed. Not every single name, however, appears in the index. You might find that something in which your ancestor was involved, such as the opening of a hospital, will appear, but that not all the

A paperboy invites people to "Read all about it!" By the mid-19th century, an increasing number of people could read.

individual people mentioned in the report will be found in the index. In cases such as these, the name of the hospital would be included, so you would need to check all the references to it in the hope that your ancestor was mentioned somewhere. Obituaries have been indexed separately.

In addition to looking up your own ancestors, who might have been involved with a big incident, you can use *The Times* index as a way of finding out when something occurred. The event might be reported at greater length in another national, regional or local paper, to which you can refer later, but you can use *The Times* index to find the exact date.

The introduction of illustrations

Although early broadsheets included woodcuts, they were not the equivalent of photographic representations. They were often standard blocks, of a hanged criminal, for example, which were reused. It wasn't until the mid-19th century that sketches of people and events began to be included. The *Illustrated London News* began in 1842.

From the beginning of the 20th century, technological advances meant that photographs could be used, but the process was expensive and time-consuming, so they were confined to publications with a large national circulation. As technology improved, local newspapers began to use photographs extensively.

Finding old newspapers

The British Library Newspaper Library is the best source of British newspapers and also has a substantial number of overseas publications. A reader's ticket is needed, but one can be issued on the spot on the production of proof of identity. Its catalogue is on-line.

CROs, local history centres and libraries usually have county and local newspapers. Find out in advance which papers they hold and for which dates: some have copies of early newspapers that are missing from the British Library Newspaper Library's collection.

Individual newspapers and periodicals also have their own archives, but they may not be willing to let you search through them.

Press guides, listing newspapers and periodicals, began in 1846. These are useful to find the titles of publications that no longer exist or to track down the kinds of periodicals to which a journalist ancestor might have contributed an article. The British Library Newspaper Library has a complete set of *Willings Press Guide*, and there may be copies in university and other libraries. The British Union Catalogue lists publications (apart from newspapers after 1799) and where copies are available in record offices and libraries.

USING PERIODICALS FOR RESEARCH

Daniel Defoe, now remembered as a novelist, most notably for *Robinson Crusoe*, was for most of his life a prolific journalist, who started the first periodical, called the *Weekly Review*, in 1704. It was followed by the *Tatler* in 1709 and a host of others.

Then, as now, these periodicals were not reporting the news so much as commenting on it for a small circle of like-minded people drawn from the same social background. Similarly, the *Gentleman's Magazine*, which contains BMD notices and obituaries, was a kind of parish magazine for the upper classes. It was published during 1731–1868 and has been indexed. These were the first of a long line of political and social weekly or fortnightly magazines.

The *Methodist Magazine* began in 1798 and was followed by other periodicals aimed at members of religious denominations. Trade journals aimed at people working in particular occupations began with the *Naval Chronicle* in 1799. Later, magazines aimed at leisure interests began to appear.

Published from 1758, the *Annual Review* is a summary of items from the previous year, taken from newspapers and magazines.

The *Illustrated London News* was one of the first publications to include pictures.

Other countries in the British Isles

The countries that make up the British Isles differ in ways that the researcher needs to know about, because they may affect the type of records that have been kept and where they are found today. Some have a different language, others have separate laws and all have traditions that must be taken into account.

Welsh records

Wales has effectively been under British rule since medieval times, so the kinds of records found are the same as in England. The exception is land inheritance. By a Welsh tradition called "gavelkind", which ceased with the Act of Union of 1536, a man's property was divided between all his sons, rather than left to the eldest son. This led to people owning smaller and smaller parcels of land, which eventually became uneconomic and had to be sold. Since 1536, inheritance laws in England and Wales have been the same, so the family historian will find the same kinds of records in both countries.

INVESTIGATING BMD AND OTHER RECORDS

BMD certificates began in 1837, and the indexes are in the Family Record Centre (FRC). Other records are much the same as in England.

ABOVE Although Wales has a strong individual identity, in its public record keeping at least it is the same as England.

BELOW Carreg Cennen is one of the many castles built by Edward I of England in his efforts to rule Wales.

Parish records

Following the 1536 Act of Union, the law was the same in both countries, and therefore Welsh parish officials had the same duties and kept the same kinds of records in Wales as their counterparts did in England.

By the mid-19th century, some 80 per cent of the Welsh population was thought to belong to Nonconformist churches, mainly Methodist or Baptist, with a small Catholic community. This means that most of them will not be found in parish registers, apart from those that married between 1753 and 1837. They will, however, appear in other parish records, such as settlement and bastardy examinations, workhouse minutes, etc.

Wills

There are four bishops' dioceses in Wales: Bangor (including Anglesey), St Asaph, Llandaff and St David. Wills not proved in the Prerogative Court of Canterbury (PCC) were mainly proved in the diocesan courts. (The archdeaconry courts were less important for probate matters than in England.) Only in the archdeaconry of Brecon, in the see of St David, was there a consistory court proving wills. There was only one "peculiar" in Wales – the parish of Hawarden, Flintshire – which had the right to prove its own wills. Some Welsh parishes fell within the diocese of Hereford, so the wills of their inhabitants are kept in the Hereford and Worcester County Record Office (CRO).

Only a small number of Welsh families remained Roman Catholic after the Reformation, but their numbers

Understanding Welsh family names

The small number of names shared by a majority of the population meant that many people acquired an extra name to distinguish them from other people with the same name in the same locality. This might be a mother's name, making hyphenated or double names quite common in Wales, or it might be a geographical location or an occupation, such as Jones of Mostyn or Jones the Baker. This helps the researcher to distinguish between individuals in records, but can become confusing with the next generation, since a child would not necessarily inherit the extra name but might acquire one of his or her own instead. This practice of using patronymics rather than fixed surnames did not fully die out until the advent of civil registration in 1837.

were swelled in the 19th century when many Irish Catholics came to the industrialized parts of Wales.

INTERPRETING THE LAW

Although Wales had its own legal system before the Act of Union in 1536, since that date the law has been the same as it is in England.

The Poor Laws

It seems that in Tudor times the Poor Laws operated only in Monmouthshire, and in many of the more sparsely

ABOVE Just as in England, Welsh counties have their own CROs, in which are held the wills of their inhabitants.

populated parishes poor rates were not collected until 1755. The poverty stricken in many places therefore relied on charity and the support of landowners rather than parish relief. The Napoleonic Wars from the end of the 18th century led to an increase in the collection of rates.

Assize courts

From 1542 to its abolition in 1830, the Court of Great Session sat twice a year in each of the Welsh counties, with the exception of Monmouthshire, which was excluded from 1689. From 1831 there were two circuits, North and South Wales, and from 1945 Wales and Chester.

LOCATING RECORDS RELATING TO WELSH ANCESTORS

Since England and Wales have the same government, many of the official records relating to Wales are found in The National Archives (TNA).

Those searching for Welsh ancestry will find the National Library of Wales (NLW) is also a good starting point. Although the Welsh counties do have individual CROs, the NLW has copies of parish registers as well as

diocesan records, court papers, newspapers and other material covering all the counties collected together in one place. Documents relating to manors, estates and other property in Wales may be here or in TNA.

RESEARCHING WELSH ANCESTORS

The ancient Palatinate of Cheshire, whose records are in TNA, included the old Welsh county of Flintshire, so it is possible you may find some relatives recorded there.

The area around the border between Wales and England is known as the Welsh Marches, and if your ancestors lived here, it is probably worth checking for missing ancestors in the records of the neighbouring English counties.

The Welsh courts went on returning coroners' inquests to the assize circuits well into the first part of the 19th century, long after the English courts ceased to do so. These records, which are in TNA, are therefore worth consulting for the genealogical information they might contain.

FURTHER HELP

Hamilton-Edwards, Gerald
In Search of Welsh Ancestry
(Phillimore)
National Library of Wales,
Aberystwyth, Ceredigion SY23
3BU www.llgc.org.uk/. A reader's
ticket is necessary to use the
library. It is one of the copyright
libraries in the British Isles, so
publishers should have deposited
a copy of all new books there.
Rowlands, John and Rowlands,
Sheila *Welsh Family History:
A Guide to Research* (FFHS)
Rowlands, John and Rowlands,
Sheila *Second Stages in
Researching Welsh Ancestry*
(FFHS)

Scottish records

Before the Act of Union in 1707, Scotland had a separate parliament from England and Wales. After nearly 300 years, its own parliament was restored in 1999. Scotland had, and still has, a different legal system to the rest of Britain, which affects the types of records that are kept.

INVESTIGATING BMD AND OTHER RECORDS

Civil registration was introduced in 1855. Scottish certificates contain the same information as those south of the border, but with a few major, and useful, additions regarding BMD.

Birth certificates

On a child's birth certificate, the date and place of the parents' marriage is entered. This was dropped between 1856 and 1860. In the first year of registration (1855) only, the ages and birthplaces of both parents and details of their other children (if any) are recorded. All birth certificates also include the time of the child's birth, not just (as in England and Wales) if it was a multiple birth. For those genealogists who are interested in astrology, this presents an opportunity to have a full birth chart drawn up. There is an index of adopted children from 1930, though this does not contain the names of natural parents, and one of stillbirths from 1939, though the latter is not on open access.

Marriage certificates

The names of both parties' fathers and mothers (with maiden names) are included on marriage certificates. They also, until 1922, state whether

New Register House in Edinburgh, designed by Robert Adam, holds BMD records and parish registers for Scotland.

the bride and groom were related and what the relationship was. In Scotland, a legal marriage could be contracted by agreement before witnesses or a sheriff, and the certificate will show whether the couple were married in church (the officiating minister would have signed the certificate) or by agreement. Certificates drawn up in 1855 only will also give details of previous marriages, any children and the birthplaces of both parties. There is a register of divorces from 1984.

Death certificates

In addition to the information given on death certificates in England and Wales, these contain the names of the deceased's father and mother (including her maiden name). In 1855, certificates also noted the deceased's birthplace and how long he or she had been resident in the place where they died, plus the names of spouses (including maiden names) and children, with their ages. For 1855–1861, details of the burial place and undertaker were noted.

Parish registers

When civil registration began in Scotland, the parish registers of the Church of Scotland parishes were called in. These are known as the Old Parochial Registers. Although some began in 1558, registers were generally not kept until about 1750 in the Highlands. Most were indexed by the original compilers, but in a variety of sometimes confusing and unhelpful ways. The Church of Jesus Christ of Latter-

---

Understanding Scottish family names

Before the 20th century, the Scots had a fairly standard pattern of naming children, which may give clues to the names of grandparents:

- eldest son was named after the paternal grandfather
- 2nd son was named after the maternal grandfather
- 3rd son was named after the father
- eldest daughter was named after the maternal grandmother

- 2nd daughter was named after the paternal grandmother
- 3rd daughter was named after the mother

It was also quite common to create girls' names by adding "-a" or "-ina" to a man's name, e.g. Jacoba, Jamesina, which in some cases seems to have been done when there weren't enough sons in the family to commemorate the male relatives.

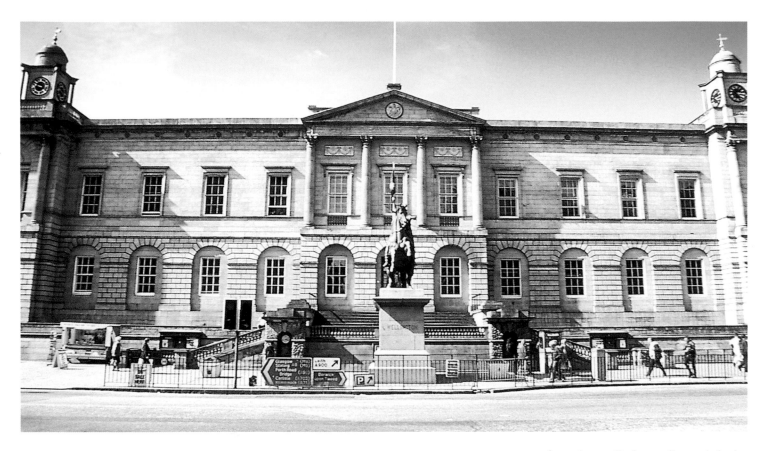

The National Archives of Scotland in Edinburgh, formerly the Scottish Records Office, holds a wealth of material on Scottish ancestors.

day Saints (LDS) has produced a better index of baptisms and marriages on CD-ROM and the internet. Many have also been published by the Scottish Record Society. Some do not include the actual details of a service but do, in the case of marriage, include notice of the intention to marry.

The registers contain relatively few burial records, but might have a note about the hiring of the mort cloth – a cloth to cover a body. They do, however, usually give the names of godparents in the entry for a baptism.

Many Scots were Nonconformists, mainly Presbyterian. There was also a strong Catholic presence in Scotland, particularly among those of Irish origin who migrated in the 19th century.

Testamentary records

The inheritance of land and buildings in Scotland was according to laid-down rules, not the owner's personal whim. This meant that only movable property could be left at death, with the details recorded in a document called the testament.

Before 1823, Scotland was divided into areas called commissariots, which were roughly the equivalent of a bishop's diocese, where testaments were proved. The Commissariot of Edinburgh had both local and national jurisdiction, as well as over those Scots who died overseas. Most testaments have been indexed. If heirs were under the age of majority, the commissary courts could appoint guardians of their interests, called tutors. Even though rules on inheritance were clear-cut, there could be disputes about the provisions of a testament, which would be heard in the court in which the wills were proved.

If someone died intestate, a testament dative, including an inventory of the deceased's possessions, was drawn up. A notice, called an edict, might be nailed to the church door requesting anyone who had an interest in the deceased's goods to attend a commissary court hearing. These notices appear in commissary court records, to which other documents relative to the matter should be attached.

Sheriff's Courts took over the administration of testaments in 1823 and continued to do so until 1876, when a national system was instituted.

Armorial bearings

The Lord Lyon King of Arms has jurisdiction over all matters relating to armorial bearings, and the records of the Lyon Court contain much information about pedigrees. Ancient heraldic material is often worth researching, as it is not only the wealthy and nobility who are entitled to bear and apply for arms.

The interior of the impressive dome of the National Archives of Scotland.

Service of Heirs and Register of Sasines

The Service of Heirs relates to the inheritance of property other than land and generally states the relationship of the person who inherited it to the deceased. The Register of Sasines relates to the inheritance of land and dates from 1617.

These are the major differences to be found between family records in England and Wales and those in Scotland. Other information relating to family history, such as apprenticeships, freemen, criminal and civil proceedings, will be found in the equivalent Scottish records.

INTERPRETING THE LAW

Scotland has a separate legal system from the rest of the UK. The differences of most interest to genealogists relate to wills and inheritance of property, but other areas, like family law, will need to be considered and investigated when doing research.

The Poor Laws

Before 1845, the Scottish Poor Laws were administered by parish officials, and references to relief may be found in the minutes of Kirk Sessions. After 1845, Parochial Boards were set up in each parish. Lists of people receiving assistance in their homes and those who had entered the poorhouse were compiled. Some children, invalids and lunatics were placed in private homes to be cared for, and the board made reports on them.

Courts

The lowest level of criminal courts is the Sheriff's Court (which also had jurisdiction over some civil matters). Appeals from here went to the High Court of Justiciary (the highest criminal court in Scotland), which dealt with serious crimes. The statements of witnesses, called precognitions, are held in the records of the Lord Advocate's Department, but there might be copies of some with the papers of the Sheriff's Court. There are few surviving precognitions before 1812.

In some places, a particular person held a franchise from the Crown that gave him jurisdiction over both civil and criminal matters in a specified area.

Before the Act of Union in 1707, which led to its abolition in the following year, the Scottish Privy Council dealt with criminal cases, generally among the higher echelons of society. The Admiralty Court, abolished in 1830, had jurisdiction over the high seas and harbours.

Fatal accident inquiries

Scotland did not have a system to investigate suspicious deaths. Any that resulted in legal action will be found in the criminal courts, but there were no investigations into deaths through, for example, suicide or misadventure.

From 1848 there are records in the Lord Advocate's department of inquiries into accidents, and after 1895 Sheriff's Courts had, by law, to conduct inquiries into fatal accidents.

LOCATING RECORDS RELATING TO SCOTTISH ANCESTORS

The genealogist tracing Scottish ancestry has a great advantage over those doing research elsewhere in the British Isles, because BMD certificates after 1855, census returns, and parish registers before 1855 of the Church of Scotland are all kept in the same record office at New Register House in Edinburgh. The records of the Lord Lyon King of Arms are also located here.

Other registers of Nonconformist and Roman Catholic churches are stored next door in the National Archives of Scotland (NAS). It also contains testamentary records (not wills) and minutes of Kirk Sessions, which contain information about illegitimacy, irregular marriages, claims for poor relief and the like. It is also the major repository for local and national government records, including law courts and business archives. The Scottish Archives Network has a database of wills covering 1500–1875.

FURTHER HELP

Ferguson, Joan P. S. *Scottish Family Histories* (National Library of Scotland): a compilation of printed books, pamphlets and articles, and where they are found, about individual Scottish families.

General Register Office (Scotland), New Register House, Edinburgh EH1 3YT www.gro-scotland.gov.uk/

National Archives of Scotland, HM General Register House, 2 Princes Street, Edinburgh EH1 3YY www.nas.gov.uk/: has information leaflets about its holdings, which are also available on-line.

Scottish Association of Family History Societies www.safhs.org.uk

Sinclair, Cecil *Tracing Your Scottish Ancestors in the Scottish Record Office* (National Library of Scotland)

Despite being housed in a historic building, the National Archives of Scotland has modern facilities and a vast collection of records.

Most, but not all, of the records of the courts dealing with testaments have been deposited in the National Archives of Scotland. From 1876 an annual calender of testaments was compiled, and this is also in the NAS.

The miscellaneous indexes at the NAS contain a Marine Register of births from 1855, listing the births of children on British-registered vessels if the father was Scottish. There are also registers of BMD in foreign countries during 1860–1965; in the High Commissioner's Returns of BMD from 1964; in Air Registers of Births and Deaths from 1948; in Service Records from 1881; in Consular Returns of BMD from 1914 and in Foreign Marriages from 1947.

After 1707, the armed forces covered the whole of the British Isles, so records relating to Scottish soldiers, sailors and airmen will be found in The National Archives of England.

Irish records

The family historian researching Irish ancestry faces a number of problems. The first is that the majority of the population was Roman Catholic, and their registers did not begin until late in the 18th century. The second is the relatively few number of surnames shared by most of the population. The third is that the Irish Public Record Office, housed in Four Courts, Dublin, was destroyed by protestors against British rule in 1922. Very few of the contents, which included about half the Church of Ireland parish registers, census returns, wills and other government records, survived.

Four Courts, Dublin, was bombarded during the 1922 uprising, and many records were destroyed.

INVESTIGATING BMD AND OTHER RECORDS

After 1922, BMD records are complete but, as the country was then divided into two, these and other records are in different places.

Civil registration

Civil registration of all BMD began in Ireland in 1864, but non-Catholic marriages were registered only from 1845 onwards. The partition of Ireland has meant duplication of material between the two General Register Offices. Records up to 1922 are held in the General Register Office (GRO) in Dublin. After that date, it holds copies of records in Northern Ireland. The GRO (Northern Ireland), in Belfast, is a separate register office. It holds BMD records for Northern Ireland from 1922 onwards and copies of indexes to pre-1922 events. There are also Marine, Consular, and Foreign Marriage Registers of BMD relating to Irish people at sea or overseas in both offices. After 1922, laws on registration of events such as stillbirth, adoption and illegitimate children were different in Eire and Northern Ireland.

Parish registers

The Church of Ireland served a small percentage of the population, mainly the Protestant middle and upper classes. As mentioned above, about half their registers from before 1870 had been deposited in the Dublin Public Record Office and were destroyed. However, others had remained in their own churches; some transcripts of these had been made before the registers were surrendered, and others had already been published. The surviving material, in addition to parish accounts and other documents, are scattered among various locations. The records of parishes that no longer exist, for example, have been deposited in the library of the Representative Church Body.

Between 1915 and 1922, proof of age in order to claim benefits might be extracted from Church of Ireland parish registers, and the forms to do this, which contain parents' names, are preserved in the National Archives.

Unlike the Church of Ireland, the Roman Catholic Church did not have a role in local government, and so it did not need to keep registers in the same way. Most baptisms and marriages took place in the priest's home or in the home of the family. Catholic registers did not begin until the middle of the 18th century in towns and the 19th century in rural areas. Most original registers remain with their churches, but the majority has been copied on to films, which are held in the National Library. Some burials of Catholics took place in Church of Ireland burial grounds, depending on the attitude of the minister.

Other denominations, such as the Nonconformists (Baptists, Congregationalists, Huguenots, Lutherans,

Methodists, Moravians, Presbyterians and Quakers) and Jews, kept their own records. Although all the original registers of the Huguenot churches were destroyed in 1922, they had already been published. Other records are deposited in various archives or remain with their congregations, but many have also been copied.

Wills

Between 1536 and 1858, wills were proved in Church of Ireland ecclesiastical courts. The senior court was the Prerogative Court of Armagh, which had jurisdiction over all the commissary courts (there were no archdeaconry courts in Ireland) but was inferior to the PCC. People with property in both Ireland and England would therefore have had their wills proved in the PCC, and those records are in the Family Record Centre in London.

After 1858, the proving of wills was taken over by the government. Transcript copies of wills proved in local registries were passed to Dublin, where an annual index was made. The original wills, before and after 1858, were deposited at Four Courts, and so destroyed in 1922, but the indexes, which give some useful information, have survived and so have the post-1858 transcript copies from the registries outside Dublin.

Between 1858 and 1876, the Principal Probate Registry in London had an additional section at the end of its indexes, which included some Irish probate records dealing with people who owned property in both Ireland and England.

INTERPRETING THE LAW

Ireland had its own parliament, but all of its activities had to be approved by the British government. Although the majority of the population was Roman Catholic, laws were passed at various times to penalize them and prevent them from holding office of any kind. This discrimination finally ended in 1829, although some provisions had been repealed at different times before that date.

Land records

The paucity of registers and the destruction of many documents mean that much information about Irish family history will come from records relating to land tenure. Most land in Ireland was owned by a relatively small number of people and let out on leases. Private estate papers may contain information about tenants. Because they are private papers, they may be with the original owners or in a number of repositories in Ireland or mainland Britain. During the famine years, many landowners abandoned their properties and left Ireland.

Registry of Deeds

The Registry of Deeds was set up in 1708, primarily to stop Catholics acquiring land. A variety of documents, including wills, land transfer documents, mortgages, marriage settlement letters and share sales, are included in these records. They mainly relate to upper-class Anglo-Irish families, and so are not typical of the average inhabitant. Registration was not compulsory, so not every transaction will be here.

As the laws on Catholics were relaxed towards the end of the 18th century, more people were able to lease or own land. The records are in the Registry of Deeds, in Dublin, where there is an index containing abstracts of the documents.

Ejectment books

Before a landlord could eject tenants from his property, he had to obtain a court judgement, and ejectment books summarizing these cases provide much information of use to genealogists, especially those whose ancestors emigrated. Not all have survived (there seem to be none, for example, from Northern Ireland), but they are worth checking out.

The famine of the 1840s created a huge increase in ejectments, but this was not entirely a case of hard-hearted

The Irish potato famine led to widespread poverty and eviction.

landlords throwing out starving people. The landlords had to pay rates on their land, and, in order to help the increasing number of poor, the amounts rose. Those with land-owning ancestors may find their problems reflected in ejectment books.

The Incumbered Estate Court

From 1849, if bankruptcy resulted, the landlords' estates were disposed of in the Incumbered Estate Court, which dealt with the auction of lands. This was renamed the Landed Estates Court in 1858. In 1877, it became part of the Chancery Division of the High Court in Ireland. Here it was called the Land Judges' Court, and continued until 1880. Records are in the National Archives of Ireland. Much valuable information, including maps, is given in the sales catalogues (called rentals) produced when landowners had to sell, these are in the National Archives, the National Library or the Public Record Office of Northern Ireland (PRONI).

Other sources

Ireland possesses records giving the same kinds of genealogical information as the rest of the British Isles, such as courts, apprenticeships, freemen, commercial and trade directories, and so on. Newspapers and magazines, especially the *Hibernian*, will provide additional facts, but it is mainly the well-to-do and criminal classes that are recorded in them.

Tithe Plotment Books

Compiled in the 1820s and 1830s, Tithe Plotment Books cover landowners and primary tenants in parishes. The LDS has filmed these records, so they are available through their Family History Centres and in a number of record offices.

LEFT **After eviction, an Irish peasant would have little with which to start again.**

Griffith's Primary Valuation

Information about landowners and occupiers in the mid-19th century was issued in stages for 1848–1864. This publication's official title is *General Valuation of Rateable Property*, but it is generally known as Griffith's Primary Valuation, after the commissioner who was responsible for carrying it out. The surveys largely took place after the Irish famine, and so are valuable for allowing the family historian to see who survived or remained in Ireland. Almost every head of a household is listed in these surveys.

Land Commission

The 1881 Land Act set up the Land Commission, which originally determined fair rents. Its work developed into helping tenants purchase their property. These records are currently in the Irish National Archives, but public access to them is restricted. A summary of the Commission's documents is held in the National Library.

LOCATING RECORDS RELATING TO IRISH ANCESTORS

Listing where in Ireland your ancestors were before and after 1922 will make locating records easier.

Census returns

A few records of censuses before 1901 survived the 1922 destruction: there are fragments from 1821, 1831, 1841 and 1851. The pre-1851 censuses in Ireland contained more information than their English or Scottish equivalents. In addition to the original records, there are some forms relating to information from searches made in the census records, which were used by elderly people to prove their ages in order to claim old age pensions after 1908. The 1901 and 1911 censuses

survived and are open to researchers, but you do need to know where your ancestors were living in those years.

Heritage Centres

The increasing growth of interest in family history led to the setting up of Genealogical Indexing Centres, also called Heritage Centres, around Ireland. These centres index and computerize church registers and other records in their area. The public is not allowed access to the databases, but information from them is provided for a fee. They are useful if you know at least the county from which your ancestors came.

Service records

Records for the Irish branches of the armed services are in TNA.

Education records

Charter schools began in 1731, and by the beginning of the 19th century there were a variety of private, Church and "hedge" schools in Ireland. Hedge schools, which dated from medieval times, educated children in Gaelic, which was the first language of most Irish people until the 19th century. They declined for a number of reasons: the growth of state-run education, which was in English; the recognition that, in order to succeed professionally, people needed to speak English; and the emigration of many of the poorer Irish citizens.

The National Board of Education (Ireland) began state-run schools in 1831. Information from school logbooks, where they survive, can substitute for the destroyed censuses. Although the schools were non-denominational, their records include a note of the children's religions. When and why children left the school is also entered, and this may give useful information about families who emigrated.

IRA forces fought a bitter struggle with the British in the streets of Dublin in 1922.

Records of university graduates from Ireland's main universities have been published. Although Roman Catholics were officially barred from universities until 1793, some seem to have received a university education before this date and are noted as "RC" in the registers.

FURTHER HELP

General Register Office, Joyce House, 8–11 Lombard Street East, Dublin 2, Eire www.groireland.ie

General Register Office (Northern Ireland), Oxford House, 49–55 Chichester Street, Belfast BT1 4HL www.groni.gov.uk

Mac Conghail, Maire and Gorry, Paul *Tracing Irish Ancestors* (Harper Collins)

National Archives of Ireland, Bishop Street, Dublin 8, Eire www.nationalarchives.ie

Public Record Office of Northern Ireland, 66 Balmoral Avenue, Belfast BT9 6NY www.proni.nics.gov.uk

Representative Church Body, www.ireland.anglican.org

RESEARCHING IRISH ANCESTORS

The destruction in 1922 of Four Courts in Dublin, which contained centralized records, means that it is essential to find out where in Ireland your ancestors originated. If they emigrated to England, Wales Scotland, or overseas, this may come from census returns (although many people simply entered "Ireland" on the return) and settlement examinations. Those who entered the armed services will also have their birthplace entered in records. It is worth remembering that the Republic of Ireland was neutral during World War II.

When civil registration was introduced in 1864, a fine was payable if a birth was not registered within three months, so poor people might have adjusted the date of a child's birth to avoid a penalty. Roman Catholics would, however, have had the child baptized within a few days of birth, either at the priest's house or their own home, so it is worth cross-referencing the civil and church records if you can.

Channel Islands records

The Channel Islands came under British rule with the accession of William the Conqueror in 1066, and they retained both a system of law very different from that of England, especially in respect of land inheritance, and a form of French as the inhabitants' first language. As a result, the majority of earlier records are in French.

Many of the islands' inhabitants were involved in the fishing industry. Their proximity to the West Country in England, where fishing was also a major industry, means that there was a fair amount of interchange between the two places.

A number of Huguenots emigrated from France to the Channel Islands, and refugees from the French Revolution also settled there. Although the islands have their own dialect, the language was similar enough for them to have integrated easily.

During the French and Napoleonic Wars, the islands were heavily garrisoned to keep them out of French

LEFT The castle above Gorey Harbour in Jersey was built to defend the island from seaborne invasion.

BELOW LEFT The French failed to gain control of the Channel Islands in the late 18th century.

hands. A number of soldiers and sailors married local women. A local militia was also raised, and many of its records are in TNA.

During World War II, the Channel Islands were occupied by the Germans. There are a number of books on this period.

Guernsey

Civil registration of births, deaths and non-Anglican marriages began in 1840, but all marriages did not have to be registered until 1919.

During the 19th century, accounts of strangers, or etrangers, were kept, which included passenger lists. These will be found among the constable's records in each parish.

The island's Archives Office, the Greffe, contains the registers of BMD and wills from 1841. It also contains the records of St Peter Port's Hospital, which was built in 1741 and served both as a place to treat the sick and a workhouse. The records cover 1741-1900. Records for the prison, known as the House of Separation, also survive.

Jersey

Civil registration of BMD began in 1842. Before that date, information was recorded in parish registers. Jersey has separate archives for civil registration from 1842 (which are in the Superintendent Registrar's) and other records (in the Judicial Greffe).

Before 1602, matters concerning land were arranged verbally in front of witnesses, generally after church services. The Land Registry was then set up to document transactions. On the death of a landowner, his estate would be divided between his children, with the eldest son receiving the largest

share. Wills of Realty, relating to land and buildings, date from 1851 and are deposited at the Land Registry, while Wills of Personality, covering money and movable goods, are in the Probate Registry. Both have been filmed by the LDS. Legal courts covered inheritance, crime, civil cases, small debts and bankruptcy.

Refugees from the French Revolution in 1789 came to Jersey. They established a Roman Catholic congregation, which was later joined by an influx of Irish immigrants. Many of these left for America from the 1870s, when there were financial problems and the work dried up in the Channel Islands. A chapel was built in 1825 and two other churches in 1867 and 1877. The surviving registers of all three have been transcribed and deposited in the Channel Islands Family History Society's archives and the Société Jersiaise. There is an index.

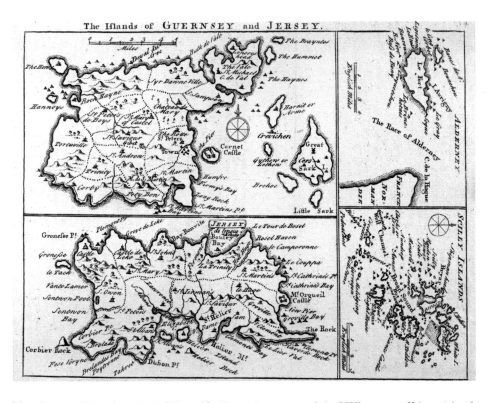

The Channel Islands and the Isles of Scilly are just some of the UK's many offshore islands.

Alderney

The civil registration of births and deaths dates from 1850, and marriages from 1886.

Many of Alderney's earlier records seem to have been destroyed during the German occupation in World War I. Those that have survived (apart from censuses) have been copied by a local volunteer. Enquiries are routed through the Greffe in Guernsey.

Sark

The island of Sark was uninhabited until 1563, when the Seigneur of St Ouen in Jersey moved there with his family and a number of followers to prevent it being taken over by the French. They were joined by other people from Guernsey and Jersey and a few from the English mainland. A small Huguenot community established itself there in 1570.

The island still has a feudal system of land tenure. Inheritance laws are very strict, so relatively few people made wills. The records of Sark are accessed through the Greffe in Guernsey. Civil registration of deaths began in 1915, marriages in 1919 and births in 1925.

RECORDS RELATING TO ANCESTORS FROM THE CHANNEL ISLANDS

Although there are copies locally, TNA holds census returns. It also has some records of BMD notified to the British authorities between 1831 and 1958. The Bouillon Papers contain information about refugees from the French Revolution who went to Jersey. The Chelsea and Greenwich Hospitals' records contain information about retired soldiers and sailors living in the Channel Islands and receiving a pension from them. A particularly useful source is the Association Oath Rolls of 1696 for Guernsey and Jersey, since they constitute a virtual census of the adult male population of the islands at that date. There are also documents relating to the rental of Crown lands in Alderney for 1832–1961.

Isle of Man records

The Isle of Man was ruled by Norsemen from the 10th century, until the King of Norway sold it to Scotland in 1266. In 1341, it came under English control, but the feudal system of land and property laws remained in force until 1867. Tenants paid for land owned by their lords by handing over part of the produce of their holding and by doing work for the landowner.

The Isle of Man is self-governing and levies its own taxes. Its legislative body, the Tynwald, is divided into an upper and a lower house. Otherwise, the Isle of Man came under English rule, so the administrative system of parishes is the same. It forms the diocese of the Bishop of Sodor and Man.

Manx, a form of Gaelic, was spoken on the island until the 18th century, but legal and official documents were written in English. This language gradually took over, hastened by the

ABOVE The Isle of Man's ancient Scandanavian heritage is celebrated at the annual Viking Festival.

BELOW Viking ship-burials are no longer practised, only recreated at festivals commemorating the Isle of Man's past.

introduction in 1872 of free elementary schools, where the teaching was in English. The last mother-tongue speakers died in the 1940s.

INVESTIGATING BMD

Civil registration of births and deaths began in 1878 and of marriages in 1884. From 1849 there are some certificates of Nonconformists' marriages, obtained by those who did not wish to be married in a parish church. Wills were proved in ecclesiastical courts until 1884, when a system of civil probate was instituted.

LOOKING FOR MORE SOURCES

As elsewhere in the United Kingdom, property records and local newspapers are a vital source of information about Manx ancestry.

Property records

The Isle of Man's feudal system of land tenure means that land records are essentially the same as manorial records. They are recorded in books called Libri (from the Latin for books): Libri Assedationis contain rent rolls, while Libri Vastarum contain details of admissions of landowners to property and the fines and rents they paid.

Composition Books contain descriptions of individual holdings and fines paid on them. They were no longer kept after 1704, when some of the more feudal rights of the lord were removed, though some remained.

Newspapers

Local newspapers started around the beginning of the 19th century. Before then, the *Cumberland Pacquet* carried

some Manx news. Copies are held in the Heritage Library, as well as in the British Library Newspaper Library at Colindale in London.

LOCATING RECORDS RELATING TO ANCESTORS FROM THE ISLE OF MAN

The National Archives holds records of the Isle of Man's government and government employees, armed services, and assize records. It also has documents relating to land rented from the Crown for 1832–1954 and pensions paid to ex-servicemen living there. It may also hold wills of inhabitants proved in the PCC before 1858.

The Manx National Heritage Library is the equivalent of the CRO and holds copies of the surviving church registers, which are all indexed on the International Genealogical Index (IGI), as well as copies of the census returns (the originals are in TNA, with filmed copies at the FRC). The 1881 census is recorded on the

CD-ROMs produced by the LDS. The Heritage Library also holds copies of wills before 1910 and property records, including a large collection of deeds between the late 17th century and 1910, which were enrolled with the local courts. Wills proved after 1916 are in the Registry, as are deeds after 1910.

When plans to destroy the majority of Merchant Navy crew lists held at the Registry of Shipping and Seamen were announced, due to lack of space, the Heritage Library managed to save those relating to Manx ports, and these have now been indexed. In addition to Manxmen, there are many sailors from Ireland and Scotland in these records.

During the two World Wars, there were internment camps on the Isle of Man holding German and Italian men. The records are in TNA.

ABOVE Germans in a camp at Douglas during World War I. These internees were kept occupied by making brooms.

LEFT Mooragh camp, an internment camp set up during World War II, is now a public park.

FURTHER HELP

A good site for the history and records of the Isle of Man is on www.ee.surrey.ac.uk/Contrib/ manx/famhist/genealgy
General Registry, Finch Road, Douglas, Isle of Man www.gov.im/infocentre
Isle of Man Family History Society www.isle-of-man.com/ interest/genealogy/fhs/
Manx National Heritage, Douglas, Isle of Man IM1 3LY www.gov.im/mnh
Narasimham, Janet *The Manx Family Tree: A Guide to Records in the Isle of Man* (Isle of Man Family History Society)

Working lives

Only a small proportion of the population did not need to work for a living. Most of our ancestors worked long hours for many years – there were no old age pensions or an official retirement age until the 20th century. From their first days at school, people were preparing to enter the workplace. What future did their working lives hold – a steady rise to professional status and wealth, or poverty and ruin resulting from accident, illness or misfortune?

Education

Before the 20th century, relatively few people needed to be able to read and write, since there were plenty of jobs that did not need literacy or numeracy. Indeed, many of the upper classes resisted plans to educate the poor, fearing that teaching them these skills would make them dissatisfied with their lives and lead to social unrest.

PRIMARY AND SECONDARY EDUCATION

Education was, until comparatively recently, not seen as the responsibility of the state. It was up to individuals to arrange for their children's education, and there were a variety of different ways to deliver it.

Early schools

There was a strongly defined hierarchy to the education provided for children in the past. Grammar schools, many of which were founded in the 16th century under Edward VI, and public schools, such as Eton, had originally been intended for poor children but were quickly taken over by the rich. The better-off sections of society employed tutors or governesses for their children. Among the middle and lower classes, it was mothers who were expected to teach their children to read and write. The children of tradesmen also learned account-keeping, either from their parents or from someone paid to teach them.

There were, in addition, a variety of schools, most of which were established as charitable foundations by either an individual or a religious organization, such as the Society for Promoting Christian Knowledge. Many

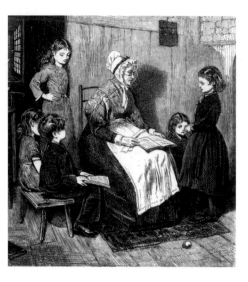

had distinctive uniforms, such as the blue coats and yellow stockings of Christ's Hospital in London. Cathedrals also had (and still have) schools for choristers, who were, until the end of the 20th century, always male. Nonconformists also established schools to educate their children. What all schools had in common was that they based their education on religious faith.

There were a few occupational schools before the 19th century. Most of these, such as Christ's Hospital in

London, were connected with the sea. Although most pupils at this establishment had a general education, the boys in the mathematical school were specifically prepared for their apprenticeship to sea captains.

Schools in the 19th century

Dame schools, usually run by a single woman, started from the 1830s. The standard of teaching was variable: some were little more than child-minding services so that mothers could work, but others did provide a basic education, mainly in reading and, for girls, sewing. It was not until the beginning of the 19th century that proposals for a national system of education were made. The first was in 1802, but the government was reluctant to get involved until 1870, when the Education Act obliged local authorities to provide education, which was made compulsory.

Schools to educate children and young people who had committed petty crimes or who were deemed

ABOVE LEFT
Dame schools provided a basic education for those whose parents could afford a few pence a week.

LEFT Sunday schools, set up by churches, were another source of education for poor children.

likely to get into trouble were started around the beginning of the 19th century. In addition, Magdelen Hospitals, which attempted to reform prostitutes, often educated the women they took in, many of whom were very young, then tried to place them as servants.

Other establishments, known as reformatories, Certified Industrial Schools or Day Industrial Schools, educated children and trained them in a skill that would help them to obtain employment. In 1933, they were renamed Approved Schools.

Schools in the 20th century

The 20th century brought various changes in education, but these largely built on the work done in the 19th century. The major difference was the 1944 Education Act, which made primary and secondary education free to all, and set up grammar, technical and

After 1887, delinquents could be sent to special schools instead of being imprisoned.

secondary modern schools for children over 11. Comprehensive schools, from the 1970s, no longer divided children according to academic ability.

The place of girls

Most education was given to boys, because they were expected to earn a living, in order to support their families, when they grew up. Girls' education was considered to be of secondary importance. Small private schools, some of which took boarders, taught girls accomplishments designed to help them attract a husband. These were set up from the late 18th century and taught reading and writing; some history and geography; a little fashionable French and/or German; and a musical instrument, usually the piano. During the 19th century, the number of these schools increased, but it wasn't until the end of the century that a few with academic ambitions for girls were started. The number increased throughout the 20th century as the need for women to earn a living, both before and after marriage, was recognized.

Significant dates in the history of primary and secondary education

1780 Sunday School Movement began.

1802 Act for the Education of Apprentices stated that apprentices should have at least an hour a week's religious instruction on Sunday. They were to be examined by the parish minister.

1810 Ragged Schools, free to very poor children and orphans, began. They encouraged practical skills and expected their pupils to earn money from a very early age by cleaning shoes or running errands.

1811 National Society for the Promotion and Education of the Poor founded with the aim of providing a school in every parish.

1814 British and Foreign Schools Society founded to provide schools with a Nonconformist ethos.

1833 The government awarded a

grant of £20,000 to introduce denominational schools. In 1839, inspectors were appointed to ensure that the money was being properly spent. The grant was increased in 1850, 1858 and 1861, when pupil teachers were introduced. These were bright pupils who were paid to work and train as teachers for five years, getting a certificate for each year successfully completed.

1857 Industrial Schools set up to educate delinquents in a trade. They were also called reformatories.

1861 Payment by results introduced. Schools received 4s for each pupil who attended and 2s 8d for each subject passed by each child in the annual examinations. This led to a national syllabus.

1870 Education Act made education compulsory for children

under 10. It was free to the poor, but others paid a small weekly fee.

1893 School leaving age raised to 11.

1899 School leaving age raised to 12.

1902 Local Education Authorities (LEAs) replaced the old School Boards and received increased powers.

1908 Borstals for delinquent children replaced reformatories.

1944 Education Act created grammar, technical and secondary modern schools. The 11-plus examination was introduced to decide which type of school each child should attend.

1947 School leaving age raised to 15.

1974 School leaving age raised to 16.

Locating school records

From 1862, all schools had to keep logbooks, and references to individual pupils can be found in them. You may also find admission books and attendance registers, which were begun in order to record the number of pupils. Some local authorities gave awards for good attendance.

The managers of the school (later known as the governors) kept minute books, which may also have survived. These deal largely with administrative matters and should include information about children punished for bad behaviour. School magazines and ex-pupils associations' newsletters may provide further useful information.

Some school records remain with the schools themselves; others have been deposited in County Record Offices (CROs), and those for Church schools may be located through the denomination's archives. Dr Williams's Library holds information on some Nonconformist schools. Many of the registers of the early grammar, charity and more up-market schools, such as Wellington and Haileybury, have also been published.

Researching school records

The following points should help you in your research:
- In census returns, school children were noted as "scholars".
- If your ancestors lived in a large town or city, you may find directories useful to locate the nearest school to their home, then find the records.
- As well as the child's date of birth, father's name, address and previous school, admission books usually record the date and reason a child left, if this was before the school-leaving age. This could give clues to when your ancestors moved house.
- Events in schools are usually well reported in local newspapers from the end of the 19th century.
- Many schools have honours boards, which list pupils who went on to higher or further education, and Rolls of Honour, which list ex-pupils and teachers who died while serving in the World Wars.

TERTIARY EDUCATION

Before the 19th century, any form of higher education at universities was the preserve of the wealthy or the very clever, who managed to get scholarships, although this would only be with considerable support from a teacher or patron. Most universities and some colleges have published lists of their graduates.

Universities

Until 1836, there were only two universities in England: Oxford and Cambridge. Scotland had four: St Andrews, Glasgow, Edinburgh and Aberdeen, and there was one, Trinity College, Dublin, in Ireland. These all had their origins before 1600. Those people who could not accept the tenets of the established Church, such as Nonconformists, Roman Catholics, Jews and others, were barred from these universities. If your ancestors were not members of the Church of England, they are unlikely to have gone to the established universities, so you need to look elsewhere for records of their tertiary education.

Catholic tertiary education

Catholics often sent their children to the Continent for both secondary and tertiary education. Some lists of

St Paul's School in London had an imposing classroom where boys received a classical education.

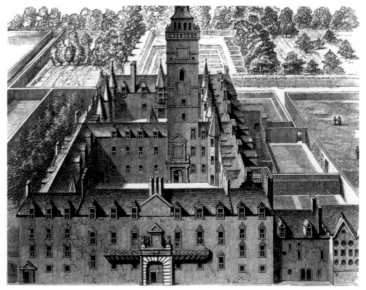

The great respect for education in Scotland meant that Glasgow University was one of four founded here before 1600.

Significant dates in the history of tertiary education

The list of institutions included here is not exhaustive: many large hospitals trained doctors and nurses, for example. Also, all the many denominational colleges are excluded.

1167 Oxford University founded.

1209 Cambridge University founded.

1411 St Andrews in Scotland founded.

1451 University of Glasgow founded.

1495 University of Aberdeen founded.

1583 University of Edinburgh founded.

1593 Trinity College, Dublin founded.

1663 First Dissenting Academy founded.

1799 Royal Military College Sandhurst set up to train Army officers.

1804 East India Company started two establishments – one for its army, the other for its civil servants.

1820s Mechanics Institutes and Working Men's Institutes started to hold classes in the evenings for men. Most were on technical subjects to help them progress at work, but there were also lectures on cultural matters.

1844 Royal Agricultural College, Cirencester, founded.

1855 The Jews' College (later renamed the London School of Jewish Studies) founded to train Orthodox rabbis. It is now part of the University of London.

1869 Girton College for women founded. It moved to Cambridge University in 1873.

1879 Lady Margaret Hall and Somerville, the first two women's colleges of Oxford University, founded.

1889 Technical Instruction Act made provision for the establishment of part-time and evening classes to provide technical and occupational qualifications.

1903 Founding of the Workers Educational Association.

Catholics who graduated overseas have been published by the Catholic Record Society.

Nonconformist tertiary education

A few Dissenting Academies were established after the mid-17th century, and from the 18th century more and more Nonconformists founded their own denominational colleges and academies. Most were started to train clergymen, but others existed to provided a university-level education for those who, for religious reasons, could not go to the established universities. London University started out by awarding degrees gained through a number of colleges and institutions, such as the Inns of Court and medical schools, which later joined together under its aegis.

The admittance of women

Towards the end of the 19th century, women began the fight to enter higher education, and colleges for them were founded within universities.

Teacher training colleges

Pupil teachers in elementary (now primary) schools started work at about 14. Some were apprentices, but most were simply children in the school who showed an interest in and aptitude for teaching.

The first teacher training college for primary teachers was started in Glasgow in 1837. From the early 1900s, Local Education Authorities set up day training colleges, and universities established departments of education, which catered for both primary and secondary school teachers.

Alternative further education

Before the advent of grants for tertiary education, most working-class people could not attend university. Even if a child was able to get a scholarship, poor families depended on their children's income, and so needed them to work. The answer was night school. Most taught commercial practical skills that would improve the students' job opportunities, but the Workers Educational Associations aimed to provide classes in a variety of subjects for those who had not been able to pursue their education while younger.

FURTHER HELP

British & Foreign Schools Archives Centre, West London Institute of Higher Education, Borough Road, Isleworth, Middlesex TW7 5DU

Catholic Education Council, 41 Cromwell Road, London SW7 2DJ

Chapman, Colin R. Basic Facts *About Using Education Records* (FFHS)

Dr Williams's Library, 14 Gordon Square, London WC1H 0AG

Methodist Church Division of Education & Youth, 2 Chester House, Pages Lane, London N10 1PZ

Ragged School Union (now incorporated into the Shaftesbury Society), 10–20 Kingston Road, London SW19 1JZ
www.shaftesburysociety.org.uk
Minutes of both organizations have now been issued on microfilm.

Apprenticeships

The majority of children started work between the ages of 12 and 14. Many went into domestic service (before World War I this was how most people began their working lives), but others were apprenticed to learn a trade.

APPRENTICESHIPS BEFORE THE 19TH CENTURY

In 1563, the Statute of Artificers laid down that no one could practise a certain occupation without serving at least seven years as an apprentice and

BELOW Apprenticeship indentures included strict conditions about how the apprentice should behave.

until reaching the age of 24. In 1768, this was reduced to 21, and the statute remained in force until 1814, although by that time enforcement of it had become rather lax. The 1563 legislation also applied only to occupations then in existence. As other trades started, the requirement that practitioners should serve an apprenticeship in full was not enforced in many cases.

If the master could not complete the full term of training, arrangements were usually made to find another master to complete the apprenticeship. This was known as "turning over".

There were three distinct kinds of apprenticeship:

- voluntary apprenticeship, where the child was placed by its parents
- Poor Law apprenticeship, where parish authorities placed a child in the master's care
- apprenticeship to a guild or livery company of a town or city

Voluntary apprenticeship

This was a private arrangement, usually made by parents on behalf of their child. They paid someone a fee to cover the cost of tuition as well as the apprentice's keep while he or she was learning. Both parties signed a legal document called an indenture, which had two parts. One part was kept by the parents and the other by the master.

If children were apprenticed to their father, mother or another relative, there was only a token fee.

Between 1710 and 1808, apprenticeship premiums over 1s were taxed. The records, which actually finish in 1811, are in The National Archives (TNA). Until around 1752 they contain the parents' or guardian's names. There are indexes up to 1774 to both masters and apprentices in TNA, the Guildhall Library and the Society of Genealogists' library. Poor Law apprenticeships were exempt, so will not appear here, nor will the apprenticeship of a child to a father.

Poor Law apprenticeship

It was the responsibility of the overseer of the poor for each parish to provide for orphans and those children whose parents were too impoverished to care for them. The 1601 Poor Relief Act allowed parish officers, with the consent of Justices of the Peace (JPs), to bind a child under the age of 14 to a master (either a man or woman). This was not a proper apprenticeship, and was called an "apprenticeship binding". Often these hapless children were simply used as unpaid labour rather than being taught a skill.

In 1696, it became compulsory to take apprentices in this way, and masters were selected in rotation or chosen by ballot. Apprenticeship bindings lasted until 1834. Since 1662, serving a full term of apprenticeship had given settlement rights in a parish, and so officials tried to find masters outside their own parish, in order to evade potential responsibility for the apprentice and any dependants. Records relating to Poor Law apprentices will be found in parish records in the CRO. The SoG has a large collection of original indentures made between 1641 and 1888, including many Poor Law apprenticeships.

There were also local charities that paid for the apprenticeship of poor children, although as time went on better-off parents sometimes managed to get their sons and daughters placed in good trades through this route. These records will be found in the CRO.

Guild apprenticeship

Members of guilds were responsible for teaching apprentices their various trades and crafts. Completing a guild apprenticeship brought all kinds of privileges, so a high premium could be charged for taking one. A record of these premiums appear in TNA's tax records, as well as in the records of the guilds themselves, which are usually in the CRO.

Guild records will also contain information about disputes over apprenticeships and the turning over of an apprentice from one master to another. Sometimes this was due to the inability of a master to continue in business, but in other cases children simply proved to have no aptitude for or interest in a craft, and so started again in a different trade or skill.

Quarter sessions papers contain many examples of apprentices petitioning to be released from their indentures because their master was either not teaching them his or her craft or ill-treating them. Some apprentices did not go to the trouble of legal proceedings: they just ran away, and advertisements for their return may be found in local newspapers. Anyone employing such a runaway was liable to prosecution. Newspapers may also contain reports of legal proceedings. Masters also went to law to cancel the indenture of an unsatisfactory apprentice.

APPRENTICESHIPS IN THE 19TH AND 20TH CENTURIES

The strict controls exercised over apprentices started to loosen in the mid-18th century. Many people did not complete their full term but still practised a trade.

In the 19th century, with the growth of large companies, apprentices were increasingly taken on by businesses, such as shipbuilders, gas companies, and motor manufacturers.

Surviving records of indentures from the 19th and 20th centuries will be found either in company archives (many deposited with CROs) or among private family papers.

RESEARCHING APPRENTICESHIP RECORDS

Completing an apprenticeship was one of the ways after 1662 in which to gain settlement in a parish, and so settlement examinations will always say whether an apprenticeship was started and if it was completed, and will give the name and parish of the master.

The dates of the beginning and end of an apprenticeship will give clues to the person's age: the standard term was seven years, ending at the age of 21 (or 24 in the 16th and 17th centuries).

Directories and advertisements in newspapers may help to locate where an ancestor served as an apprentice.

FURTHER HELP

TNA Domestic Records
    Information 80 *Apprenticeship Records as Sources for Genealogy*
Some guild records, including apprenticeships, have been published.

Guilds and freemen

The guilds of cities and towns began in the Middle Ages. They were originally made up of reputable merchants, tradesmen and craftsmen who organized themselves into groups to maintain occupational standards and agree prices. They also arranged many welfare services for their members, such as insurance, burial clubs and financial support for widows and orphans of members.

Someone who had successfully completed an apprenticeship to a member of one of the guilds became a freeman, which usually gave the right to vote in local elections.

BECOMING A FREEMAN

At the end of his or her guild apprenticeship, the aspiring guild member produced an example of the skills that had been learned. This was often a miniature article, such as a piece of furniture, and was called the "masterpiece". If this masterpiece was considered satisfactory, the person paid a fee to be enrolled into the guild as a freeman and could practise his or, much more rarely, her trade.

Most men then became journeymen. This name is not connected to the fact that they travelled around, which they often did, but comes from the fact that they were paid by the day. (It comes from the French word *journée*.) They worked on a casual basis until they had the means to set up their own businesses, hire other workers and take on their own apprentices. The more prudent ones waited until they found somewhere that needed their skills before settling down and starting a family.

There were three other ways of becoming a freeman:

- by redemption or fine, i.e. paying to join a guild or livery company when you had not completed an apprenticeship in its trade or craft
- by patrimony, if your father was a freeman at the time of your birth. In some places, therefore, the freedom of a guild or borough could be inherited and passed down through the generations, although this usually applied only to eldest sons. This inherited freedom still operates in some of the ancient boroughs, so you may find that you or your eldest son are entitled to become a freeman.
- by marrying a freeman's widow or daughter (this was only practised in some guilds)

These different methods meant that a man might have a different trade from that of the guild he entered.

If someone was expelled from a guild, he would not be allowed to trade within the radius of the city or town. This is where the expression "sent to Coventry" may have originated.

Freemen had certain rights granted to them by the city or town:

- to take apprentices
- to trade
- to vote for officials such as the Mayor and Aldermen, and also in national elections.

In addition, freemen were responsible for local government functions, such as the running of schools and care of the poor, as well as the administration of both civil and criminal law within their borough, including inquests. Many guilds supported local charities and educational establishments.

The guilds and livery companies of the City of London have their own crests (from left to right: the Mercers, Merchant Tailors, Grocers and Ironmongers), which may appear on heirlooms and provide the family historian with clues about an ancestor's membership.

CITY OF LONDON GUILDS

Outside London there was usually a single guild to which all traders and craftsmen belonged, whatever their business. In the City of London, however, there were different livery companies and guilds, which originally had their basis in specific occupations. (The livery companies are chartered companies that originated from the craft guilds.) There are 102 companies, of which 77 are ancient and 25 modern. Before about 1700, people tended to belong to the same company as their trade. From 1750, the other methods of gaining the freedom of the City became more common. The cost of apprenticeship to a citizen of London meant that skilled people who could not afford to become a freeman tended to live in the parishes around the Square Mile.

CITY OF LONDON BROKERS

Commodity brokers who wanted to trade in the City of London had to be freemen (until 1856) and be licensed by the City authorities (until 1886), although some evaded being licensed from the 19th century onwards. They were issued with a medal to prove their credentials. The numbers of Jews and other aliens were strictly limited. Between 1738 and 1830, Jews were not admitted to the freedom of the City, but twelve were allowed to become brokers.

KING'S/QUEEN'S FREEMEN

Between 1784 and 1873, discharged servicemen and their wives and children had the right to trade in any town in the British Isles. They were called King's/Queen's Freemen, and received a certificate. Relatively few seem to have taken advantage of this, because, from the beginning of the 19th century, strict control started to decline. Fewer and fewer men chose to pay the

The Stock Exchange was set up in 1760 by a group of men thrown out of the Royal Exchange for rowdy behaviour. By Victorian times, it was a respectable place to work.

costs of guild membership, especially if they had done their apprenticeship in a city or town but decided to set up in business elsewhere, so King's/Queen's Freemen had no special advantages.

HONORARY FREEMEN

City and borough councils could grant someone who had done their community some special service the title of honorary freeman.

RESEARCHING GUILD RECORDS

Electoral registers and poll books before about 1835 will list those who had the right to vote in local and national elections. They usually state how the individual was qualified to vote, including if they were freemen. If your City of London ancestor was a grocer, he may not have joined the Grocers' Company. The variety of ways of becoming a freeman means that he could also have belonged to any of the other companies. Wills usually state whether a person was a member of a City of London livery company.

The archives of most of the City of

London's livery companies and guilds are in the Guildhall Library, but a few remain with the companies themselves. There is a complete list of freemen between 1681 and 1915, which includes the guild to which they belonged. City of London apprenticeship records are in the process of being published. The guild records of many provincial cities and boroughs have been published, at least up to 1800.

FURTHER HELP

Aldous, Vivienne E. *My Ancestors Were Freemen of the City of London* (SoG)
CLRO *City Freedom Archives* (CLRO Research Guide No. 1)
CLRO *Sworn Brokers' Archives* (CLRO Research Guide No. 2)
GL *City Livery Companies and Related Organisations* (Guildhall Library Research Guide No. 3)
GL *Searching for Members or Those Apprenticed to Members of the City of London Livery Companies at Guildhall Library*
Ward, Harry *Freemen in England* (self-published)

The professions

The British practice of leaving land and money to the eldest son meant that the other children had to make their own way in the world. Within the upper classes, there was sometimes enough money in the family to ensure that younger sons didn't have to do anything so vulgar as work, and the lower middle classes had businesses or trades to pass on to their sons, but there were many families where profitable occupations had to be found for their sons. (The daughters were expected to marry well.) Some purchased commissions as Army officers or went into the Navy; others became clergymen, lawyers or perhaps doctors but not, until the late 19th century, surgeons, who were not held in such high respect.

THE CHURCH

Clergymen of the Church of England usually went to university, then, having obtained their degree, were appointed to a parish, either as the incumbent or as a curate. Many parishes, or livings, were in the gift of the bishop of a diocese or an individual, such as a lord of the manor. In the 18th century, it was common for a clergyman to have more than one living: he would pay a curate to look after the parishioners of the less glamorous parish, or parishes, and live elsewhere.

There were often complaints about clergymen neglecting their duties or committing other sins; these are found in the records of the Church courts in either the DRO or CRO. From 1792, all clergymen and preachers had to be licensed by the bishop, who also issued licences for a number of other matters,

George Whitefield, one of the founders of Methodism, joined the society while at Oxford in 1735 before it broke away from the Church of England.

such as holding more than one living, or engaging in a trade. Not all clergymen became the incumbent of a parish: some became chaplains, others missionaries. Information about chaplains will be found among surviving papers of the organizations they served. There were a number of missionary societies linked to different denominations. Since they depended on subscriptions and voluntary contributions, they usually produced annual reports, which contain information about individuals' activities.

The Clergy List, published from 1841, lists the names of all the Anglican clergy and gives details of their livings, including when they were appointed, how much each living was worth per annum and who was the patron. From 1858 this list was taken over by a man called Crockford, and it continues as Crockford's Clerical Directory to the present day. There are other sources of information: most dioceses issued publications listing the personnel in them, and DROs and CROs may hold ordination papers for individual clergy, containing letters of recommendation, references and other useful documents.

Nonconformist clergy

After the restoration of Charles II in 1660, Nonconformist clergy faced official persecution. From 1672, they had to be licensed, but it was not until the 1689 Toleration Act that they and their congregations had complete freedom of worship.

Nonconformist clergy tended to come from a lower social class than Anglican clergy, and, as they did not have parish tithes to support them, they depended on what their congregation could give them and what they could earn themselves. Most, therefore, had another occupation. Surviving records will be found in the denomination's archives. From the mid-19th century, most produced both magazines and directories, which contain obituaries and other biographical material on ministers.

Researching clerical records

Look first at the lists of Oxbridge alumni, which contain biographical details. From there, you can go on to the records of the organizations or places where your ancestor(s) worked.

If your ancestor isn't an Oxbridge graduate, look at the records of Nonconformist colleges in the 19th century, or records of licences.

THE LAW

There was, and still is, a distinction between solicitors (known as attorneys until 1875) and barristers. Only the latter could appear in court to plead for their clients. Attorneys conducted legal business, such as drawing up marriage settlements and wills or dealing with property matters. Some also dealt with other estate business, such

as collecting rents, and were involved with manorial courts. Attorneys could also carry out their clients' business in those courts to which they were admitted to practise.

Qualifying for the law

People wanting to become barristers mainly went to university, either Oxford or Cambridge, and then to the Inns of Court in London, where they had to remain for a certain period of time before qualifying. An examination was introduced in 1853. Those wanting to become solicitors might also go to university, but the majority were apprenticed. The period of apprenticeship was fixed at five years in 1728.

Researching legal records

Most of the admission registers of the Inns of Court have been published. Surviving records that have not appeared in print are still with the individual Inns, apart from those of Clement's Inn, which are held by TNA. It's also worth checking the registers of the chapels attached to the inns: barristers were sometimes married or had children baptized there.

TNA holds records of attorneys admitted to the various courts: Common Pleas, King's/Queen's Bench,

Exchequer, Equity, Chancery, Bankruptcy, the Palatinate Courts, High Court of Admiralty and the Prerogative Court of Canterbury. Lawyers practising in the last two courts were called "proctors". An oath had to be sworn before they could be admitted, which effectively disbarred Catholics from practising in these courts before 1791. Judges also had to take an oath.

The Law List, containing attorneys, was published from 1780, and the Law Society was founded in 1828. The society also holds records relating to their members dating back, in some cases, to 1790. Between 1710 and 1811 there was a tax on apprenticeship premiums, so attorneys will appear in these records too.

Some lawyers, of course, completed their training but did not practise, so if you find an ancestor in the records of the Inns of Court or apprenticeship records, don't assume that he necessarily became a lawyer. An education in the law was regarded as good preparation for life.

LEFT Judges' wigs and gowns date from the late 17th century, when they were everyday wear.

Calling in a doctor was expensive, and before the mid-19th century he had few effective remedies for illness.

Apothecaries dispensed medicines and offered advice to those too poor to pay for a doctor.

MEDICINE

Since the medical profession deals with life and death, it has, for obvious reasons, been strictly regulated. Before the 19th century, when there were considerable advances in both medical science and public health, the profession was not highly specialized. Women were largely responsible for their families' wellbeing and any nursing that needed to be done. Calling in a doctor might be expensive and, in many cases, there was little that he could do. Some of the drugs in common use, like mercury, might be almost as harmful to the patient as the diseases they were meant to cure. Many people relied on folk medicine, like wrapping an old sock or stocking around the neck to cure a sore throat, or went to people who had a reputation for herbal medicines (but no formal qualification or licence).

Physicians and surgeons

From medieval times, there was a sharp distinction between physicians and surgeons. Before anaesthetics made invasive surgery possible, only minor operations, blood letting and amputations could be carried out, and their familiarity with razors meant that barbers carried out these operations. In London, surgeons belonged to the same company as barbers until 1745, when a separate Company of Surgeons was established. Training was by apprenticeship.

Surgery was considered only one step up from butchery, so the men who went into this branch of medicine were (and still are) called "Mr", rather than "Doctor". Medical men who went to sea were almost invariably surgeons: the ability to carry out amputations was vital in battle. The Royal College of Surgeons was founded in 1801.

Physicians treated all illnesses not requiring surgery: indeed, some prided themselves on not touching their patients at all. Before the late 18th century, they were apprenticed, but increasingly went to university, especially in Scotland. Lists of university graduates have been published. From 1512, all medical men practising in London had to be licensed by the Bishop of London.

Apothecaries

Apothecaries, who dispensed drugs and medicines, and chemists and druggists, who made them, came into the medical profession through apprenticeship. Both doctors and surgeons might also have training as apothecaries. From 1815, they had to be licensed by the Society of Apothecaries, whose records are in the Guildhall Library.

Dentists

In early years, dentistry consisted of little more than extracting teeth. Any strong person could set himself, or more rarely herself, up as a tooth-puller. The first dental hospital, which also carried out training, was founded in London in 1858.

Nurses and midwives

Women have been involved in caring for the sick since before records began. From medieval times, many orders of nuns were involved in this work. After the dissolution of the monasteries, a few hospitals remained, and women worked in them, but they were rarely those who had gone into nursing because of a religious vocation. Most were elderly widows, for whom the alternative was starvation, and they were paid a pittance for their work. Workhouses and parish infirmaries usually employed a matron and occasionally other women, often one of the paupers in the workhouse, to care for the sick.

Hospitals were very unhygienic and dangerous places to stay in, so most people preferred to be cared for at home and might hire nurses to look after them there, especially after childbirth. There was no recognized training for nurses, and those who undertook such work had the unwelcome reputation of being drunken, slovenly and incompetent.

Florence Nightingale transformed both the image and the training of nurses. After her experiences in Scutari during the Crimean War, she came back to Britain determined to make nursing a skilled and respectable profession. The first training school for nurses was set up at St Thomas's Hospital in London in 1860. State registration of nurses began in 1919.

Researching records of medical practitioners

Since 1845, an annual directory of practitioners has been published as the *British Medical Directory*, and this is the best starting point for the family historian. Dentists were included from 1886. Local and trade directories list medical practitioners before and after these dates. Records of apprenticeships can be found in TNA for 1710–1811.

FURTHER HELP

History of Nursing Society, Royal College of Nursing www.rcn.org.ik/learning/archives
Magg, Christopher *Sources for the History of Nursing in Great Britain* (Kings Fund Project Paper No. 46)
The Wellcome Insitute for the History of Medicine www.wellcome.ac.uk

Before the mid-18th century, physicians, surgeons and midwives had to be licensed by the bishop of their diocese, because they might have to baptize a newborn child in danger of dying. Records will be found in Diocesan Record Offices (DROs) or CROs.

The United Kingdom Central Council for Nursing, Midwifery and Health Visiting (UKCC) holds a list of registered practitioners, but this has only their date of registration. To go further, you need to know in which hospital your ancestor trained. Photographs may help, as hospitals had their own, distinctive uniforms. Records relating to military and naval nurses will be in TNA.

ABOVE Until the 20th century, most women gave birth at home.

RIGHT Florence Nightingale's efforts made the nursing profession respectable.

Other occupations

It would, of course, be impossible to give information about every job that every person in everyone's ancestry might have done. This section covers some of the occupations for which good records exist, because the people who did them were public servants.

STARTING THE SEARCH
First you need to find out what your ancestor did, using sources such as:
- apprenticeship records
- BMD certificates
- burgess or freemen's rolls
- censuses

Domestic service was a major form of employment for women before World War I.

- directories
- newspapers
- quarter sessions (when licences were granted)
- wills

Before about 1830, occupations were not given for a large number of people. In rural areas, you can suspect that they were agricultural labourers (usually listed as "ag. labs." in records). Before the mid-19th century, more people lived in the countryside than towns, and farming employed many generally unskilled labourers.

Other unskilled or semi-skilled labour was required in the factories that were established by the Industrial Revolution, which started at the end of the 18th century. In industrial areas, those people whose occupation is not given are likely to be factory hands or general labourers.

While many jobs could be done in any part of the country, some areas had concentrations of particular trades, such as miners. Coal was mined in South Wales and in various places in the north of England and Scotland. Tin mining was a speciality of Cornwall, and lead of Derbyshire. Fishing was an important source of employment in coastal areas and along major rivers.

SERVANTS
Until the end of World War I, the majority of people spent some or the whole of their lives as servants. Even lower-middle-class people expected to employ at least one servant to help the mistress of the house, and on a large estate there might be a staff of up to a hundred. Some lived in; others came in on a daily basis.

The word "servant" covered a range of jobs. Farm servants were not necessarily domestic workers: they were unmarried men and women who lived on the premises. Once married, and living in a separate dwelling, the men were known as agricultural labourers. (Their wives invariably worked too, but on a casual basis as the demands of raising a family permitted.)

THE POLICE
In addition to the armed forces, there were other occupations that required the wearing of a uniform, of

The uniformed bobby on the beat became a familiar sight during the 19th century.

which a photograph might help to identify an ancestor's job. Among these jobs was membership of the police force.

Before the early 19th century, law enforcement was largely the responsibility of individual parishes. They had a constable, whose policing duties extended to little beyond locking up apprehended criminals and ensuring their attendance at court. The constable was also charged with ensuring that market stall-holders and shopkeepers obeyed the trading laws. In towns and cities, watchmen, usually elderly men, might be hired to patrol the street at night to deter lawbreakers. There was very little in the way of detective work done – it was largely the person against whom a crime was perpetrated who had to bring the criminal to justice.

In London, the problems of crime were much more pressing than elsewhere. The magistrate Sir John Fielding set up the Bow Street Runners, who were paid constables. In 1829, the first police force was set up in London, covering an 11-km (7-mile) radius from Charing Cross but excluding the City of London.

Miners, such as this Yorkshire pitman, played an important role in the creation of Britain's wealth through the Industrial Revolution.

Before World War II, many towns and boroughs might have had their own police force. Since then, they have been amalgamated into larger geographical units. In addition to those dealing with street crime, there are other divisions, such as forces policing ports, rivers, railways (including the London Underground) and airports.

Researching records relating to the police

The records of London's Metropolitan Police are in TNA. Other forces' records will be with the CRO or the relevant force's museum. Some may remain in the force's headquarters. The Police History Society covers all aspects of police history, and many individual forces have their own museums and societies whose members have published histories.

There are several publications of use to the family historian. *Hue and Cry*, published from the early 19th century, became the *Police Gazette* in 1828. Both listed deserters, the names of criminals who had absconded and unsolved crimes, and often included

the names of the officers in charge of cases. The *Police Service Advertiser* was published between 1866 and 1959. *The Police Review (and Parade Gossip)*, published from 1893, has been indexed. *The Illustrated Police News* (1864–1938) was a sensationalist magazine that described the more lurid crimes and trials and often included sketches of the policemen involved. In addition to these specialist magazines, local and national newspapers reported in detail crimes and trials at which police officers gave evidence.

Before mechanization, agricultural labour employed many unskilled workers.

> **FURTHER HELP**
>
> Bridgeman, Ian and Emsley, Clive *A Guide to the Archives of the Police Forces of England and Wales* (Police History Society)
> Police History Society www.policehistorysociety.co.uk
> Royal Humane Society, Brettenham House, Lancaster Place, London WC2E 7EP
> Shearman, Anthony *My Ancestor Was a Policeman* (SoG)
> Waters, Les *Notes for Family Historians* (Police History Society)

The introduction of the penny post meant that even the less well off could keep in touch with their families.

FIREFIGHTERS

Early firefighters were either employees of the fire insurance companies or volunteers. The insurance companies employed firemen and porters (the latter carried out the salvage operation after a fire). Records relating to fire brigades are usually deposited in the CROs.

AWARDS FOR BRAVERY

Many of those in the above-mentioned uniformed services behaved heroically in the course of their duties and might have received recognition of this. There are various awards for particular services.

Ordinary people were also given awards for bravery. There are a number of organizations that might have issued some token, such as a medal or certificate. One of the main bodies involved in this is the Royal Humane Society, which was established in 1774, originally as a way of encouraging people to bring drowned bodies to two doctors who were interested in

researching resuscitation techniques. It grew into a charity that both employed rescuers stationed at places, such as rivers and lakes, where drowning was a danger, and gave awards for bravery. Some of its records date back to its founding, and it has a list of awards made from 1823 onwards. These have not been indexed, so the date of the event, which would have been covered in newspapers, is necessary to get further information.

THE POST OFFICE

In 1636, Charles I allowed the general public to use the royal mail services, and the Post Office was born. In 1840 the practice of requiring the sender, rather than the recipient, of a letter or package to pay began. An adhesive stamp, the first being the Penny Black, showed that the sum had been paid.

Although most of its records were destroyed in the Great Fire of London in 1666, the Post Office's archives include some records dating back to 1636. From 1719, many Post Office employees received pensions, and their application forms are indexed. In addition to information about employees'

appointments and careers, there are copies of union publications, company newsletters and magazines, and an extensive collection of photographs and artwork. Records relating to telegraph and telephone services are now with British Telecommunications, and these include telephone directories dating from 1880.

RAILWAYS

Originally the railway system in Britain consisted of individual private companies. In 1947, the whole railway system was nationalized, and the vast majority of surviving records of all the different companies were deposited in TNA or the Scottish Record Office (SRO), though a few may be in CROs. There are many books available on aspects of the railways and their history.

OTHER COMPANY ARCHIVES

Histories of many individual companies have been written and published, but they usually mention only the higher echelons of employees. Archives may have been deposited in CROs, while others remain with the company. Many large organizations,

The vast amount of waste produced in cities needed an army of refuse collectors and cleaners, many of whom were women.

including department stores and hotels, have their own archives. Among their records may be personnel details and company newsletters, which usually mention people's retirements and carry obituaries.

RESEARCHING ANCESTORS INVOLVED IN A PARTICULAR OCCUPATION

There are a large number of occupational indexes. Some are in the possession of individuals who have, through a personal interest, set them up; others are attached to specialist museums. Local historians may also have set up an index of everyone in their area of study, which will include the occupations of all the people there. It is quite difficult to find out where all these indexes are located, as many people have compiled them mainly for their own interest.

The title and further information about companies, particular occupations and directories of those engaged in them can be found by typing an occupation into the search engine of the British Library's on-line catalogue. The book can then be ordered through your local library's service or, if this is impossible, read at the British Library or the nearest library that holds a copy, which your library should be able to discover for you.

If the occupation was a skilled trade that generally required a period of apprenticeship, or needed some kind of licence to practise the trade, there will be a variety of sources you can check with.

It is worth remembering that every trade or occupation has its own association and specialist magazine. Some professional societies, including the livery companies, date from medieval times, but from the 19th century onwards trade associations for other

Working for a railway company was regarded as a prestigious job and brought a pension, which meant a secure old age.

occupations were set up. Records of members may still be with the relevant association; if not, the association should be able to tell you where they are now deposited.

Many of the skills learned by people in the past no longer exist or have been replaced by machines. If you find that a reference to your ancestor's occupation is something you don't understand, and a dictionary does not contain it, look at a book such as the *Book of Trades or Library of Useful Arts* (pub. 1811–18 and reprinted by Wiltshire Family History Society), which describes pre-19th-century occupations, or Colin Waters' *A Dictionary of Old Trades, Occupations and Titles*.

FURTHER HELP

BT Group Archives, Third Floor, Holborn Telephone Exchange, 268–270 High Holborn, London WC1V 7EE www.btplc.com/ Corporateinformation/BTArchives/ Appointment needed.

The Directory of British Associations (CRD Research) and other similar directories publish all those in existence today and usually give the date of foundation.

Harvey, C. *Business Records at The National Archives* (TNA)

Hawkings, David T. *Railway Ancestors: A guide to the staff records of the railway companies of England and Wales 1822–1947* (Alan Sutton Publishing)

Heritage Services, The Post Office, Freeling House, Phoenix Place,

London WC1X 0DL www.consignia.com/heritage/ has information sheets about genealogical research. A reader's ticket and an appointment are not necessary, but proof of identity is required.

Jewell, Andrew *Crafts, Trades and Industries: A book List for Local Historians* (National Council Social Service 1964)

National Railway Museum, Library Archive, Leemans Road, York YO26 4XJ www.nrm.org.uk

Raymond, Stuart *Occupational Sources for Genealogists: A Bibliography* (FFHS)

Torrance, D. Richard *Scottish Trades and Professions: A Selected Bibliography* (Scottish Association of Family History Societies)

Licences

Anumber of occupations required the practitioner to have a licence. Sometimes it was a matter of ensuring competence, as in the case of gamekeepers. In other instances, such as printers, it was to ensure that laws were not broken.

VICTUALLERS

There can be very few families who do not have someone connected with the manufacture or sale of alcohol in their ancestry. (In some places, every third house was licensed to brew or sell alcohol, in the times when water was too dangerous to drink.) The Crown also made money by selling licences to import and sell wine and spirits.

Different regulations applied to alehouses, taverns and inns. An alehouse was usually a small establishment where ale, beer or sometimes cider was made on the premises and sold to customers. Often this was a single person working from his or her own home. Taverns, which were in towns, boroughs or cities, offered wine as well as ale and might also have sold spirits. Inns sold alcoholic drinks and had rooms where travellers could stay.

The first law regulating the sale of alcohol was passed in 1553. Licences to sell alcohol had to be granted by JPs, which remains the case today. People who wanted to provide entertainment as well as sell alcohol on their premises needed a licence from 1752, and if they also wanted to hire out horses they had to get a separate licence from 1784.

In 1828, the laws were revised and different types of licences to sell beer, wine and spirits on and off premises

LEFT Anyone selling alcohol needed a licence, which could be withdrawn if customers became too rowdy.

were granted. From 1830, those selling only beer and cider could get a licence from the local excise office rather than in court.

Locating records of alcohol-related licences

The National Archives holds records relating to licences to sell wine in the 16th and 17th centuries, and some licences for this period are also found in quarter sessions held in CROs. From the 18th century, matters to do with licences - both the granting of them and cases involving illegal sales - were dealt with at petty and quarter sessions. Recent records relating to licences may still be with the magistrates' courts that granted them.

GAMEKEEPERS

Between 1710 and the middle of the 20th century, the men who looked after the game birds on a country estate were supposed to be registered at the local quarter sessions, though it seems that this was not always observed. Court records may also contain legal proceedings relating to

poachers apprehended by gamekeepers. Estate records mentioning gamekeepers may remain with the owner or may have been deposited in CROs or other repositories. Local directories may also list gamekeepers in their area.

COACHMEN AND DRIVERS

Coachmen in general did not have to have a licence or be registered anywhere, but hackney coachmen, the taxi-drivers of the 19th and early 20th century, did have to be licensed. Records of these licences, which do not include the licences themselves, are in TNA. Sometimes hackney coachmen gave the number of their licence in census returns.

London taxi-drivers are now licensed by the Public Carriage Office, but records of individual cabbies are destroyed six years after their death or

---

FURTHER HELP

Gibson, Jeremy and Hunter, Judith *Victuallers' Licences: Records for Family and Local Historians* (FFHS)

retirement. Other local authorities generally license taxi-drivers in their own area, and the survival of records depends on their policies.

From 1903, drivers of motor vehicles, including motorcycles, had to have a licence issued by the local authorities, so surviving records will be in CROs.

PAWNBROKERS AND CHIMNEYSWEEPS
From 1786, pawnbrokers in all parts of the country had to have annual revenue licences. Records before the Pawnbrokers' Act of 1872 are sparse, but after this date there are some records in CROs, since the licence was dependent on a certificate granted by a magistrate. Chimney sweeps were given similar certificates after 1875.

TRAVELLING SALESPEOPLE
Itinerant sellers of goods had to be licensed by a magistrate from 1698 to 1772. They had to wear a badge showing that they were licensed, and so were sometimes called "badgers". These records will be in the CRO, and there are also lists of licences granted in TNA among the Exchequer records. There was a fine line between sellers of some goods, such as matches, and beggars. From 1531, beggars had to be licensed by JPs or mayors.

DROVERS
Before railways and motorized transport, the only way to get cattle and other animals, such as sheep, pigs and even geese, to market was to drive them there. Most, of course, went to the nearest market town, but others were taken much longer distances to cities, especially London. The men engaged in this trade were known as drovers, and they, like other itinerants, were licensed.

BARGEES AND RIVER SAILORS
Boats had always been used to transport goods around Britain's coastline and along the navigable rivers inland. The first canals were constructed in the late 18th century by private companies. There were no common agreements between them about the width and depth of these waterways, so barges could be used only on particular canals, which was restrictive.

Between 1795 and 1871, owners of barges had to be licensed. Records of christenings, marriages and burials (CMBs) of bargees, river sailors and their families should be found in the parishes along the route of canals. Some families actually lived on their barges, while others had a home on land instead.

The 1861 census uniquely required additional details about ships in port to be included, and, since this would include river and canal boats delivering or collecting goods to or from ports, respectively, it is a useful source of information. There is an index to ships' names in TNA. In 1877, an Act required registers of canal boats to be kept, and those that survive are usually in CROs.

PRINTERS AND PUBLISHERS
The government has always worried about what is published, especially if it criticizes them, but also if it contains material defined as seditious, blasphemous or obscene. Since 1834, all printed material has had to contain the name and address of the printer. Between 1799 and 1869, the owners of printing presses had to be licensed.

GUN OWNERS
Not surprisingly, a strict eye was kept on those who owned guns (a situation that has not changed today), and the manufacturers of guns were also carefully regulated. Initially most gunsmiths worked in and around the City of London and belonged to one of the livery companies there. After the Civil War, the Midlands, especially Birmingham, became another centre of arms manufacture. The government was a major customer, and employed some gunsmiths through the Board of Ordnance, whose records are in TNA. The arms they made had to be tested in proof houses, which still exist. The one in Whitechapel, East London, dates back to 1675.

Before the growth of railways and motor vehicles, the waterways were an important form of transport. Barge owners needed a licence.

Elections, poll books and electoral registers

Until the 20th century, the majority of people did not have the vote, which usually depended on owning property as a qualification.

PARLIAMENTARY ELECTIONS

Before the 19th century, Members of Parliament were returned for three types of constituency: counties, boroughs (burghs in Scotland) and the universities of Oxford and Cambridge.

County MPs

The franchise was largely based on property qualifications. Before 1832, the vote was restricted to those who possessed land or a house worth 40s or more in annual rent.

Borough franchises

Only those towns that had an ancient charter were boroughs. This is why many of the northern and Midlands towns that grew out of the Industrial Revolution had no individual MPs but were included in the county elections until after the 1832 Reform Act.

Only a small section of the population could vote, and they cast their ballots in public until 1872. Allegations of bribery and vote-rigging were common.

The vote in these boroughs depended on local customs. In some, all freemen had the franchise but in others, it was only those who were resident there that qualified. In some boroughs, ratepayers could vote. The lists of people entitled to vote in boroughs are called burgess or freemen's rolls.

The City of London

All the Acts that gradually eroded the rights of freemen in boroughs to elect their own MPs and officials have always excluded the City of London, where a system of government, relatively unchanged since medieval times, still operates.

The right to vote

Until the 20th century, the majority of people did not have the right to vote. At various times, certain people were not allowed to vote in parliamentary elections:

- women (until 1918, and even then there were certain restrictions)
- peers of the realm (though peeresses could vote between 1918 and 1963)
- those under 21

- lunatics
- sentenced criminals in prison
- aliens who had not been naturalized
- those in receipt of public alms, i.e. those receiving outdoor relief (money given to poor people not living in a workhouse) or those living in parish workhouses
- anyone convicted of bribery at an election
- those not included in an

electoral register (after 1832, when they were introduced)

Certain occupational groups were also excluded:

- serving policemen (before 1887)
- postmasters (until 1918)
- customs and excise men (until 1918)

Conscientious objectors in World War I were also forbidden to vote in the 1918 and 1923 parliamentary elections.

Significant dates in the history of the franchise in England and Wales

1429 All men over the age of 21 who held land or property with a rental value of 40s or more per annum in a county, and were resident there, could vote in county elections.

1774 Men no longer needed to be resident in the county where their property was situated in order to vote.

1832 Reform Act revised constituencies and extended the county franchise to tenants of land worth between £2 and £5 per annum (p.a.); to those paying more than £50 p.a. in rent; and to those with a long lease on land worth more than £10 p.a. All the varied qualifications in the borough franchises were standardized to those who had property with a ratable value of more than £10 p.a. All voters had to have paid their rates and taxes. This Act also introduced electoral registers.

1867 Representation of the People Act gave the vote to all men paying £10 or more p.a. for housing in towns (but not in rural areas), reduced the property value in counties to £5 and extended the franchise to all men paying £50 or more per year in rent for a building or land. The right afforded to Oxford and Cambridge to elect their own MP was extended to the University of London.

1869 Municipal Franchise Act gave unmarried women who paid rates the right to vote for certain local officials.

1870 Electoral rights of unmarried women ratepayers extended to school boards.

1872 Secret ballot introduced.

1888 County Electors Act allowed women with property qualifications to elect county councillors.

1894 Married women allowed to vote for local officials on the same basis as unmarried women.

1918 Women over 30 allowed to vote in national elections if either a householder or married to a householder.

1928 All men and women over the age of 21 given the vote.

1971 Age of majority (and therefore the right to vote) reduced from 21 to 18.

University seats

Oxford and Cambridge returned two MPs each. They were elected by the universities' legislative assemblies.

POLL BOOKS

In 1696, the sheriff of a county was given responsibility for compiling a list of all those who voted in a county election and for whom they cast their vote. This was to be made available to anyone who wanted to consult it. In 1843, a similar Act was passed relating to borough elections, but, unfortunately, most of these manuscript documents have been destroyed.

The poll was not secret before 1872, and poll books were published. They often include an account of the electoral campaign, though they are not always completely accurate. There is also no standard format. People who were not able to vote, for example those whose religion meant that they could not take the oath of allegiance, might or might not be listed. The candidate's political party might not be recorded, so you will have to look at a parliamentary history book to find out whether he was a Whig or a Tory. It is a good idea for family historians to investigate the policies of the individuals for whom their ancestors voted.

Researching poll books and electoral registers

These usually state individuals' addresses, occupations and qualifications for voting, which will give you further avenues to explore.

After 1774, when voters no longer had to be resident in the counties where they had property, land tax records were often used to prove their qualifications. Copies made of these might be found among quarter sessions records in CROs.

If you find that your ancestor appears in one poll book or electoral register but not the one before, don't automatically assume that he had only recently moved into the county. Check the date to see whether the franchise qualifications had changed in that time, as new legislation might have brought him into the electorate. In a borough, for example, he might have only recently become a freeman, either by completing his apprenticeship or by one of the other ways of gaining entry to a guild.

FURTHER HELP

Gibson, Jeremy and Rogers, Colin *Poll Books c.1696–1872: A Directory to Holdings in Great Britain* [FFHS]

Gibson, Jeremy and Rogers, Colin *Electoral Registers Since 1832 and Burgess Rolls: A Directory to Holdings in Great Britain* [FFHS]

In addition, there are a number of books about individual boroughs, counties and elections, which are listed in the Gibson Guides.

Trade unions and friendly societies

The government has always been highly suspicious of working men gathering together. At the end of the 18th century, the ruling class was afraid of revolution – a fear that the French Revolution largely confirmed – and it is true that many of the "corresponding societies" set up at about that time, ostensibly for social reasons and to discuss current affairs, did want changes in society. The two types of organization had much in common, especially in the early days: trade unions concentrated on pay and working conditions, while friendly societies concerned themselves with benefits for the unemployed and sick.

Another kind of revolution, the Industrial Revolution, began in this period, and changed the way people had previously worked. The scope for exploitation was now much greater, and workers realized the benefits of concerted action. The government responded with a series of laws against "combinations" – both trade unions and friendly societies.

TRADE UNIONS

From the mid-19th century, the government began to accept the right of people to form unions to negotiate with employers. Some unions were highly specialized, while others had a more general membership.

Throughout the 19th and 20th centuries, the number of unions grew. In many industries, membership became mandatory – the so-called "closed shop". Those who refused to join or who were rejected or expelled could not work in a particular company or occupation. This situation lasted until

the last quarter of the 20th century, so if you have ancestors in certain occupations, they will have been members of the relevant union. The Trades Union Congress (TUC), founded in 1920, is an association to which the majority of individual unions belong. Unions were an important factor in the founding, growth and development of the Labour Party.

Researching trade union records

The TUC Library Collections holds books and documents relating to the trade union movement. These largely relate to its history, but active and prominent members of unions may also appear in them. Its own archive holds records relating to the development of the TUC itself. Individual unions' records may still be with the

ABOVE Members of the Ancient Order of Foresters carry tools of agricultural trades.

LEFT Women were expected to support their menfolk when they went on strike.

union itself or may have been deposited in a separate archive, often within a university.

FRIENDLY SOCIETIES

Before the 20th century, illness and unemployment meant penury for not only the average working man but also his family. The workhouse was a grim experience, and, although there were charities to help, not everyone qualified for their assistance. To avoid the threat of the workhouse, groups of people would get together and pay into a fund designed to assist any of their number in financial trouble. Such benevolent and fraternal associations did, however, run the risk of being seen as a cover for political subversion. In 1793, the Friendly Societies Act regularized their position by requiring such clubs to draw up a set of rules and get themselves approved by local JPs, but this did not prevent official suspicion of their activities.

The major friendly societies were the Ancient Order of Foresters and the Independent Order of Oddfellows, but there were a number of other, smaller, ones. Individual branches were called "courts" in the Foresters and "lodges" in the Oddfellows, and, at the beginning, their members usually met at a local inn. Each member, who had to live within walking distance of the inn, received a certificate, which may survive in family papers. The courts or lodges retained the services of a medical man to provide treatment for its members. Those who were ill received sick pay, and a lump sum was paid to their families on death. As the trade union movement gathered strength, the membership of friendly societies declined.

Initially the Oddfellows met in public houses, but, during the mid-19th century, as the temperance move-

By the 20th century, the trade unions had become a powerful political force, as well as supporting their members in times of unemployment.

ment grew, lodges began to build their own halls to keep their members away from the demon drink. The Oddfellows had a system whereby members could be issued with a document to allow them to stay overnight in any Oddfellows Hall. This was of great use to members looking for work. Emigrants took the principles of the society overseas, and Oddfellows lodges were founded in America and the Commonwealth. The American soci-

ety (which split from the British organization in 1834) founded lodges in many European countries.

Researching friendly society records

Surviving records may be with local branches, in record offices or with the individual societies' archives. There were also annual published accounts, which often included the names of officials and of members who had left or died in the preceding year.

FURTHER HELP

Foresters Heritage Trust, Ancient Order of Foresters, College Place, Southampton SO15 2FE
Independent Order of Odd Fellows, Oddfellows House, 40 Fountain Street, Manchester M2 2AB www.oddfellowsco.uk/
Logan, Roger *An Introduction to Friendly Society Records* (FFHS)
People's History Museum (formerly the National Museum of Labour History), 103 Princess Street, Manchester www.nmlhweb.org/ houses the Labour History Archive and Study Centre (LHASC), which has records

relating to working-class political organizations from the early 19th century onwards.
The Labour Party and the Communist Party of Great Britain site at www.a2a.pro.gov.uk has an index of archives.
TUC Archive, Modern Records Centre, University of Warwick Library, Coventry CV4 7AL http://modernrecords.warwick.ac.uk
TUC Library Collections, Learning Centre North Campus, London Metropolitan University, 236 Holloway Road, London N7 6PP www.unl.ac.uk/library/tuc/

Bankruptcy and insolvency

There is a distinction between someone who was bankrupt and someone who was simply an insolvent debtor. Before 1868, bankruptcy, which wipes out the debts and allows the person to begin trading again, was available only to people who owed more than a specified amount of money. Anyone owing less than that sum was an insolvent debtor and continued to be liable to repay debts.

BANKRUPTCY

Between 1571 and 1841, bankruptcy was possible only if a trader owed more than £100. This was a comparatively large sum at a time when the average income was about £1 a week. After 1842, the sum was reduced to £50, and after that the figure was amended from time to time. It was not until 1862 that all insolvent debtors were liable to bankruptcy proceedings. Until 1844, only individuals or partners in a business could be made bankrupt: companies could not.

Before 1832, creditors wanting to have a person declared bankrupt, so that they had some hope of recovering at least part of their debts, applied to the Lord Chancellor for a commission of bankruptcy to handle the sale of assets and distribution of the resulting proceeds. In 1832, the Court of Bankruptcy was set up so that creditors could go directly to it.

Outside London there were district bankruptcy courts, which functioned between 1842 and 1869. Thereafter matters were dealt with by the county courts, which might transfer cases to the London Court of Bankruptcy, which became part of the Supreme

The entrance to the Fleet prison was a chilling sight to those whose business careers ended in debt: many might never be released.

Court as the High Court of Justice in Bankruptcy in 1883. This court might transfer cases to and from county courts. Since 1869, there have been various other changes about how bankruptcy is administered, which affect where records will be found. It's a complicated area.

People who owed money to the Crown between 1314 and 1947 might have their property and goods valued by a county sheriff and jury. This valuation was called an Extent of Debt.

Sometimes, of course, bankrupts had committed a crime, such as fraud, or refused to pay, even though they had the means to do so, and they would be imprisoned for this rather than the fact of owing money.

INSOLVENCY

Those who owed less than the amount in force were insolvent debtors and so could not apply for bankruptcy, which would allow them to start again. The only redress their creditors had was to apply to the courts to have them put in prison until the debt was paid. This seems self-defeating – a person in prison was not able to work and therefore was even less likely to be able to repay debts - but the situation continued until 1869, when imprisonment for debt ended. The position of these prisoners was not helped by the fact that warders charged them for superior lodgings, food and bedding, so they incurred further debts. Some spent the rest of their lives in gaol. The only consolation was that wives and children could usually join them there.

Outside London, debtors were held in local prisons. In London, they might be found in a number of places. Those imprisoned for small debts were usually held in the Palace Court. The better-off went to the King's/Queen's Bench Prison or Fleet Prison. Others went to the Marshalsea or Newgate, where they had separate quarters from the criminals. There were other, less well-known, prisons, such as Giltspur Street Compter, Poultry Compter and Whitecross Street in the City of London. Prisoners had to submit a petition to be discharged to the relevant court.

LEFT Some prisons allowed wives and children to join the husbands who had been imprisoned for debt.

RESEARCHING BANKRUPTCY RECORDS

Notices of proceedings against bankrupts in England were published in the *London Gazette*; in Scotland, where such notices were called sequestrations, the details appeared in the *Edinburgh Gazette*. *The Times* also published information about them, often giving details of the cases. Information on cases in county courts might be published in local papers, either by the courts themselves or as reports of proceedings.

County court records will include cases of people being imprisoned for debt and will mention if a person was later released, implying that the debt had been paid in full. There may also be lists of people imprisoned for debt among prison papers. These records will be found in CROs.

There was supposed to be an inquest on everyone who died in prison, so there may be records or reports in newspapers of inquests if your ancestor died while they were imprisoned for debt.

Records held in TNA relate to:
- proceedings in the national courts
- official bankruptcy
- Extent of Debt valuations
- petitions for discharge (1813–69) made to the Commissioners of Bankrupts (before 1832) or the Court of Bankruptcy (after 1832) for the release of insolvent debtors
- a register of petitions for protection against bankruptcy (from 1854)

The SoG has two directories of bankrupts, 1774–86 and 1820–43, and TNA holds copies of them.

FURTHER HELP

TNA Legal Records Information 5
Bankrupts and Insolvent Debtors: 1710–1869
TNA Legal Records Information 6
Bankruptcy Records After 1869

Physical and mental illness

Before the mid-19th century, the care of the physically and mentally ill was largely the responsibility of their families, though if this was beyond their abilities, charities or the parish authorities would step in.

THE CARE OF THE PHYSICALLY ILL

Originally hospitals could do little but keep their patients warm, dry and better fed than they would have been otherwise. Their transformation into the high-tech establishments we know today is comparatively recent.

Early hospitals

Medieval hospitals, which cared for both the aged and the sick, were run by religious foundations. With the dissolution of the monasteries in England, responsibility passed to the local parish, which either took people into the poorhouse – later the workhouse – or paid for treatment in their own homes. There was no great distinction between those who could not work because of illness and those who could not work because they were old. Details about the poor sick will therefore be found in workhouse minutes and parish accounts. In cities, where there were a large number of people, parishes might have a separate infirmary to treat their paupers.

The first teaching hospitals

Although a few medieval hospitals survived the dissolution of the monasteries, it was not until the beginning of the 18th century that dedicated hospitals were set up in London, and, by the mid-18th century, other cities had fol-

LEFT Before the introduction of sterile theatres, an operation was undergone only as a last resort.

lowed. The first were for pregnant women and were known as Lying-in Hospitals. They were established largely as teaching hospitals to educate doctors and midwives, who also delivered women in their own homes. Many had their own baptismal registers.

Dispensaries

In 1770, dispensaries catering specifically for the poor began, again initially in London but quickly spreading to the provinces. These were places where people could get advice and medicines and could be visited by the staff in their own homes, though they did not take in-patients.

Subscription hospitals

During the 18th century, the better-off members of society were treated in hospitals that were funded by public

subscriptions and individual contributions. According to how much each person paid, they were entitled to nominate a certain number of in- and out-patients per year. This was how the relatively wealthy got treatment for themselves, their family and their servants, rather than having to mix with the destitute in the workhouses and parish infirmaries.

Most hospitals, because they were essentially charitable institutions, also admitted people who could not pay at the discretion of the medical staff, which is how those without money or useful contacts but with an interesting medical condition got treatment. The hospital staff were generally not paid: they also had to have a private practice to earn their living. Hospitals were very much used as training grounds in those days.

Specialist hospitals

The first specialist hospitals, treating only one part of the body, date from 1805 with the creation of London's Moorfields Eye Hospital. The introduction of anaesthetics and asepsis (the method of achieving a germ-free condition) in the middle of the century made many more surgical operations possible, increasing the number of patients who could be treated. In response, the number of specialist hospitals grew.

Private hospitals

From the middle of the 19th century, hospitals started to take in private patients. This mixture of charitable contributions and payment for treatment continued until the creation of the National Health Service (NHS) in 1948, but private healthcare continued.

Workhouse infirmaries

After the 1834 Poor Act, the Boards of Guardians of each Poor Law Union had an important role in the administration of workhouse infirmaries. Some of these became hospitals under the NHS.

Isolation hospitals

Until the beginning of the 19th century, there were separate hospitals only for those suffering from smallpox, or recovering from inoculation against it, and venereal diseases. The latter were called Lock Hospitals. From the late 19th to the middle of the 20th century, people infected with childhood diseases, such as chicken pox, measles and scarlet fever, were often sent to isolation hospitals to prevent an epidemic. Such diseases seem to have changed over the years and become less virulent. In port towns and cities, the possibilities of more dangerous diseases, such as typhoid, cholera,

The Smallpox Hospital was built in open fields at St Pancras to isolate sufferers who might spread the deadly disease among the population.

malaria, enteric fever, even plague, meant there was a need for an isolated place to treat infected people.

Tuberculosis and sanatoriums

Tuberculosis, also called TB, consumption or phthisis, was one of the great scourges of the past. Until the introduction of antibiotics in the

Queen Anne (1665–1714) was the last British monarch to touch people in the belief that this would cure scrofula.

1940s, pulmonary tuberculosis, which affected the lungs, could be treated only with cold, pure air. The rich went to mountainous countries in Europe, particularly Switzerland. The poor went to sanatoriums in the higher parts of the British Isles.

TB could also affect other parts of the body. When the lymph nodes in the neck were affected, it was called scrofula, or the king's evil, and people believed that they could be cured by the touch of the king or queen. Thousands came forward. The last monarch to do this was Queen Anne, who died in 1714. Parish officials sometimes paid expenses for people to travel to London for the royal touch, and their names may be found in the relevant churchwarden's accounts.

Convalescent and nursing homes

Patients who had been weakened by a period of illness at home or who were not ill enough to remain in hospital after treatment but not well enough to go home, might spend time in a convalescent home. Nursing homes were mainly for women having babies.

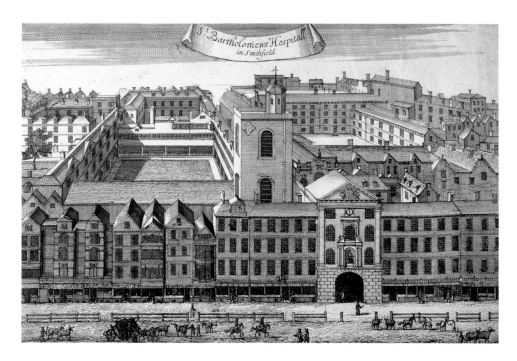

St Bartholomew's Hospital in Smithfield, London, has records dating back to medieval times and still treats patients today.

Researching hospital records

Both TNA and the Wellcome Insitute for the History of Medicine have databases on the internet that contain details of where surviving records of hospitals are held. Most have been deposited with CROs but some remain with the original hospital.

Hospital records on individual patients are closed for 100 years. Workhouse infirmaries, however, come under a different ruling, and their records are closed for only 65 years. Although access to these records may be allowed under certain conditions, it is generally not given for genealogical research.

Individual patient files that are more than 100 years old have generally not survived. What the family historian might find, however, are the names of patients who were admitted to a hospital and on whose authority they were admitted. There are rarely specific details of their illnesses.

Hospitals linked to a religious foundation, such as St Bartholomew's Hospital in London, might have their own baptismal registers, which often contain adult baptisms carried out on patients thought to be in danger of death.

In addition to information about patients, hospital records contain information about the medical staff, such as training and promotion, as well as details of those who supported the hospitals through subscriptions.

THE CARE OF THE MENTALLY ILL

Beliefs in the causes of mental illness went through as many fashions in the past as they do today. The distinctions between mental handicap, temporary insanity and psychosis - a long-term and incurable mental state - were well understood, but before the 19th century there was little public provision for the care of the insane.

Private and public treatment

Mentally handicapped children from better-off families might be cared for privately. For the disturbed, or temporarily insane, there were a number of "mad doctors" who had their own theories about the causes and treatment of insanity. They ran private institutions of various sizes, but care in them was expensive. Finally, for those who were a danger to themselves or others, incarceration on a warrant from two JPs was the only remedy.

The Hospital of St Mary of Bethlehem, in London, known as "Bethlem" (hence "bedlam"), is the best known of the lunatic asylums, where the violently deranged were detained. One of these asylums – the York Asylum – had a very brutal regime, and William Tuke (a Quaker merchant) was so shocked by this that he set up the York Retreat in 1796, which pioneered more gentle treatment, based on modifying behaviour, than was available in most mental hospitals.

Unfortunately, most people could not pay to have their mentally handicapped or ill relatives looked after, and so they had to join all the other unfortunates in the parish workhouse.

The government took an increasing interest in the treatment of the mentally ill from the early part of the 19th century. In 1808, permission for counties to set up asylums for lunatic paupers was granted, but it was not until 1845 that this was made compulsory. Some county asylums were converted prisons that had been used in the Napoleonic Wars.

Commissions of Lunacy

When a wealthy person was unable to function properly, from the mental point of view, the state became involved to protect his or her interests. From medieval times, the assets of a lunatic became the property of the Crown, but by the last part of the 18th century a procedure was established whereby the next of kin of someone mentally afflicted could petition the Chancery Court to have the person declared a lunatic and appoint trustees to administer his or her estate. There were, of course, abuses of the system: families might try to get someone committed to an asylum in order to take control of their money and possessions. Visitors in lunacy were appointed by the court to visit each "chancery lunatic" every year and to write a report on the person.

In 1842, this system was put on a statutory basis, and the Chancery Commission in Lunacy was established. This department was renamed the Masters in Lunacy in 1845. Their inquiries, called Commissions of Lunacy, were occasionally reported in newspapers, but the names of those involved were not always given, since, by the 19th century, mental instability had become a social stigma extending to the whole family.

Criminal lunatics

Although it was always recognized that many people who committed murder were not responsible for their actions, it was not until 1800 that legal provision was made for the care of the criminally insane. In 1840, an Act was passed that allowed all criminal lunatics to be put into an asylum rather than a prison.

Locating mental health records

Some mental hospitals retain their records; other records have been deposited in the usual repositories: CROs, denominational archives and specialist libraries.

TNA holds some asylum registers and returns (surveys) of lunatics in workhouses and asylums (1834-1909), as well as some records relating to naval lunatics. It has a database of the location of the records of county lunatic asylums, and a copy of an unpublished thesis containing TNA sources that can be consulted there.

Researching mental health records

From 1851, census returns have a column to note whether a person was deaf, dumb, blind or lunatic, but after 1871 there was a separate record of those who were lunatic, imbecile or idiot. When you are using census returns, it is always worth checking the parish workhouse, prisons, hospitals and asylums in the area where your ancestors lived to see whether a member of the family might be there. Unfortunately, in the earlier censuses, hospital patients' full names may not be given, simply their initials.

Distinctions were made between the different types of mental state:

- a *lunatic* had periods of sanity
- an *imbecile* was someone who had, later in life, become demented
- an *idiot* was mentally handicapped from birth
- a *moron* had a mental age of 8–12 years
- a *cretin* had mental retardation caused by thyroid deficiency

These words have, over the years, lost their medical connotations and simply become terms of abuse, but they were originally used as fairly precise definitions. They will help you to understand exactly how members of your family were afflicted.

Many lunatic asylums have been closed, but those that remain as mental hospitals tend to be on the same sites as their original incarnations. Most have, unsurprisingly, changed their names. Directories and maps will help you to find out what they are called today. Many, however, have been converted to another use, often divided up into luxury apartments.

The workhouse was often the only place where the poor, whether they were physically or mentally ill, could find shelter.

FURTHER HELP

Faithfull, Pamela *Basic Facts About Lunatics in England and Wales for Family Historians* (FFHS)
TNA *Lunacy and the State*
TNA Domestic Records Information 104 *Lunatic Asylums*

For Crown and Country

There can be very few people who do not have an ancestor who was a member of the armed forces. It has been estimated that during the whole of recorded history there have been only a few years when there was no warfare anywhere in the world. As a major power, Britain was almost constantly at war with European nations until the mid-19th century and needed military personnel to defend and maintain its empire during the following one hundred years. The two World Wars in the 20th century also involved thousands of servicemen and women, from Britain, from the Commonwealth and from the United States. Did your ancestors serve? Were they rewarded with a medal, perhaps for bravery? Did they die in the service of their country, or did they survive to draw a pension and tell their children stories of their experiences?

Members of the armed forces

The creation and maintenance of the British Empire needed considerable numbers of armed personnel. They were also called on to keep order at home before the advent of police forces from the mid-19th century.

SERVICEMEN AND WOMEN

To research service personnel, you need to think about what could have happened to a serviceman or woman. Every stage of his, or her, career would have generated records. The National Archives (TNA) has detailed leaflets giving the class marks of surviving records for the three branches of the services of all the events listed below, and more:

- joining up, either on a voluntary basis or through conscription
- training
- transferring from one unit to another
- wages
- commissions and promotion
- being awarded a medal or other distinction
- being taken prisoner
- dying in battle or while serving
- deserting
- getting court-martialled
- being discharged from the service
- pensions for those who survived
- widows', children's and dependants' pensions
- war memorials and graves

There was always a sharp distinction between officers and other ranks, and their records are generally kept separately. Promotions of officers were published in the *London Gazette*, and lists of officers in the three services were published as the Army List, the Navy List and the Air Force List. The

Recruiting Sergeants at Westminster in 1877 wait for potential recruits. Their aim was to enlist all who were able to serve.

family historian must do more research work to find out about those lower down the hierarchy.

In addition to the soldiers, sailors and airmen, the armed forces needed support staff, and you may find your ancestors among them. They could be medical personnel, chaplains, spies or government employees of the Board of Ordnance, which was responsible for weapons, ammunition and stores. This division employed craftsmen, such as carpenters or smiths. Unfortunately, there are no records specifically relating to the craftsmen and others who supplied goods to the forces (though their names may appear in account books), because they were not directly employed by the government.

The East India Company had its own army and naval officers until 1858, when the company was wound up, so if you don't find a military or naval ancestor in the regular forces, consider the searching the East India Company records.

Any bookshop will reveal that military, naval and airforce history are subjects of enduring interest, and the family historian will find a great deal of background information in them. Some are, of course, academic tomes on the causes and tactics of a war, but others are more concerned with the individuals involved in campaigns and battles. One or more of these books may even include some research concerning your ancestor.

CONSCIENTIOUS OBJECTORS

In both World Wars, those who were opposed to fighting on moral, political or religious grounds, such as Quakers or Jehovah's Witnesses, had to go before a Military Service Tribunal to explain their reasons. Other people, who claimed that they were medically unfit or that their work was too valuable to stop, had to attend tribunals that were held locally. Special Tribunals were held for medical practitioners (including dentists) or vets who wanted to avoid conscription on the basis of their profession. There was also an Appeals Tribunal in almost every county for people who wanted to appeal against the local tribunal's decision. Some conscientious objectors were imprisoned and some were court-martialled.

Unfortunately, most of the government papers relating to World War I tribunals were destroyed in 1921, so TNA has only a few records relating to conscientious objectors. The minute book of the Central Tribunal, which dealt with appeals from the Special Tribunals, was kept, and the records of the Middlesex Appeals Tribunal and the Lothian and Peebles Local Tribunal were retained as samples. Not all other local tribunal records were destroyed, and those that did survive are now stored in either County Record Offices (CROs) or local record offices.

Some people avoided conscription in other ways – by fleeing to Ireland, by bribing officials or by taking drugs to make them appear medically unfit – and a few files relating to these people can be found in TNA.

LEFT Temporary grave markers were made of wood until more permanent memorials could be erected.

BELOW World War I soldiers rest in the trenches.

COMMONWEALTH WAR GRAVES COMMISSION

Founded in 1917 as the Imperial War Graves Commission, this organization aims to care for the graves of members of the armed forces who died on or as a result of active service, and to commemorate those who have no known grave or who died as a result of enemy action. It maintains cemeteries all over the world and publishes lists of the dead buried there. Casualty lists were also published at the time in local newspapers and recorded on war memorials erected to commemorate those who died.

PRISONERS OF WAR

In earlier times, the majority of defeated enemies were usually put to death or enslaved. People of higher rank, however, might be ransomed.

By the mid-18th century, most captives were released after a period of imprisonment. TNA holds some lists of British POWs held in France and French POWs held in Britain during the French Revolution (1789–93) and Napoleonic Wars (1793–1815). The other 19th-century wars for which there are records relating to POWs in

TNA are the Crimean War (1853–55) and the Boer War (1899–1902).

There are very few records in TNA relating to POWs from either of the World Wars: some records were destroyed by bombs, others, unfortunately, were destroyed as a result of official policy, and other records were passed to the International Committee of the Red Cross for safekeeping. The TNA leaflets listed on the following page give information about the records it holds.

INTERNMENT OF CIVILIANS DURING THE WORLD WARS

There was a great fear that nationals of countries against which Britain and her allies were fighting might be used as spies and saboteurs. Germans in World War I were rounded up (in some cases for their own protection) and interned in various places in Britain and Ireland. There was also a camp on the Isle of Man, which was used again in World War II for Germans and Austrians, many of whom

Wars, campaigns and military actions involving British forces from 1538

1587–1603	War against Spain	*1838–42*	1st Afghan War	*1914–18*	World War I
1642–46	English Civil War	*1839*	Opium War (against China)	*1919–21*	Ireland
1652–54	1st Anglo-Dutch War			*1936–39*	Palestine
1665–67	2nd Anglo-Dutch War	*1843–48*	1st Maori War (in New Zealand)	*1939–45*	World War II
1702–13	War of the Spanish Succession	*1845–46*	1st Sikh War	*1945–48*	Campaign in Palestine
1739–42	War of Jenkins' Ear	*1846*	Maori insurrection	*1946–47*	Withdrawal from India
1740–48	War of the Austrian Succession	*1846–47*	War against the Bantu (in South Africa)	*1948–60*	Malayan Emergency
1753–63	Seven Years' War	*1848–49*	2nd Sikh War	*1950–53*	Korean War
1755–63	French and Indian War (in North America)	*1852–53*	2nd Anglo-Burmese War	*1952–60*	Mau-Mau Revolt (in Kenya)
1775–83	War of American Independence	*1853–56*	Crimean War	*1955–59*	Campaign in Cyprus
1775–82	War with Marathas (in India)	*1856–60*	Anglo-Chinese War	*1956*	Suez
1779–83	Siege of Gibraltar	*1857–58*	Indian Mutiny	*1956–63*	Northern Ireland
1793–1802	French Revolutionary War	*1873–74*	1st Ashanti War	*1962*	Brunei
1803–15	Napoleonic Wars	*1875*	3rd Anglo-Burmese War	*1963–66*	Borneo
1808–14	Peninsular War	*1878–80*	2nd Afghan War	*1964–67*	Aden
1812–15	War in America	*1879*	Zulu War	*1969–*	Northern Ireland
1824–26	1st Anglo-Burmese War	*1880–81*	1st Boer War	*1982*	Falklands Campaign
		1882	Occupation of Egypt		
		1896	2nd Ashanti War		
		1899–1902	2nd Boer War		

British forces have been, and still are, involved as peace-keepers in a number of places around the world. The more recent the conflict, the easier it is to trace individuals.

were refugees, and Italians, most of whom had arrived as economic migrants during the 1930s. The Manx Museum contains many records relating to those internees who were held on the Isle of Man.

Other camps were set up elsewhere in the British Isles, and a number of internees were sent to Canada and Australia. The initial panic had died down by 1941, and most of those held in camps were gradually released. British territories overseas also interned foreign nationals during World War II.

INTERNATIONAL COMMITTEE OF THE RED CROSS

Very few records about internees are held in TNA, as the British government passed information to the International Committee of the Red Cross in Geneva. This organization has compiled records of prisoners of war and internees from all nations during both World Wars. Researchers cannot consult these, but the Red Cross will supply information in response to written requests and the payment of a fee. At TNA there is also a list of internees' names and an index to World War II internees.

FURTHER HELP

Commonwealth War Graves Commission, 2 Marlow Road, Maidenhead, Berkshire SL6 7DX. The Debt of Honour Register, listing those killed and where they are buried (if known) during the two World Wars, is available on CD-ROM and on the website www.cwgc.org

TNA Military Records Information 12 *British Prisoners of War c.1760–1919*

TNA Military Records Information 16 *First World War: Conscientious Objectors*

TNA Military Records Information

26 *Intelligence Records in the TNA*

TNA Military Records Information 27 *Prisoners of War and Displaced Persons 1939–1953*

TNA Military Records Information 29 *Prisoners of War in British Hands, 1698–1919*

TNA Military Records Information 55 *Military Nurses and Nursing Services*

TNA Military Records Information 66 *Records of the Board of Ordnance*

TNA Military Records Information 74 *Records of Women's Services: First World War*

Army records

Before 1660, there was no standing army: soldiers were recruited as the need arose. Each regiment was generally known by the name of the colonel who commanded it, until the early 18th century, when they acquired more permanent names. Since then, the Army has been reorganized several times, and regiments have been renamed and amalgamated. There are histories of the Army and individual regiments that will help researchers.

FOREIGN SOLDIERS

Men from many different nationalities joined the Army, but, in addition, there were regiments composed of foreign soldiers commanded by white British officers. The most famous is the brigade of Gurkhas, originally formed in 1815, which comprises soldiers recruited from Nepal in North

ABOVE Cavalry troops took part in battles until World War I.

BELOW Armies depend on men willing to die for their country's cause.

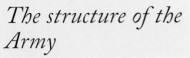

The structure of the Army
Brigade
Battalion/regiment
Company
Platoon/troop

Cavalry are mounted troops
Infantry are foot soldiers

India. Others were the West Africa Regiments, raised from 1800, and the West Indian Regiments, from 1795. The latter had their origins in the Carolina Black Corps established in America during the War of Independence. On the independence of their various countries, the West African and West Indian regiments ceased to be part of the British Army.

ABOVE Women and children were among the "camp followers" who went on military campaigns with the army.

WOMEN IN THE ARMY

Women didn't officially join the Army until 1949, when the Women's Royal Army Corps (WRAC) was formed, although there had been a few women's units in World War I. As long as there were soldiers, however, there were women, including wives, accompanying them. They were called camp followers, and they did the laundry, nursed casualties and provided other services. This was semi-acknowledged: the Army kept records of births of children to serving soldiers whose wives were attached to the regiment while on a campaign. Surviving registers from 1761 are in TNA and have been indexed.

RECRUITMENT AND TRAINING

Until 1871, commissioned officers were almost exclusively drawn from the upper classes or wealthy families, because they had to pay for their appointments and promotion. Non-commissioned officers came up through the ranks. Conscription was introduced only in World War I. Before that, recruiting officers toured the country to encourage young men to join the Army. Criminals might also be offered the option of joining up, especially in wartime.

Until the establishment of the various Army colleges, beginning in 1802 with officer training, any instruction needed was given by the unit to which a soldier was posted. As equipment became more specialized, especially in the 20th century, apprenticeships were offered to those wishing to acquire a particular skill.

LOCATING ARMY RECORDS

Finding and putting together records relating to Army ancestors is not easy: this is a highly specialized area of research. Although there are many records (mainly pre-20th century) in TNA, individual regiments may have their own archives and many also have museums where papers may be lodged. There is also the National Army Museum in London. Many records relating to soldiers in the World Wars

---

Army ranks

Commissioned officers
Field Marshal
General
Lieutenant General
Major General
Brigadier
Colonel
Lieutenant Colonel
Major
Captain
Lieutenant
Second Lieutenant

Non-commissioned officers and other ranks
Warrant Officer 1st class (Regimental Sergeant Major)
Warrant Officer 2nd class (Company Sergeant Major)
Sergeant Major
Staff Sergeant
Sergeant
Corporal
Lance Corporal
Private (also called a Gunner in the Artillery, a Sapper in the Engineers and a Trooper in the Cavalry)

Significant dates in the history of the Army

Note that the establishment and name changes of all the different regiments, as well as many support departments, have been omitted.

1660/1 Standing army established.
1716 First separate artillery regiment created.
1717 Corps of Engineers formed.
1741 Royal Military Academy created at Woolwich, East London, initially to train artillery officers and later engineers and signals personnel.
1796 Chaplains' Department formed.

1802 Royal Military College created at Great Marlow and later moved to Sandhurst, Berkshire, to train officers of the cavalry and infantry divisions.
1857 Military Music School (currently Royal Military School of Music) created at Kneller Hall, Middlesex.
1858 Staff College created at Camberley, Surrey.
1858 Veterinary Medical Department (currently the Royal Army Veterinary Corps) formed.
1877 Military police introduced.
1897 Army Nursing Service (currently Queen Alexandra's Royal Army Nursing Corps) formed.
1916 Tanks introduced into warfare.
1920 Separate Corps of Signals created.
1939 Conscription introduced.
1940 First Parachute Corps formed.
1947 National Service introduced (abolished in 1961).
1947 Royal Military Academy amalgamated with the Royal Military College at Sandhurst.
1949 Women's Royal Army Corps (WRACS) formed.
1952 Special Air Service Regiment formed.

RIGHT Flags, furled while marching, provide a rallying point for soldiers who have become lost or cut off from their comrades on the battlefield. The crests on the flags originated in the days when most people could not read.

were destroyed by bombing. The majority of recent records are still with the Ministry of Defence; they are not on open access, and a fee is charged for research. The family historian researching a soldier ancestor must therefore find out where he served and, for both World Wars, his service number, if possible.

FURTHER HELP

Cantwell, J. *The Second World War: A Guide to Records in the Public Record Office* (HMSO)

Fowler, Simon *Army Records for Family Historians* (TNA Readers' Guide No. 2)

Pimlott, J. *The Guinness History of the British Army* (Guinness 1993). This has an appendix summarizing the histories of divisions and regiments (detailing name changes), which is useful for the family historian trying to work out in which modern-day regiment an ancestor was serving at a particular time.

TNA Military Records Information 3 *Civil War Soldiers 1642–1660*

TNA Military Records Information 4 *Army: Officers' Records, 1660–1913*

TNA Military Records Information 5 *Army: Soldiers' Discharge Papers, 1660–1913*

TNA Military Records Information 6 *Army: Soldiers' Pension Records, 1702–1913*

TNA Military Records Information 7 *Army: Muster Rolls and Pay Lists c.1730–1898*

TNA Military Records Information 9 *First World War, 1914–1918: Soldiers' Papers 1914–1920*

TNA Military Records Information 10 *First World War: Army Officers' Service Records*

TNA Military Records Information 11 *First World War: Army War Diaries*

TNA Military Records Information 14 *Army: Other Ranks: Useful Sources if You are Getting Nowhere*

TNA Military Records Information 15 *First World War: Disability and Dependants' Pensions*

TNA Military Records Information 17 *The Army Lists*

TNA Military Records Information 22 *Army: Courts Martial 17th–20th Centuries*

TNA Military Records Information 23 *Army: Campaign Records, 1660–1714*

TNA Military Records Information 24

Army: Campaign Records, 1714–1814

TNA Military Records Information 25 *Operational Records of the British Army, 1816-1913*

TNA Military Records Information 68 *Second World War: Army Operations*

TNA Military Records Information 73 *Army: Officers' Commissions*

TNA Military Records Information 75 *Army: Courts Martial: First World War 1914–1918*

TNA Military Records Information 76 *Armed Service: Campaign Medals and Other Service Medals*

TNA Military Records Information 77 *Armed Services: Gallantry Medals*

TNA Military Records Information 78 *Armed Services: Gallantry Medals, Further Information*

The Ministry of Defence's website has a section with links to various Army and regimental museums www.army.mod.uk/ceremonialandher itage/museums_main.html-ssi

Royal Air Force records

The Royal Air Force (RAF) was created comparatively recently, and so researching family members who served in it can be simpler than working on other branches of the armed forces. By the beginning of the 20th century, bureaucrats were better at record-keeping, and there are fewer records to search.

THE BEGINNING OF AERIAL WARFARE

As early as 1804, experiments using balloons were being conducted at the Royal Military Academy in Woolwich, London, and they were used in wars in Africa and China at the end of the 19th century. There was even a School of Ballooning at Aldershot, Hampshire. These balloons came under the responsibility of the Royal Engineers, which were part of the British Army, so any records relating to ancestors who worked with them will be in Army records.

It was not long after the first flight in a heavier-than-air machine in 1903 that the potential for aeroplanes and,

Royal Airforce pilots in an overseas airfield in 1964. A photograph such as this in a family member's archives might be where your research in military records begins.

later, airships in warfare was recognized. On 1 April 1918, the Royal Air Force was formed by the amalgamation of the Royal Flying Corps and the Royal Naval Air Service.

The RAF is divided into commands – different sections responsible for particular types of activity. There are currently only two (Strike Command, and Personnel and Training Command),

but in the past there were more, such as Bomber Command, Fighter Command, Training Command, etc. Each of these Commands contained a number of groups, divided into squadrons. A squadron consisted of a number of airplanes, the crews (pilots, navigators, gunners and signallers) who flew in them and the ground crew who maintained and repaired them. The airfields

RAF ranks

Commissioned officers
Marshal of the Royal Air Force
Air Chief Marshal
Air Marshal
Air Vice-Marshal
Air Commodore
Group Captain
Wing Commander
Squadron Leader
Flight Lieutenant
Flying Officer, Pilot Officer

Non-commissioned officers and other ranks
Warrant Officer/Master Aircrew
Flight Sergeant
Sergeant
Corporal
Senior Aircraftman/woman
Leading Aircraftman/woman
Senior Technician
Junior Technician

The shark's mouth was a motif used by 211 squadron in World War II.

Significant dates in the history of the RAF

1912 Royal Naval Air Service (RNAS) and Royal Flying Corps (RFC) established.
1918 RNAS and RFC merged to form Royal Air Force (RAF).
1918 RAF Nursing Service created, becoming Princess Mary's RAF Nursing Service in 1923.
1918 Women's Royal Air Force (WRAF) created (abolished in 1920).
1920 RAF College opened at Cranwell.
1939 Women's Auxiliary Air Force (WAAF) created.
1994 WAAF integrated into the RAF.

from which they flew also needed medical and administrative staff, stores, transport – all the usual back-up involved in any large organization.

WRAF AND WAAF

The Women's Royal Air Force (WRAF) was formed at the same time as the Royal Air Force in 1918. It was disbanded in 1920, but re-established as the Women's Auxiliary Air Force (WAAF) in 1939. In World War I, the role of women was confined to administration, but in World War II they did work in some technical and mechanical grades as well. They were not allowed to join operational aircrews, although there were women pilots in Ferry Command and the Air Transport Auxiliary (ATA), which flew aircraft from one place to another.

Very few records relating to women officers from World War I have survived, although ordinary airwomen's records are in TNA, where there is an index to all Air Force personnel, which includes women, and gives service numbers.

RESEARCH AND DEVELOPMENT

The government played a great part in the research, development and manufacture of aircraft, airships and radar systems. Many of the records are in TNA, and the RAF Museum also has a substantial collection, as well as many old aircraft.

NURSING SERVICES

At the outbreak of World War I, advertisements were placed in nursing journals to recruit personnel for the Royal Air Force Nursing Service (RAFNS). At first this service was intended to last only as long as the hostilities, but after the war the government decided to make it a permanent part of the RAF. In 1923, it became Princess Mary's Royal Air Force Nursing Service.

If your ancestors were among the very first volunteers, information about them might be in TNA, which mainly holds documents relating to the establishment of the RAFNS and the decision to continue it. Otherwise their records will be with the RAF.

Nursing staff on an exercise to learn to help air crash victims.

LOCATING RAF RECORDS

Records relating to servicemen whose service number was between 1 and 329000 (largely those who served in the RAF during World War I) are mainly in TNA, where there is an index of service numbers. The records of anyone who was still serving in the RAF at the outbreak of World War II, however, will still be with the RAF's records.

The RAF Museum at Hendon, North London, holds many records, including log books and officers' diaries, as well as a card index of every aircraft belonging to the RAF.

FURTHER HELP

Fowler, S., Elliott, R., Nesbit, R.C. and Goulter, C. *RAF Records in the PRO* (TNA Readers' Guide No. 8)
TNA Military Records Information 28 *Royal Air Force: Research and Development*
TNA Military Records Information 49 *Royal Air Force: Airmen's Service Records*
TNA Military Records Information 50 *British Air Forces: Tracing an Individual*

TNA Military Records Information 74 *Records of Women's Services, First World War*
Royal Air Force Museum, Aerodrome Road, Hendon, London NW9 5LI www.rafmuseum.org.uk
Williamson, H.J. *The Roll of Honour, Royal Flying Corps and Royal Air Force for the Great War 1914–18* (Naval and Military Press) lists officers and men of the RFC and RAF who died in World War I.

The militia, posse comitatis and volunteers

In addition to regular or professional soldiers, a reserve of men who could be called upon in times of war was needed. In England, these reserves, or militia, date from Saxon times. In the Middle Ages, all healthy men between the ages of 15 and 60 were required to do archery practice on Sundays and, according to their income, to provide themselves and their sons over the age of 7 with armour and weapons. Lists of men who could be called upon to serve and those who could give money were made by each county. These were called muster rolls.

With the introduction of a standing army in 1660, these volunteers were stood down, but they were revived in 1757 as a force to protect the country in case of invasion.

THE MILITIA

Each year parishes drew up a list of men capable of serving, and a ballot was held to provide militiamen. They were then trained by the parish, often under the leadership of a member of the local gentry, and the term "trained bands" is often used in records to describe them. Many categories of people, such as clergymen, magistrates, apprentices and parish constables, were exempt. Service was also unpopular among people who had businesses to run, so the better-off members of the community often paid substitutes to serve in their place.

Men served for three years between 1757 and 1786, and for five years after that. They were based at home, except in times of war. While they were away on service, their wives and children were paid an allowance.

A Loyal London Volunteer chose to serve rather than be conscripted.

THE POSSE COMITATIS

During the panic caused by the prospect of invasion at the time of the Napoleonic Wars, a list of the posse comitatis for each county (the strength, or able-bodied men, of the county, effectively the medieval muster) was drawn up in 1798. In addition to listing all the men in the county capable of bearing arms, the list included bakers and owners of barges, horses and wagons. Buckinghamshire is the only county for which a complete record survives, and this has been published, but a number of individual parishes' lists survive from elsewhere. In 1803–4 the Levée en Masse, literally "mass enlistment", collected similar information. With the end of the Napoleonic Wars, fear of invasion declined, and no more general surveys of this kind were made.

VOLUNTEERS

In addition to the militia, in which most men were forced to serve (although there were some volunteers), a number of purely voluntary forces were created. These included the Volunteers, who would not be obliged to serve abroad, and the Yeomanry, who were a cavalry force. Along the coastline, forces of Sea Fencibles (seafaring men under the command of a naval officer) were raised to defend the country against invasion. The various voluntary forces came under the aegis of the Lords Lieutenant of the counties.

19TH-CENTURY DEVELOPMENTS

The end of the Napoleonic Wars in 1815 brought a period of comparative peace to Britain. As a result, it was no longer considered necessary to conscript men to serve in the militia, and the last ballot took place in 1829; thereafter, it was a completely voluntary force. In 1881, militias became linked to local regiments and were renamed as battalions or reserve units. The Rifle Volunteers, a separate organization, was founded in 1859.

20TH-CENTURY DEVELOPMENTS

The two World Wars meant that there was a continuing need for voluntary forces to serve at home.

Territorial Army

In 1908 the militia became the Territorial Army (TA), which continues to the present day, and at the same time the Yeomanry became part of the TA.

Home Guard

During World War II, the militia was revived under the name Local Defence Volunteers – later renamed the Home Guard – in which men between the ages of 17 and 62 were called upon to serve their country.

LOCATING RECORDS OF THE MILITIA, POSSE COMITATIS AND VOLUNTEEERS

Finding references to individual militiamen is not easy, as the records are scattered between a number of repositories. Lists of militia officers were published from 1794, and records relating to them are held in TNA, along with muster and pay books for everyone. Militiamen were eligible to become Chelsea Pensioners after a certain length of service or if they were invalided out, and these records are also in TNA, as well as information on deserters and those who were court-martialled. CROs hold miscellaneous papers, including the ballots.

Other material may be in the regimental museums to which the various volunteer and militia forces were linked after 1881, when a large-scale reform of the Army and auxiliary forces was made.

Local newspapers often covered the activities of the militia in detail. Family History Societies and individuals have produced booklets and microfiche listing individuals who served in their area, which should be in CROs.

USING MILITIA AND POSSE COMITATIS RECORDS

During the period of the ballots to provide militiamen, most parishes listed every man between the ages of 18 and 45, and noted those who were unfit through blindness or other disability. A few lists also included children. Consequently, they form a kind of local census and should be consulted both to locate ancestors and to see whether they had any physical or mental problems.

Unusually long gaps between the births of children can, of course, be due to a number of reasons, but a three- or five-year gap during times of war may suggest that your ancestor was serving in the militia away from home. Women often had to apply to parish officials for support while their husbands were serving, and their appeals will be found in parish records in the accounts of either the overseer of the poor or the churchwarden.

Posse comitatis lists are useful because they can help you to gauge your agricultural ancestors' level of wealth from the number of horses and carts they owned. People's occupations are also often given.

FURTHER HELP

Gibson, Jeremy and Dell, Alan *Tudor and Stuart Muster Rolls* (FFHS)
Gibson, Jeremy and Medlycott, Mervyn *Militia Lists and Musters* (FFHS)
TNA Military Records Information 18 *The Militia 1757–1914*
TNA Military Records Information 72 *Auxiliary Forces: Volunteers, Yeomanry, Territorials and Home Guard, 1769–1945*
Spencer, William *Records of the Militia & Volunteer Forces 1757–1945* (TNA Readers' Guide No. 3)

RIGHT Each county was responsible for raising a militia force. These soldiers are from Buckinghamshire.

Royal Navy records

Known as the Senior Service, the Navy is the longest-established branch of the armed services, having its roots in the 9th century. There are some medieval and Tudor records relating to it, but most date from the post-Commonwealth period. Samuel Pepys, the famous diarist, was from 1660 a civil servant who rose to the top of the Navy Board. He reformed many aspects of naval practice and introduced many of the systems that survive today. He also laid down methods of record keeping for which the genealogist should be grateful.

The *Henry Addington*, festooned with flags of many nations, fires her guns on a ceremonial occasion in 1802 at West India Docks, London.

SECTIONS OF THE ROYAL NAVY

The Royal Navy (RN) is divided into four sections: Ships, Royal Marines, Fleet Air Arm and Submarines. In addition, there is the Women's Royal Naval Service, which has formed a permanent part of the Royal Navy since 1939.

Ships

The history of the vessels themselves is largely one of developments in technology, as ships changed from being made of wood to metal. They were first powered by sails, then steam, then diesel, and, in the case of submarines, nuclear power. With the changes in technology came the need for more specialized and trained personnel, which led to a variety of job titles.

Royal Marines

The Marines were originally soldiers who served at sea. They were founded in 1664 as the Admiral's Regiment. In 1755 they came under the control of the Admiralty and were, like sailors, entitled to enter the Greenwich Hospital after discharge.

The Marines, first formed in 1755, had four divisions, depending on where they were based, and they usually remained with the same division throughout their career. The first three bases were Chatham, Portsmouth and Plymouth, and during 1805–69 the fourth was at Woolwich. Records for 1793–1925 are in TNA, but those relating to officers after 1925 are held at the Royal Marines' Historical Office. There are also some 20th-century records in the Fleet Air Arm Museum. The Royal Marines

Navy ranks

There are a bewildering number of titles and ranks in the Royal Navy, which have changed over the years. The following is an abbreviated list.

Commissioned officers
Admiral
Commodore
Captain
Commander
Lieutenant
Mate/Sub-lieutenant
Master (after 1808)
Midshipman

Other ranks
Warrant Officer
Boatswain/Bosun
Gunner
Carpenter
Chaplain
Purser
Schoolmaster (18th century)/
Naval instructor
Cook
Rating (the ordinary seaman)

Museum at Southsea also has many documents, diaries and other records relating to individuals' experiences.

Fleet Air Arm

This section of the Navy is responsible for aircraft of all kinds launched from on board ship. In World War I, it also operated armoured cars transported by ship to the battlefields.

Submarines

The first British submarine was launched in 1901, and by the outbreak of World War II there were 74 submarines in service.

Women in the Royal Navy

From early times, women were frequently, but unofficially, found on board ship. Between the mid-17th century and the mid-19th century, warrant officers were allowed to take their wives to sea, but they rarely appear in the muster books. During battles, women carried ammunition and tended to the wounded. Petitions requesting financial help if their husbands were killed in action and as recompense for their own work as nurses may be found at TNA.

Reports of women disguising themselves as men to serve on board ship are occasionally found. They were immediately discharged when their gender was discovered. It was not until World War I that the Women's Royal Naval Service (WRNS – pronounced "Wrens") was formed. It lasted only a year (1918–19) but was reformed in 1939 for World War II.

MUSTER BOOKS

Ships' muster books, to be found in TNA, list all members of a crew on a particular ship when it began a new voyage, and this is the main way of tracing a rating's career. Ships had to take their support services with them, and so, in addition to the officers and sailors, crews would include surgeons, chaplains, cooks and carpenters, who might all be found in muster books.

Until 1853, commissioned officers and sailors were paid off at the end of each voyage, although warrant officers were generally regarded as belonging to a particular ship. Officers were put on half-pay until they received a new commission, but the ratings had to fend for themselves. Many ratings would try to remain in the service of a particular captain because they had become accustomed and loyal to him.

APPRENTICESHIPS

Before 1794, naval officers could begin an apprenticeship when they were only 7 years old. They were generally known as midshipmen, and after a period of on-the-job training and study in navigational skills, they passed an examination to qualify as a lieutenant. Ships usually had someone on board to educate children and

---

Significant dates in the history of the Navy

As an island, England has always needed ships for defence, so the Navy's origins pre-date the Norman Conquest.

1642 Permanent Navy structure established.

1652 Creation of the post of "able" seaman, senior to and more experienced than the "ordinary" kind.

1660 Samuel Pepys became Clerk of the Acts at the Navy Board. Between this date and his resignation in 1689, by which time he had been promoted to Secretary of the Admiralty, he created an administrative system that lasted into the 19th century.

1694 Foundation of Greenwich Hospital.

1733 Royal Naval Academy founded (became Royal Naval College in 1806).

1755 Royal Marines transfer from Army to Navy control.

1795 Issue of lemon juice to prevent scurvy introduced.

1820 RN began surveying and mapping the seas.

1824 First attempts to standardize uniforms.

1825 Rum ration halved.

1831 Beer ration abolished.

1830 Gunnery School created.

1835 Register of Seamen introduced.

1840s Steam-powered ships introduced, requiring stokers to feed coal into the engines.

1859 Royal Naval Reserve established.

1871 Flogging in peacetime suspended (1879 suspended totally, but not actually abolished).

1873 Royal Naval College transferred to Greenwich.

1880 Royal Naval Engineering College opened.

1901 Submarines introduced.

1903 Osborne section of the Royal Naval College opened on the Isle of Wight.

1918 Women's Royal Navy Service (WRNS) created.

1937 Fleet Air Arm transferred from RAF to RN control.

1963 First nuclear-powered submarine introduced.

1994 WRNS integrated into the RN.

NAVY WEEK The Dockyards will be open to the Public every Weekday from Saturday. August 1st to Saturday. August 8th. inclusive.

VISIT THE DOCKYARDS
CHATHAM. PORTSMOUTH. DEVONPORT
CHEAP DAY TICKETS BY SOUTHERN RAILWAY

Devoting a whole week to celebrating the Navy shows how important it was in the nation's consciousness in the 1930s.

young sailors. From the early 19th century, some chaplains were also acting as schoolmasters. Warrant officers could also become lieutenants. Promotion thereafter was largely through ability, though the patronage of senior officers was also essential. Midshipmen received certificates, called Passing Certificates, on becoming qualified, and these are held at TNA.

ROYAL NAVAL COLLEGE
A training school for young naval officers was founded at Dartmouth in 1863. It was initially based in two hulks moored on the River Dart, but in 1905 a college was built. The junior section of the Royal Naval College was set up at Osborne on the Isle of Wight to educate boys who would progress to the College at Dartmouth.

As well as attracting the sons of the middle and upper classes, who were sent there to learn to be officers, the Navy provided a convenient way of providing for orphans, and various organizations and charities sent boys into the service.

PRESS GANGS AND THE ROYAL NAVAL RESERVE
Although attracting naval officers was relatively easy, it was not quite as simple to get ordinary sailors, or ratings, to serve. In times of war, young men condemned to death for a crime might be offered the alternative of enrolling in the Navy, and men might be legally pressed into service, which was effectively kidnapping.

Not all men were in danger of this, however, because the last thing the Navy needed was those who were unaccustomed to the sea and who might imperil their fellow sailors or the ship through seasickness or ignorance. Press-ganged landlubbers were therefore usually released if taken on board, while the press gangs went in search of merchant seamen and fishermen. If an

ancestor working in a marine occupation suddenly disappears, this may be because his ship sank, but it might also be because he was press-ganged into the Navy, so it is worth checking out both possibilities.

Local papers in maritime areas might report riots or fights caused by people trying to prevent their menfolk being taken. This might also have led to criminal proceedings.

After 1859, this unusual recruiting practice was regularized through the formation of the Royal Naval Reserve, whereby merchant seamen could be called up into the Royal Navy as the need arose.

NAVAL DOCKYARDS
Naval dockyards, where ships were built and equipped, employed a range of skilled workmen: shipwrights, ropemakers, carpenters, and so forth, as well as general labourers. The ships also had to take their food with them. Both sections came under the ultimate authority of the Admiralty. Supplying guns, however, came under the Board of Ordnance. Surviving records for Britain date from the late 18th century. In addition to establishments in Britain, the Navy maintained dockyards all over the world, and some of these records go back to the beginning of the 18th century.

RESEARCH AND DEVELOPMENT
Most naval R&D was carried out by private firms under the patronage of the Admiralty. It is possible that some information may exist in company archives, but, since the development of ships and weapons would have been confidential, most records will be in TNA. Patents on inventions before 1853 are also held in TNA. After that they are with the Patent Office.

GREENWICH HOSPITAL

The Greenwich Hospital was opened in 1694 and closed in 1869. Until then, seamen who had served in the Royal Navy (but not the Merchant Navy) were entitled to live there. The rules were stringent – basically no wine, women or song – so many sailors who had reached retirement age or had been invalided out of the Navy chose to live outside but still collect their naval pensions. The records are in TNA.

LOCATING RECORDS OF THE ROYAL NAVY

Printed lists of officers were published as the Navy List during 1782–1914. Records relating to officers entering the service after 1890 and ratings after 1892 remain with the Ministry of Defence Royal Navy records. Before that date, most are in TNA. The National Maritime Museum holds a large collection of naval portraits and photographs of ships and sailors. The Royal Naval Museum holds many private documents, pictures and photographs, donated by former and serving men and their families, which date back to the late 18th century. These show what life at sea was like over the years.

Lists were kept of those protected from being press-ganged.

FURTHER HELP

Commissioned Sea Officers of the Royal Navy 1600–1815 (National Maritime Museum 1954)

Fleet Air Arm Archive 1939–1945 www.fleetairarmarchive.net

Fleet Air Arm Museum, Royal Navy Air Station, Yeovilton, Ilchester, Somerset BA22 8HT www.fleetairarm.com

National Maritime Museum, Greenwich, London SE10 9NF www.nmm.ac.uk also contains the Caird Library

TNA Military Records Information 30 *Royal Navy: Officers' Service Records*

TNA Military Records Information 31 *Royal Navy: Ratings' service records 1667–1923*

TNA Military Records Information 32 *Royal Navy: Log Books and Reports of Proceedings*

TNA Military Records Information 33 *First World War: Naval Operations*

TNA Military Records Information 35 *Operational Records of the Royal Navy 1660–1914*

TNA Military Records Information 38 *Naval Research and Development*

TNA Military Records Information 41 *Naval Dockyards*

TNA Military Records Information 43 *Ships Wrecked or Sunk*

TNA Military Records Information 45 *Royal Marines: Other Ranks' Service Records*

TNA Military Records Information 46 *Royal Marines: How to Find a Division*

TNA Military Records Information 47 *Royal Marines: Officers' Service Records*

TNA Military Records Information 48 *Royal Marines: Further Areas of Research*

TNA Military Records Information 56 *Royal Navy: Nurses and Nursing Services*

TNA Military Records Information 60 *Royal Navy: Pay and Pensions Records: Commissioned officers*

TNA Military Records Information 61 *Royal Navy: Pay and Pension: Warrant officers*

TNA Military Records Information 62 *Royal Navy: Pension Records: Ratings*

TNA Military Records Information 69 *Royal Navy: Operational Records 1939–45*

TNA Military Records Information 71: *The Royal Naval Volunteer Reserve 1903–1919*

TNA Military Records Information 79 *Royal Navy: Officers' Service Records, First World War and Confidential Reports 1893–1943*

Rodger, N.A.M. *Naval Records for Genealogists* (TNA Handbook No. 22)

Royal Marines Museum, Southsea, Hampshire PO4 9PX www.royalmarinesmuseum.co.uk

Royal Naval Museum, HM Naval Base (P66), Portsmouth, Hants PO1 3NH www.royalnavalmuseum.org

Royal Navy Submarine Museum, Haslar Jetty Road, Gosport, Hampshire PO12 2AS www.rnsubmus.co.uk

Merchant Navy records

Although merchant seamen were not officially part of the Royal Navy, in practice men worked for both, particularly in wartime. As a maritime nation, exporting and importing goods over the globe, merchant seamen played an important role in the development of British history.

LOCATING RECORDS OF MERCHANT SEAMEN

Surviving records of ships' musters from 1747 and crew agreements for 1835–60 are held by TNA. Thereafter records are divided among a number of repositories. Ten per cent of crew agreements and those for famous vessels are held by TNA. The National Maritime Museum holds the remaining 90 per cent for 1861, 1862 and every year thereafter that ended in "5", until 1939. Some local record offices took documents from the other years, but the majority went to the Maritime

History Research Collection at the Memorial University of Newfoundland in Canada. The Manx National Heritage Library took those records relating to ports on the Isle of Man. Crew agreements for 1939–50 are held by the General Register and Record Office of Shipping and Seamen in Cardiff.

SHIPS' NUMBERS

In order to access the records, you need to know the official number of the ship on which your ancestor served, and the dates. From 1786, each ship above a certain size had to be registered by its owner with the customs office of its home port. It was given a number, which remained the same as long as it was in service, and a certificate. A copy of the certificate was sent to Customs House in London. In 1814, a fire destroyed these centrally held copies. CROs or local record

During World War II, the Merchant Navy kept Britain and her allies in supplies.

offices may hold original port documents including details of the certificates. The TNA holds post-1814 records. These are useful in researching ship-owning ancestors, as well as mariners, because many merchant ships were owned by a number of people from a variety of professional backgrounds with shares in its profits (or, of course, losses).

In 1825, all ships had to be re-registered, but at any time an individual vessel might need a new certificate if there was a change in ownership or it moved to a new port. There is an index of ships giving their numbers on microfiche, which is held by a number of repositories. Two annual publications, Lloyd's Register of Shipping and the Mercantile Navy List, also contain lists of ships with their official numbers.

Seafarers might work on local fishing boats before joining the Merchant Navy and then serving in the Royal Navy.

LLOYD'S OF LONDON

As an insurer of ships and cargoes, Lloyd's of London compiled registers of captains and mates of merchant vessels who held masters' certificates and who were working during 1869–1947. These Captains' Registers contain details of each man's career, and some information recorded in them goes back to 1851. Details of men who held masters' certificates but did not serve as captains or mates in 1869–1911 and 1932–47 are also included. These registers generally do not contain information about men working on fishing vessels, coasters, colliers and ferries, but they do include those who were involved in foreign trade, who needed different certificates.

Lloyd's List, published since 1697, is a newspaper produced by Lloyd's of London containing news about commercial shipping. Issues from 1741 survive in a number of archives. Over

Food from overseas being unloaded near Tower Bridge in London.

the centuries it has changed in format and name and has had supplements added, which are of great use to family historians, enabling them to track the journey of merchant seamen ancestors and, perhaps, discover records of their deaths in wrecks and losses.

RANKS

The hierarchy on board merchant ships is not quite as complicated as that on Royal Navy vessels. Master mariners, mates and engineers were the officers on board merchant ships, and seamen were the equivalent of the ratings in the Royal Navy. No qualifications were needed to work on merchant ships until 1845, and they were initially voluntary.

Masters and mates who wished to pilot their own vessels in and out of British ports without a pilot were examined by the Corporation of Trinity House in order to receive an exemption certificate. Registers of certificates for 1850–1957 and examination results for 1864–1986 are all held in the Guildhall Library.

FURTHER HELP

Guildhall Library Leaflet No. 1 *Lloyd's "Captains Registers" at Guildhall Library and Related Sources Elsewhere*

Guildhall Library Leaflet *The Corporation of Trinity House – Family History Sources at Guildhall Library*

Hogg, Peter L. *Using Merchant Ship Records for Family Historians* (FFHS)

Manx National Heritage, Manx Museum and National Trust, Douglas, Isle of Man IM1 3LY www.isle-of-man.com/interests/genealogy/sources.htm

Memorial University of Newfoundland, St Johns, NF A1C 5S7, Canada www.mun.ca/

NMM Research Guide No. C1 *The Merchant Navy: Tracing People: Crew lists, agreements and official logs*

NMM Research Guide No. C2 *The Merchant Navy: Tracing People: Master mariners, mates and engineers*

NMM Research Guide No. C3 *The Merchant Navy: Bibliography*

NMM Research Guide No. C4 *The Merchant Navy: Sources for Enquiries*

NMM Research Guide No. C5 *The Merchant Navy: Sources for Ships' Histories*

NMM Research Guide No. C6 *The Merchant Navy: The Mercantile Navy List*

NMM Research Guide No. C7 *The Merchant Navy: Shipping Listed in Parliamentary Papers*

NMM Research Guide No. C8 *The Merchant Navy: Wrecks, Losses and Casualties*

NMM Research Guide No. C9 *The Merchant Navy: World War One*

NMM Research Guide No. C10 *The Merchant Navy: World War Two*

NMM Research Guide No. C11 *The Merchant Navy: The Handy Shipping Guide*

NMM Research Guide No. C12 *The Merchant Navy: Ship Registration and Custom House Duties*

NMM Research Guide No. H1 *Lloyd's:*

Lloyd's List: Brief history

NMM Research Guide No. H2 *Lloyd's: Resources at the National Maritime Museum*

NMM Research Guide No. H3 *Lloyd's: Captains' Registers*

NMM Research Guide No. H5 *Lloyd's: Registers Held at the National Maritime Museum*

TNA Source Sheet 38 *Merchant Seamen Records in TNA*

TNA Military Records Information 37 *Merchant Seamen: Royal Naval Reserve*

Registrar General of Shipping and Seamen, PO Box 165, Cardiff CF4 5FU

Smith, H., Watts, Christopher T. and Watts, Michael J. *Records of Merchant Shipping and Seamen* (TNA Readers' Guide No. 20)

Watts, Christopher T. and Watts, Michael J. *My Ancestor Was a Merchant Seaman: How Can I Find Out More About Him?* (SoG)

Other maritime occupations

As a collection of islands, the United Kingdom was dependent on the sea for imported and exported goods, and so a fair proportion of its inhabitants have at some time been involved in maritime occupations.

THE ROLE OF TRINITY HOUSE

The Corporation of Trinity House, which received a royal charter in 1514, has been responsible for overseeing a range of activities linked to the sea. Officers of the Royal and Merchant Navies were eligible to become members, called Younger Brethren. From their numbers, a ruling council, called Elder Brethren, was elected. In addition to the responsibilities listed below, the Elder Brethren were

ABOVE A boatman ferries a couple across the Thames in 1804.

involved in the examination of Royal Navy pilots and pupils of the mathematical school at Christ's Hospital, who trained to be sea captains. They also oversaw the ballasting of ships on the River Thames and heard cases in the Court of Admiralty involving collisions.

CHARITIES

Trinity House maintained almshouses for ex-seamen and their widows. It also gave financial assistance, in the form of pensions or other payments, to mariners and their families anywhere in the United Kingdom. Those who wanted to take advantage of these services had to submit a petition, and the records of these petitions for 1787–1854 have been indexed.

A major port such as Liverpool needed hundreds of workers to support its shipping trade .

WATERMEN AND LIGHTERMEN IN LONDON

Until the 19th century, there was only one bridge, London Bridge, across the Thames, and so people used boats to cross the river instead. They also used them to travel along the Thames, since roads then were as crowded as they are today and in a far worse state of repair. The operators of these boats, called watermen, were regulated either by Trinity House, which licensed mainly ex-mariners, or by the Company of Watermen, one of the London livery companies, which was also responsible from 1700 for lightermen, who unloaded and loaded goods on ships. The company's area of authority extended from Gravesend to Windsor.

Like the other companies, the Company of Watermen had an apprenticeship system. Since 1721, an annual race for the prize of Doggett's Coat and Badge has been rowed on the Thames by six watermen within a year of completing their apprenticeships. (The prize was named after Thomas Doggett, an actor who initiated the race, and the winner receives a coat bearing an embroidered badge.)

LIGHTHOUSES

As the general Lighthouse Authority for England, Wales, the Channel Islands and Gibraltar, Trinity House was, and still is, responsible for supplying and maintaining lighthouses, light vessels, buoys and beacons. Before 1841, some lighthouses were privately owned. Ships had to pay a sum of money when entering or leaving port, which went to maintain the lights.

PILOTS

Ships coming into port needed pilots – men who knew the currents and the physical hazards, such as sandbanks – to guide them. Trinity House was

The only access to Beachy Head lighthouse, off the south coast of England, was by aerial railway.

responsible for examining and licensing about two-thirds of the pilots working in England, Wales and the Channel Islands. Its main area of responsibility was London and the River Thames from the estuary to London Bridge (for which it had responsibility from 1604), but there were forty other ports for which it issued pilots' licences after 1808. Masters and mates in the Merchant Navy could be granted exemption certificates by Trinity House if they wanted to pilot their own vessels and were qualified to do so.

Trinity House was not responsible for pilots working at Liverpool, Bristol and some of the ports in the northeast of England. In addition, it had no responsibility over the river pilots needed along the major inland waterways, such as the Thames.

LOCATING THE RECORDS OF TRINITY HOUSE

Since its founding in 1514, Trinity House has occupied a number of different buildings within London. Some were burned down, and in World War II the surviving records relating to

lighthouses and light vessels were destroyed by a bomb. Most of those that remain are in the Guildhall Library in London, but access to the 20th-century records is restricted.

Scotland, with the exception of the port of Leith, and Ireland did not come under Trinity House's aegis, and so records relating to these two countries will be found in their own national or local archives. Leith's Trinity House records are in Edinburgh.

LIFEBOATS

Lifeboat stations were originally run by local authorities, and any surviving records before 1824 will be with CROs. In 1824, the Royal National Lifeboat Institution (RNLI) was set up to co-ordinate the provision of stations around the coast of Britain. The crews were, and still are, volunteers, so information about individual crewmen, especially in the early days, is sparse. They were simply fishermen who could be called out in the event of an emergency. The RNLI does, however, have records of coxswains (helmsmen) and the honorary secretary of each station, as well as lists of those killed and medals awarded for bravery. Newspapers reported cases of shipwrecks and rescues.

FURTHER HELP

Guildhall Library leaflet *Records of the Corporation of Trinity House*
Guildhall Library leaflet *The Corporation of Trinity House: Family History Sources at Guildhall Library*
Guildhall Library leaflet *Records of Watermen and Lightermen*
Guildhall Library leaflet *Doggett's Coat and Badge Race*
Royal National Lifeboat Institution Headquarters, West Quay Road, Poole, Dorset BH15 1HZ www.lifeboats.org.uk

Lifecycle checklist

On the opposite page is a list of the events that occur in most people's lives. It is included as a reminder of the kinds of records the family historian needs to look for, with an indication of where they are most likely to be found. Of course there is no such thing as an "average" life – everyone's is different in some way from the norm – but the following points may help in your research.

ADOLESCENCE

Men were at their most mobile between the ages of 15 and 21, at the time of taking up apprenticeships or beginning work. They also moved the greatest distance during this period in their lives. In Victorian times, servants aged 12–15 were the most mobile of all male workers.

MARRIAGE

Contrary to popular belief, our ancestors rarely married before the age of 20. There were child marriages (or, more precisely, betrothals), but these were arranged between landowners for financial and dynastic purposes, and the couples concerned rarely lived together until they were in their mid- to late teens.

In the early 17th century, the average age at first marriage was 28 for men and 25 for women. These figures dropped over the 18th century, and by the beginning of the 19th century they were 26 and 24 respectively. By the early 20th century they had fallen again, but since the last quarter of the 20th century they have been rising again. These figures seem to have been linked to economic factors, such as industrialization, which meant that young people could earn a comparatively good wage at a younger age. Couples waited until they had accumulated enough money to set up a separate home – multi-generational households, or those consisting of extended families, were rare. A widowed parent might live with a child and in-law, especially in industrial areas where women needed to work, and would provide childcare.

Marriage was the time at which women were at their most mobile. Although they tended to marry in their home parish, they usually went to live in their husband's place of residence. Most couples lived within 32km (20 miles) of each other, presumably because they met at fairs and markets, and 16km (10 miles) was about the limit of how far people were prepared to walk.

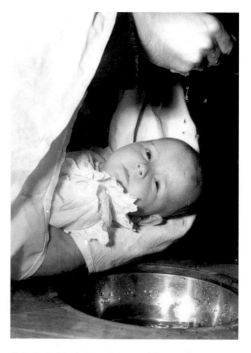

A baby's birth is celebrated by its family, and recorded by the state.

FAMILY SIZE

The high death rate among babies and young children in the late 18th century meant that the average number of children a couple could expect to survive was six. This number had dropped to five in the mid-19th century. By the 1920s the average number of children in a family was just two, but this figure represents a deliberate decision to limit family size rather than a massive growth in child mortality.

LIFE EXPECTANCY

Until the 20th century, the average life expectancy at birth was roughly 30–40 years at different times during the preceding centuries. This apparently low figure is because so many babies died in the first two years of life. A person who survived to the age of 20 could, however, expect to live to 50; at 30, people could expect to reach 60; and those who survived to 60 had a good chance of reaching 70 or even 80. A few then achieved 90 or even 100. These figures were for the country as a whole, disguising the difference between a relatively wholesome life in the country and life in cities, which, until the Victorian era brought improved sanitation, was dangerous.

Clean water, efficient sewage disposal systems and better personal hygiene had a greater effect on increasing life expectancy than advances in medical treatment until the last half of the 20th century. The introduction of antibiotics after World War II brought the next leap in public health improvement. Further advances mean that today more and more people live to 100 years and beyond.

From the cradle to the grave

AGE	EVENT	RECORDS	LOCATION OF RECORDS
0	BIRTH	After 1837 – birth certificate	FRC
		Before 1837 – parish registers	CRO
0+	BAPTISM	Church of England parish registers	CRO
		Nonconformist churches	FRC or CRO
		Roman Catholic churches	Church or DRO
4-18	SCHOOL	Public schools	Published or with school
		Church schools	CRO/denominational archives
		Local Education Authority	CRO
14+	UNIVERSITY	Alumni lists	Published
14-21	APPRENTICESHIP	Indentures	Private papers
		1710–1811 Apprenticeship tax records	TNA
		Poor Law records (for parish apprentices)	CRO
7+	WORK	Directories	Published
		Censuses	FRC
	PROFESSIONS	Published lists/membership of professional bodies	Libraries
	BUSINESS	Company archives	Libraries/CRO
	ARTISANS	Guild membership	CRO
7+	MILITARY SERVICE	Service records	TNA/museums
15+	MILITIA SERVICE	Militia ballot	CRO
		Pay and musters	TNA
	VOLUNTEERS	Pay and musters	TNA/CRO
21+	PROPERTY	Deeds	TNA/CRO
	ACQUISITION	Ratebooks	CRO
		Directories	Published
	FRANCHISE	Poll books	Published
		Electoral registers	CRO/British Library
12/14+	MARRIAGE	After 1837 – marriage certificate	FRC
		1753–1837 – Anglican parish church	CRO
		Before 1753 – denominational church	CRO/FRC
		Marriage licence	CRO/DRO
	CHILDREN	After 1837 – birth certificate	FRC
		Before 1837 – church records	CRO
		Illegitimate children – bastardy examinations	CRO
	LEGAL	Crime	CRO/TNA
	PROCEEDINGS	Property disputes	TNA
	INTERNAL	Settlement certificates/examinations	CRO
	MIGRATION	Removal orders	CRO
	EMIGRATION		
	Voluntary	Government schemes	TNA
	Transportation	Crime and prison records	TNA/CRO
	ILLNESS	Hospital records	CRO/other repositories
		Workhouse records	CRO
	DEATH	After 1837 – death certificate	FRC
		Before 1837 – burial registers	CRO/FRC
		Obituries in newspapers/periodicals	CRO/British Library
	INQUEST	Coroners' records	CRO/TNA
		Newspaper reports	CRO/British Library
	WILL	After 1858	Probate Registry
		Before 1858	CRO/DRO/TNA

Migrant Ancestors

Before the 20th century, Britain had always had a relatively open-door policy, though it did keep a fairly close eye on immigrants and foreigners once they were here. This is fortunate for the family historian, because references to immigrants can be found for the last 600 years or so.

Researching migrant ancestors

Conditions in their home countries, such as religious persecution, political upheavals or recessions, brought foreigners to Britain, so the family historian needs to be aware of what was happening both in Britain and abroad in order to deduce when ancestors might have arrived, and why. This will give clues about which records to investigate.

DENIZATION AND NATURALISATION

People who arrived from overseas could apply either for a patent of denization, which was granted by the sovereign and gave the right to live in Britain, or

Naturalisation certificates can provide details about the applicant and their family.

for naturalisation, which was conferred by an Act of Parliament and gave foreigners citizenship (i.e. the full rights of the native-born). These applications were not necessary for those coming from the expanding British Empire, who were automatically citizens and therefore did not need any special arrangements to be made. It was not until the middle of the 20th century that there were limits put on immigration from the Commonwealth.

It was not obligatory to get either denization or naturalisation, and many people, especially the poorer ones, did not bother.

Original documents are in The National Archives (TNA), but denizations and naturalisations before 1800 have been published by the Huguenot Society of London and include all foreigners, not just Huguenots. After 1800 there are indexes in TNA.

LEGISLATION

It is usually a war that makes governments aware of aliens (people who come to a foreign country but do not intend to settle there) and immigrants (people who come to a foreign country in order to settle there), who might be spies or potential trouble-makers. For this reason, new legislation is usually connected with some form of hostilities and tends to be most enthusiastically applied in times of crisis. In times of economic hardship, restrictions may be brought on foreigners' employment in order to protect the interests of the indigenous population. These restrictions also produce useful records.

The 16th century

There was relatively little legislation affecting the registration of foreigners in Britain during this period. Most of the laws that applied to people from other countries concerned money and their property and employment rights under the law. Regular surveys were made of strangers in London, but elsewhere very little official government documentation of immigrants survives.

Guilds varied in their willingness to admit strangers to the freedom of their towns and cities, and the records of the guilds, particularly those in the City of London, contain a number of cases of enrolled immigrants.

Acts of naturalisation in this period often related to the children of English people born abroad, as there was uncertainty about whether it was the parents' nationality or the child's place of birth that was more important in establishing the child's legal position.

The 17th century

Fears that foreigners would work for less money than native-born British people continued, especially in London. There was an economic crisis in the early years of the century, and this caused old laws that had fallen into disuse to be reapplied. Aliens, and those people employing them, may therefore be found in records from Quarter and Borough Sessions.

A survey of strangers was carried out in 1622, and lists for several provincial towns, as well as London, do still survive in TNA. The London returns have been published by the Huguenot Society.

The 18th century

In 1793, the French Wars brought the first requirement for foreigners arriving in ports to register themselves immediately. They also had to notify the local Justices of the Peace (JPs) of their presence. In 1797, householders had to tell parish officials of any aliens in their homes. This information was recorded at Quarter Sessions, which should be found in CROs.

The 19th century

The Napoleonic Wars ended in 1815, but regulations about registration in ports and notifications to JPs continued. In 1826, the Aliens Act introduced certificates for those arriving in Britain, which had to be completed by the master of the ship on which they arrived. The certificates themselves have not survived before 1836, but there is an index to them in TNA.

The 20th century

In 1914, the outbreak of World War I brought in a requirement for all aliens to register with the local police force. Surviving registration cards will be with police records, most of which have been deposited in the relevant CRO, apart from the Metropolitan Police records, which are in TNA.

RESEARCHING MIGRANT ANCESTORS

The regulations applying to immigrants changed over the years, so the most important fact to establish, therefore, is the approximate date of an ancestor's arrival in Britain.

If the birthplace of a child is somewhere in Britain, but his or her parents are recorded as having been born overseas, then census returns in the 19th century may help in estimating the date of their arrival. If you find "British subject" as an entry in the

A certificate of arrival shows from which port an immigrant sailed, but this may not be the country of origin.

"birthplace" column in the census returns, it should also state the country of birth. If it doesn't, check the indexes to denization and naturalisation in TNA. If your ancestor is not there, he or she could well have been born in British territories overseas.

Before the Act of Union in 1707 (which united England, Wales and Scotland to create the United Kingdom of Great Britain), and a further Act in 1801 (which created the United Kingdom of Great Britain and Ireland), Scots and Irish people were also regarded as aliens and so can be found in lists of strangers.

The certificates of arrival completed between 1826 and 1905 state the last overseas port from which the people sailed. This may not, however, have been where they originally came from, since emigrations were often undertaken in stages.

The larger foreign communities had charities to assist their compatriots, so these records should also be consulted. The French Huguenots, for example, established charities to care for the old and infirm, to educate children and to provide money to help Huguenots from particular areas of France. It

was usually on first arrival or at the end of their lives that people needed most assistance.

Information supplied to the government relates only to people arriving by sea until 1951. There are no records of airline passengers in TNA.

Those intending to research their immigrant ancestors in the country from which they originated should try to find a book written for genealogists in that country, since this is likely to contain the best advice and information.

FURTHER HELP

Currer-Briggs, Noel *Worldwide Family History* (Routledge & Kegan Paul) contains a broad outline of records of interest to the family historian intending to do research in overseas archives. It has a large section on immigrants in America.

Huguenot Society of London Quarto Series Vols VIII, X, XVIII, XXV. XXVII, LVII

Kershaw, Roger and Pearsall, Mark *Immigrants and Aliens* (TNA 2000)

TNA Domestic Records Information 49 *Grants of British Nationality*

TNA Domestic Records Information 50 *Immigrants*

Jewish ancestors

Jewish ancestry is inherited through the female line, which is very logical, since, as genealogists agree, maternity is a matter of fact, paternity a matter of opinion. Judaism, unlike Christianity, does not seek converts. Until the 20th century, Jews married mainly within their own communities. Those who "married out" were those who had decided to leave their faith. This was sometimes because certain professions were barred to them, and sometimes because of genuine conversion.

THE ARRIVAL OF JEWISH MIGRANTS

Until World War II, Jews faced at best discrimination and at worst active persecution in Europe. Britain was relatively tolerant, so many Jews found refuge here, either permanently or as a staging post on the way to America.

The Middle Ages to the 17th century

There was a Jewish community in Britain in medieval times, but in 1290 they were expelled from the country. Some 350 years later, they were allowed to re-enter. In the intervening years, a few came illegally from Spain and Portugal and pretended to be Roman Catholics: they attended Mass for show, while practising their own religion secretly. They were known as New Christians. The declaration of war against Spain in 1654 was the triggering factor in revealing their true faith, as the Government now believed them to be enemy aliens as well as Catholics, who were always regarded with fear and suspicion. In 1656, Jews were allowed to settle in Britain legally.

The interior of the Spanish and Portuguese synagogue in London in the 18th century.

The 18th century

In 1701, the first arrivals built a synagogue in Bevis Marks, just outside the city wall in London. They were followed by others, who settled in other parts of Britain, though the main community was in London.

There were two main branches of Jewish immigrants. The first branch was the Sephardim, who were largely of Portuguese and Spanish origins. After being expelled from the Iberian peninsula, they went to Holland and then to England, where they settled in London. The second branch was the Ashkenazim, who came from Eastern Europe, particularly Poland. All the communities outside London were Ashkenazim.

Jewish people brought with them a range of skills, but there were many obstacles to their existence in London. They were forbidden by city ordinances to be apprenticed to a craft (and therefore excluded from the freedom of the City of London), and the number who could trade as city merchants was limited. This meant that most of their work had to be done outside the square mile. Their inability to comply with the requirement for public officials to take the sacrament in an Anglican church and to swear an oath of allegiance also restricted their employment possibilities.

There was a sizeable Jewish presence in Devon and Cornwall, and the next synagogue to be built was in Plymouth, Devon, in 1762. In the north of England, the first settlement, by 1753, was in Liverpool, and there were communities in the north-east, of which Sunderland (around 1770) was the first. The need for a minimum number of ten men to establish a religious prayer group (called a *minyan*) meant that the Jews tended either to settle together in small communities, where they could establish a *minyan*, or, having settled separately, to choose a particular area in which to meet for their *minyan*.

The 19th century

Following political upheavals in the mid-19th century, more Jews fled to Britain as a first step to emigrating to America. Some remained in Britain rather than going on across the Atlantic. Jews from the Baltic States took advantage of the Baltic trade routes to come to Britain, landing at ports in the north-east, such as Newcastle (1830) and the Tyneside area, and Hull, where they set up communities.

The Industrial Revolution in Britain, which began around 1810, brought new employment opportunities in cotton and wool mills, so Jews began to move away from ports to places further inland, such as Leeds, Birmingham and Manchester (which remains the largest Jewish community in Britain outside London).

Political tensions and persecutions in Russia after 1881 brought the next influx of Jewish refugees. Although most of these settled in London, especially Whitechapel, some joined communities elsewhere. Before the middle of the 19th century, all Jews in Britain followed the Orthodox tradition. The first synagogue of the Reform movement was built in 1870 in London.

The 20th century

The third major wave of immigration began in the 1930s, as anti-semitism revived in Germany. The end of World War II brought some survivors of the concentration camps to Britain, while many others went to America. Postwar, there has been a trend towards assimilation of Jews into the mainstream of secular British society.

RESEARCHING JEWISH ANCESTORS

Britain was almost permanently at war with Spain before the 19th century, and, although relations were better

Many Jewish refugees fled from Germany before World War II.

with Portugal, relatively few non-Jewish people outside the royal court or diplomatic corps came from either country. A Spanish or Portuguese name from this time therefore suggests Sephardic origins.

The various synagogues served different communities, so finding out when Jewish ancestors came to Britain, and where they came from, will help to identify the synagogue most likely to have records of them.

Jewish records use a different calendar. To find the Jewish calendar number for the current year, add 3760 to it. When trying to work out in which year of the Gregorian calendar a Jewish document was written, subtract 3760.

The main types of records relating to Jewish rites of passage are the circumcision record (for boys), kept by the person (the *mohel*) who carried it out, the marriage contract, or *ketubah*, which was generally kept by the wife's family, and the burial certificate.

Like other immigrant groups, the Jews set up their own charities and schools. The first school, the Jews' Free School, was opened in London in

1732. Numerous Jewish charities were established to help their communities, such as Food for the Jewish Poor, which was started in Spitalfields in London in 1854.

Jewish people can be found in the same civil and criminal records as everyone else, such as returns of aliens, denization and naturalisation papers, wills, coroners' inquests, trials at the Old Bailey and in other courts. They are also mentioned in newspapers, of course, including the *Jewish Chronicle*, which began in 1844. Other records relating to the London communities, such as those of the synagogues, are stored in the London Metropolitan Archives (LMA), but they can be seen only with the permission of the Office of the Chief Rabbi or the person who deposited them. The LMA produces a leaflet with details.

Some Jews asked for their children to be recorded in parish registers in order to establish their right to settlement under the Poor Laws. These children were not, of course, baptized, but details of their births were entered. A few were converted to Christianity and baptized as adults.

FURTHER HELP

Gandy, Michael *My Ancestor Was Jewish: How can I find out more about him?* (SoG)
London Metropolitan Archives *Archives of the Anglo-Jewish Community at London Metropolitan Archives*
TNA Domestic Records Information 76 *Anglo-Jewish History: Sources in the PRO, 18th–20th centuries*
Steel, Don and Samuel, Edgar R. *Sources for Roman Catholic and Jewish Genealogy and Family History* (Phillimore for SoG)
Jewish Museum, Woburn House, Upper Woburn Place, London WC1E 6BT

French ancestors

The English Channel, which separates England and France, is, at its narrowest, only about 80 km (50 miles) wide, so it's hardly surprising that many people in Britain have French ancestry.

THE ARRIVAL OF FRENCH MIGRANTS

Many people have family legends that they came from France "with the Conqueror", the "evidence" being that they have a surname, such as Gascoigne, that suggests that their ancestors came from places in France. It is possible that they were among William's followers, but people came from England to France over the centuries for a variety of reasons. They came for trade purposes or as servants, and there are those who were driven out by religious or political persecution.

The first arrivals

When William the Conqueror arrived in England in 1066, he brought not only his Norman followers but also his language, which quickly became the legal jargon of his adopted country.

The 16th to mid-18th century

The biggest group of French people that came to Britain were the Huguenots (Protestants driven out of their country because of their refusal to convert to Roman Catholicism). Some Huguenots were from France; others (the Walloons) were from the Low Countries (the part of Europe today occupied by the Netherlands, Belgium and Luxembourg).

The first influx came in the last half of the 16th century, but a greater number arrived between the 1680s and the

Huguenots who fled religious persecution in Europe faced a dangerous sea journey before they arrived in England.

middle of the 18th century. They settled mainly in the south of England, with communities in London, Kent, Southampton, the West Country and East Anglia. Records from these places have been published. Individuals and small groups who went to other parts of Britain joined local parish churches. Records relating to them are found in the usual genealogical sources.

Some went to Scotland, where they formed a community in Edinburgh, whose records are lost. Their Protestantism, which was much stricter than that of the Church of England, was close to the Scottish Calvinists and Presbyterians. As a result, most Huguenots seem to have joined the local church communities rather than set up separate places of worship, as they did in England.

Those who settled in Ireland went initially to Dublin. Later, as a reward for

their help in fighting for William III, they were given land at Portarlington.

Some Huguenots went to the Channel Islands, which were French-speaking. They also settled in America, Canada and South Africa.

By the middle of the 18th century, Huguenot immigration had virtually ceased because persecution in their own countries had stopped.

The late 18th century

The next influx of French refugees came for political rather than religious reasons, fleeing from France to escape the Reign of Terror that formed part of the French Revolution. While the Huguenots had come mainly from the middle-classes or were skilled tradesmen, these new émigrés were typically from the aristocracy and were Roman Catholics. Unlike the Huguenots, they did not set up separate communities. Many had links with the British aristocracy, who helped them and took them into their own houses. In London, they gravitated to the parish of St Marylebone, where there was a Catholic church. As aristocrats, they did not have the practical skills that a lot of Huguenots had, and, as a result, many of them became teachers.

RESEARCHING FRENCH ANCESTORS

It is important to note that the boundaries of European countries have changed over the centuries, so places in present-day France might not have been in the country at different times in the past.

There is no such thing as a "Huguenot name". Their surnames were the same as their compatriots in France or the Low Countries. This makes it difficult to distinguish the people who left their homes for religious reasons from those who left for other purposes. The British struggled

FURTHER HELP

Currier-Briggs, Noel and Gambier, Royston *Huguenot Ancestry* (Phillimore & Co.)
Huguenot Society of Great Britain www.huguenotsociety.org.uk/ publishes a series of books, including transcipts of surviving registers, and the *Proceedings of the Huguenot Society*, a regular journal of articles on aspects of Huguenot history and genealogy.
TNA Military Records Information 29

Prisoners of War in British Hands, 1698–1919
TNA Domestic Records Information 50 *Immigrants*
Huguenot Library, University College London, Gower Street, London WC1E 6BT
www.ucl.ac.uk/library/huguenot.htm
Anglo-French Family History Society www.anglo-french-fhs.org/home.htm (for those with non-Huguenot French ancestry).

with foreign surnames, which may be misspelled or appear in different documents in their French or English forms.

The Huguenots set up charities to help the poor of their community and schools to educate their children, and they kept minutes of their church activities. Most of the surviving records and registers of their churches have been published in over fifty volumes by the Huguenot Society. It also has an extensive library of material, documents and private papers.

There is less material on later French immigrants. Some papers relating to those who fled the French Revolution, and also records detailing pensions and charitable payments, are in TNA. Information on French prisoners of war is also held at TNA. Most records relate to the Revolutionary and Napoleonic Wars, but there are some on people taken in previous hostilities.

Very few of the Huguenot churches had their own burial sites, so members of their congregations were interred in the Anglican parish churchyards.

Significant dates in the history of French immigration into Britain

1066 William the Conqueror arrived from Normandy to take the English throne.
1550 Edward VI granted a charter permitting immigrants and strangers of the reformed religion (the Church of England) the right to hold their own services in England. Most immigrants at this time were from the Low Countries, though some came from France. French churches were established as a result of this charter.
1550 French Church in Threadneedle Street in the City of London founded.
1565 Walloon Church in Norwich established.

1572 Massacre of St Bartholomew's Eve in France brought many Protestant refugees to England.
1598 Edict of Nantes granted French Protestants a measure of toleration, so some refugees returned. Immigration to Britain slowed down.
1661 Erosion of the rights granted to French Protestants under the Edict of Nantes began. Refuguees again started to leave France.
1685 Revocation of the Edict of Nantes. Main wave of French Huguenot immigration began.
1750s Local persecutions in the south of France, especially in the Dauphiné, brought the last French

Huguenot refugees.
1789 French Revolution began.
1793–4 Reign of Terror, when anyone thought to oppose the regime's government was executed. This was when most refugees left.
1793 French Revolutionary War declared against Britain, the Netherlands and Spain. This merged into the Napoleonic Wars, which lasted from 1799 to 1815. During this time, some prisoners of war were held in England. Most returned to France, but a few decided to remain.
1945+ Following World War II, many French people settled in Britain, mainly in the London area.

German and Dutch ancestors

The map of Europe changed many times over the centuries in response to wars. The frequent boundary changes mean that some places in present-day Germany and the Netherlands might have been in other countries at some time in the past.

GERMANY AND THE LOW COUNTRIES

During the 16th and 17th centuries until 1648, most of the Low Countries (today's Netherlands, Belgium and Luxembourg) were under Spanish rule, and much of present-day Germany was part of the Hapsburg Empire, ruled from Austria. Other parts of Germany were ruled by Poland. In 1871 Germany was united – previously it had been a collection of independent states.

Belgium, an area ruled first by the Spanish and then by the Austrians, did not exist in its present form until 1839. Today the two communities in Belgium – the Flemings and the Walloons – have different languages and cultures reflecting their separate histories. There was a Flemish community in the City of London in medieval times. In 1550, the Flemings were given their own church at Austin Friars, in the City.

THE ARRIVAL OF GERMAN MIGRANTS

Miners from Germany were invited to come to Wales in the 14th century and to Cumbria in the 16th century, but the largest German community was in London. Most Germans were Lutherans, so the majority of their churches were for this denomination.

In 1707, the Elector of Hanover, one of the German states, became George I. Two years later, wars on the Continent brought a wave of immigration from Germany. Most immigrants remained in Britain for a relatively short time, preferring after a few decades to go to America.

George I, and the kings who followed him, remained rulers of Hanover as well as Britain, so there was a lot of immigration, both from Hanover and the other German states that continued to experience social and economic problems. Although the link with Hanover was severed when Victoria became Queen (women were barred from the Hanoverian throne), her husband, Prince Albert of Saxe-Coburg and Gotha, was another German, and so the close ties between the two countries continued until World War I.

The first Lutheran church was founded in the City in 1669 and served mainly merchants and other business people. Part of Whitechapel, where most immigrants started their lives in Britain, was known as Little Germany. Other German Protestant denominations set up churches in London, but none has survived. There was one German Catholic church (still in existence today). Before it was built German Catholics attended services in the Austrian and Bavarian legation chapels. There was even a German hospital in Dalston, north London, which existed between 1845 and 1948, and a German school in Islington.

Outside the capital, there were German churches in Hull, Bradford, South Shields, Sunderland, Liverpool and Manchester, indicating the locations of other major German communities.

The Dutch king, William of Orange, became King of England in 1688 and was co-ruler with his wife Mary.

Significant dates in the history of German and Dutch immigration into Britain

12th century Flemish community of merchants formed in the City of London.

1281 Hanseatic League formed by a group of German merchants in London.

1550 Church of the Austin Friars in the City of London given to the Dutch Protestant community.

1688 William of Orange invited to take the throne as William III. Ruled Britain with Mary.

1714 The Elector of Hanover became George I, who founded the house of Hanover.

1838 Queen Victoria, whose mother was German, became Queen.

1914 Outbreak of World War I led to internment of Germans resident in Britain.

1930s Political tensions in Germany led to Jewish immigration.

1939 Outbreak of World War II again led to internment of Germans and also the setting up of camps for prisoners of war, some of whom remained in Britain after 1945.

THE ARRIVAL OF DUTCH MIGRANTS

From the early 16th century, Dutch people were brought to East Anglia, where their experience was invaluable in a scheme to drain the Fens, and low-lying land in Essex. When James II was deposed in 1688, his daughter Mary and her husband, William of Orange, who came from the Netherlands, reigned as William III and Mary. Many of his compatriots followed him to Britain, settling especially in East Anglia, where they found other Dutch people and also Dutch-speaking Huguenot communities.

RESEARCHING GERMAN ANCESTORS

In the Returns of Aliens, compiled in the 16th and early 17th centuries, people born in German towns are often called "Dutch".

Ports on the east coast of Britain had long-established links with northwest Europe. Apart from London, Hull was the major trading port with Germany, and most immigrants came through these two ports. So from 1836, aliens' certificates and passenger lists of people arriving through these ports may include your ancestors. As well as people emigrating from Europe, individual sailors from ports in Germany, Scandinavia and the Baltic States might have settled in ports in northeast England and Scotland.

Many German immigrants were actually intending to go on to America. Some never managed to raise the fare, or decided to remain in Britain, but others stayed just long enough to earn the money to travel across the Atlantic. This might have taken some years, so there may be information about them in official sources.

In addition to Christians (Protestant and Roman Catholics), there were many Jewish immigrants from Germany and Eastern Europe, so Jewish records are worth checking too.

Between 1753 and 1837, marriages of Germans living in Britain would have taken place in Church of England parish churches rather than the denominational churches.

Registers of various German chapels and churches were surrendered to the government after 1837, and the originals are in TNA. Transcripts and indexes of some are in the Family Record Centre (FRC); others have been published. Indexes to the four main German churches in London are also available.

When World War I broke out with Germany, there was immense hostility to Germans in Britain, many of whom anglicized their names. Personal announcements of these changes were made in newspapers as a way of proving loyalty to Britain.

RESEARCHING DUTCH ANCESTORS

There was a fairly continuous flow of merchants, sailors and others moving between Britain and the Netherlands. Inevitably, many Dutch people settled in Britain.

As they did not arrive as refugees from problems in their own country (apart from the Huguenots), there are none of the kinds of records generated by mass immigration. Instead, they arrived separately, probably worshipping with their compatriots, marrying and assimilating into British society. Note that the Dutch would have said that they came from the Low Countries or the Netherlands.

From 1753 to 1837, marriages of Dutch living in Britain took place in Church of England parish churches instead of the denominational churches.

FURTHER HELP

LMA Information Leaflet No. 17
The German Community in London
The Anglo-German Family History Society www.feefhs.org.uk/frgagfha.html

Black ancestors

Genealogists are usually aware that they might have ancestors from mainland Europe because of the trade and social links with Britain. Black ancestry is also a distinct possibility.

THE ARRIVAL OF BLACK MIGRANTS

Black people in Britain have a long history: there is evidence that some African soldiers arrived with the Roman army. Britain did not become involved in the slave trade until the middle of the 17th century (although John Hawkins, an Elizabethan naval commander, made three not very successful attempts in the late 1500s to trade in African slaves). There are, however, occasional references to black people from the reign of Henry VIII

LEFT An elaborately dressed black pageboy was fashionable among the wealthy in the 17th and 18th centuries.

BELOW LEFT Ships involved in the slave trade did not bring black people directly to Britain.

onwards. Most were probably captured from the Spanish and Portuguese, who began dealing in African slaves in the 15th century.

The 16th and 17th centuries

When Britain started to colonize America and the West Indies, from the late 16th century, labour was needed to develop the land. At first, indentured servants and criminals were used, but they found the climate difficult and there were not enough of them. The solution was to import slaves from Africa, and in 1662 the Royal African Company was formed from groups of merchants who had begun to trade in slaves and was given a charter to operate. In 1697 its monopoly was withdrawn.

The 18th century

The removal of the Royal African Company's monopoly meant that the 18th century saw a great increase in the number of

black people shipped from Africa to British possessions in the New World. There the majority worked in the fields on plantations, but others became domestic servants and sailors. It was people from these latter groups who came to Britain. The domestic servants were brought by plantation owners returning home, either on business or to settle here.

In 1772, Lord Mansfield ruled that black servants could not be sent back to the colonies without their consent, and a few years later the American War of Independence (1775–83) took place. These two events combined to produce a great increase in the number of black people, particularly men, who arrived in Britain. Some of these were Loyalists who had fought on the British side during the war, others were the servants of white Americans who decided to remain British, but most seem to have come because it was widely believed that the Mansfield Judgement had freed black people in Britain.

The 19th century

With the end of the British slave trade the number of black people coming to Britain fell. Slavery in the colonies was finally abolished in 1834. During the 19th century, therefore, the majority of people of African origin in Britain were sailors or students, and so they tended to be transient visitors.

The 20th century

Soldiers from the colonies served in the British Army during the two World Wars, and there were long-standing communities in ports such as London, Liverpool, Bristol and Cardiff. Some of the mariners here were Afro-Caribbeans, while others were from Africa.

It was after World War II that the major immigration of black people from the Caribbean began. In 1948, the *Empire Windrush* arrived, the first of a number of ships bringing workers to Britain. Most of the first arrivals settled in areas of London, mainly related to the island from which they came, such as the Jamaicans in Brixton.

In 1948 the *Empire Windrush* was the first ship to bring Caribbean workers to Britain.

RESEARCHING BLACK ANCESTORS

Most black people settled in ports. London, Bristol and Liverpool were the main ones involved in the slave trade, but, because many black immigrants were sailors, they can be found in almost every coastal parish. However, because it was fashionable in the 17th and 18th centuries for wealthy people to have black servants, isolated individuals can be found throughout Britain. These were mainly men who married white women, but there were also black women who married white men. The latter are far more difficult to research, as women took their husband's settlement status on marriage.

If the trail comes to a dead end in the 18th century, consider whether your ancestor might have been black. There are a number of clues that, put together, can indicate black ancestry. The clues are:

- adult baptism
- a surname that is the same as the employer or the place where he or she lived
- birthplace in the Caribbean or (before 1783) America

Check employers' wills: sometimes they mention the colour of a servant. If the will mentions property in America (before 1783) or the Caribbean, this is evidence of a link.

In the 19th century, birthplaces given in census returns and physical descriptions in official documents and newspapers are the main ways of identifying black ancestors.

In the 20th century, family memories and photographs will be the best indication. In addition, local libraries in areas with a large black community may have history projects that will give background information about your ancestors' lives. It is difficult to identify black people in official records,

because there was never any legal discrimination or segregation in Britain, as existed in its overseas colonies. Colour and/or ethnic origin were mainly given in baptism and burial registers, because birthplace was relevant under the Poor Laws. Generally such information does not appear in marriage register entries, wills or criminal indictments.

Documents that give a physical description, such as prison, Army and Navy records, may say that someone had a "black" or "brown" complexion, but these words were also used for dark-skinned British people. Newspapers consistently identify black people. Census returns up to 1991 asked for birthplace, not ethnic origin. There are therefore no records specifically related to black people.

FURTHER HELP

Fryer, Peter *Staying Power* (Pluto Press) This is the standard work on the history of black people in Britain.

Before 1948, small black communities lived in British ports, such as Tiger Bay, Wales.

Indian ancestors

Today curry is one of Britain's favourite foods and India has contributed many other things to British culture. Chutney, bungalows, verandahs, chits (an official piece of paper) are only some of the hundreds of words of Indian origin in everyday use.

THE ARRIVAL OF INDIAN MIGRANTS

Britain's long involvement with the Indian sub-continent means that Indian servants and sailors regularly travelled to Britain. They seem, however, not to have intermarried with British women in the way that men of African origin did. There appear to have been fewer baptisms of Indian servants, too. The reasons why are not clear, though it was probably partly to do with religion and partly to do with caste. The Indian caste system was as rigid as the British

class system, and marrying a white woman was frowned upon.

What is certain, however, is that many British men in India married or had children by local women. In the

ABOVE A colonial household during the period of the British Raj in India c.1910.

1780s, a third of the wills left by men in India mention local wives or mistresses and children by them. This does not mean that a third of all men there had interracial unions, because those who left wills were from the wealthier section of the community, but it is an indication of how common such relationships were. Children were generally sent to Britain to be educated.

The 19th century

Racial prejudice grew in the Victorian period, so the practice of interracial unions had greatly reduced by the mid-19th century. Eurasians were looked down on by both British and Indians, so it was people further down the social hierarchy, mainly soldiers, who married these mixed-race women in the 19th century. Even so, there were a number of interracial unions at all levels of British Indian society.

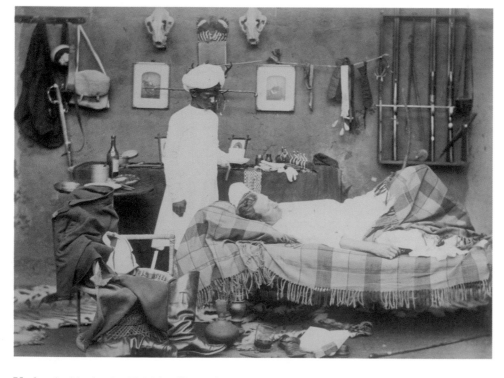

Under the blanket is a British officer whose servant might travel with him to Britain, either on visits or on retirement.

FURTHER HELP

London Metropolitan Archives has a database of black and Asian people from its records on-line.

During World War I a great many troops were brought from India to fight for the allies, including these Sikh soldiers.

In addition to these mixed-race children, a number of Indians came here as servants or sailors. The latter were known as lascars, and there were boarding houses for them in all the major ports. The Strangers Home for Asiatics, Africans and South Sea Islanders was opened in Limehouse, London, in 1857, but there were many others. Christian missions were also set up in ports to care for lascars. A few, of course, settled down with local wives.

Christian missionaries in India set up schools and orphanages. Their brighter students often came to Britain to study. Indian princes visited England, especially for state occasions, and many sent their sons to Britain for their education. A few princes, having lost their thrones in India, settled in England. Others chose to stay on in Britain after receiving their degrees. Their children and grandchildren married British people.

Other Indians came as entrepreneurs, and what might be called the first Indian restaurant (actually a coffee-house serving Indian food) opened in London in the early 19th century. It must have catered mainly for British people who had acquired a taste for these dishes in India and any expatriates homesick for their native land. Itinerant Indian pedlars and street sellers were also a fairly common sight.

The 20th century

World War I saw a great number of troops brought from India to fight in Europe. At the end of the war, many, particularly sailors, remained in Britain. Students continued to arrive, and many of them became drawn into political activities from suffragism to the development of the unions. After graduation, those who stayed in Britain usually retained their interest in politics and became involved in local councils. Many married British women.

Indians also fought in World War II, but fewer troops came to Britain than in World War I. There were, however, a substantial number of sailors in the Royal Navy. Even after India achieved independence in 1947, people from the sub-continent continued to arrive, mainly because of the post-war need for labour.

RESEARCHING INDIAN ANCESTORS

The problem with trying to trace Indian ancestors in Britain is that, unlike many other nationalities, they did not need to take out denization or naturalisation: they were already British. Reference to them may be found in ships' passenger lists, but tracking these down does depend on knowing when and where they entered the country.

Another problem is that it is difficult to distinguish between Africans and Indians in parish records: "black" seems to have covered both, and there are references to "negroes" whom the clerks noted were born in India.

Students will be found noted in universities' published lists of alumni; soldiers, sailors and airmen in the British armed forces will be located in the records of TNA. Indians in other professions will be found in the usual records relating to them.

Other overseas ancestors

People from all over the world have come to Britain. They have formed large and small communities, but, over the centuries, they have assimilated themselves into the British way of life. Family historians must therefore be prepared to find an amazing range of ethnic diversity among their ancestors, particularly if they lived in London, which has always been a magnet for immigrants, or other ports.

AMERICANS

The fact that Britain and the USA share a language has always made it easy for Americans to settle in Britain, and strong business links have led to a constant flow of people across the Atlantic, in both directions.

Before the American War of Independence, many British people moved between the two countries because they owned property in both places, but after the war those who had been loyal to the Crown, both white and black, came to the mother country. For some, it was only a temporary sojourn before they went to Canada or (in the case of whites) the West Indies, but for others it became a permanent settlement. The separation of the two countries involved the setting up of a diplomatic legation, and many Americans came to Britain as part of it.

During the 19th century, the anti-slavery movement led to a number of black Americans coming to Britain to speak at public meetings, and some decided to remain. There was also a fashion for black musicians, such as the Fisk Jubilee singers (a choir that introduced Negro spirituals to Britain) and minstrel bands.

Joseph Grimaldi (1778–1837) was born in London, the son of an Italian dance master.

Both World Wars, particularly World War II, brought American servicemen to Britain, where they were dispersed in bases all over the country. The majority went home when the war ended (often taking British brides with them), but a few settled in Britain.

ARABS

Records have used the term "Arab" to describe people from a number of Middle Eastern countries, rather than giving the actual country of origin, which is what the family historian wants to know. In addition, up to the end of the 17th century, the word "tawney" seems to have been particularly used to describe Arabs, though they were also called "Moors". Since the latter term also referred to people of African origin, it is not of much help to the family historian. Many immigrants were Turks who arrived as captives from the Mediterranean,

where piracy was rife. (Though it should be noted that the Turks were also taking British sailors prisoner.) In parish registers, the occasional conversion from Islam may be represented by an adult baptism.

British involvement in the Middle East in the 19th century meant an increase in the number of people coming from these parts of the world. The Merchant Navy also recruited sailors, particularly Yemenis, who settled in ports such as London, Cardiff, Liverpool and South Shields.

CHINESE

China largely remained closed to outsiders until the 19th century, but a few Chinese men came to Britain in the 18th century, when Chinese servants were fashionable. Some of these servants may have married British women, but there were too few of them to form a community.

Before World War II, Chinese people in Britain were overwhelmingly sailors, working on board East India Company ships initially and then, as trade with China opened up in the last half of the 19th century, on ships of all kinds. The docks in London's East End probably had the largest community (by the early 20th century, the Chinese had their own shops, clubs and friendly societies), but there were other groups in ports such as Liverpool, Cardiff, Bristol and Glasgow. The population was almost exclusively male, so they chose to marry local women.

In addition to working as sailors, the Chinese established laundries and restaurants at about this time. The restaurants they opened catered largely for their compatriots until the 1950s, when British people's eating habits became much more adventurous. These later establishments were usually opened by Hong Kong Chinese. Some of the present-day Chinese community, however, are the descendants of labourers recruited to work in the West Indies after the ending of slavery there. There are therefore several possible routes by which you may have Chinese forebears.

ITALIANS

There has always been a steady flow of immigrants and visitors from Italy. In medieval times, they came to the City of London as bankers, and Lombard Street commemorates where most of them could be found. Later on, fashions for Italian music, painting and architecture brought singers, musicians, artists and architects to Britain.

Political upheavals in Italy caused the arrival in Britain of a number of refugees in the early 19th century, among them well-educated political activists who contributed to intellectual life. Later came a number of poorer people, who, like so many immigrants, started out by selling food to their compatriots and the British, who are usually willing to try a new culinary experience. Ice cream was a particularly successful speciality.

In the 1930s, economic problems in Italy encouraged many Italians to migrate to Britain. They, too, initially sold the food of their country. London, Glasgow and Cardiff had large numbers of Italians, but smaller communities also existed in many other cities. The outbreak of World War II caused men to be interned. Some were offered the choice of returning to Italy but decided to stay, as did many who were captured as prisoners of war.

After 1945, labour shortages led the British government to recruit Italian workers, mainly from southern Italy.

RESEARCHING ANCESTORS FROM OTHER COUNTRIES

These are only a few of the immigrant communities in Britain. Most immigrants form cultural associations, which allow them to meet fellow countryfolk, give help and advice to each other, lobby on behalf of their community members and establish places of worship. The records relating to them may have been deposited in repositories such as CROs, universities or libraries, or they may remain with the association in question.

ABOVE Among the first Chinese people to come to Britain were servants, who replaced black servants as a fashion accessory in the 18th century.

LEFT Italian street vendors brought the pleasures of ice cream to poor people in the 19th century.

Gypsies and other travellers

There were many groups of people whose itinerant lifestyle makes it difficult to trace them. Before the 19th century, there was a deep distrust of people who did not have a regular job – "masterless men", as they were called – and many did their best to avoid the authorities. Note that, although performers are not immigrants, they are included in this chapter because the problems of tracing them are the same as those encountered when looking for Gypsy ancestors.

GYPSIES

The word "Gypsy" is an abbreviation of "Egyptian", as these people were thought to come from Egypt, although it seems that their origins lie in 9th-century India. Today the word "Romany" is also used. They have their own culture and traditions, such as marriage ceremonies, which run in parallel to the practices of British people, so entries relating to Gypsies are rarely found in parish records.

They were often not distinguished from Scottish and Irish tinkers, who also had a nomadic lifestyle, selling crockery and mending pots and kettles, which some true Romanies also

Romanies' and other travellers' distinctive caravans were a common sight until the 20th century, but their owners faced prejudice and official harrassment.

did. The Gypsy families had a number of distinctive surnames, which might give family historians a clue to their origins (see box below).

Horse-dealing was an important part of Gypsy life, so they travelled around the horse fairs, but they also made and sold clothes pegs, and dealt in rabbit skins and rugs. Marriage outside their community was frowned on, but, inevitably, many did marry non-Romanies, settling down in villages rather than continuing an itinerant life.

By World War I, their numbers were reducing, and mechanization, brought about by the development of cars and farming machinery, reduced the need for horses, so further contributing to their decline. There was a great interest in their way of life in the last part of the 19th century, and books published then are a good source of information.

ACTORS AND SINGERS

From the 16th to the middle of the 18th century, the aristocracy had their own companies of musicians or performers who would entertain their guests. Any surviving records of them should be among the papers of the

Gypsy surnames

Some characteristic gypsy surnames were: Ayres, Cray, Herne, Heron, Lee, Lock, Lovell, Loveridge and Stanley, as well as many others, such as Cooper and Smith, which were shared with a large proportion of the rest of the population.

Romanies sold goods, such as wooden clothes pegs, from door to door.

employer. Actors, too, needed the patronage of an influential man, or they ran the risk of being whipped as rogues and vagabonds as they toured towns and villages acting at inns or in the open air.

Following the Restoration in 1660, only two theatres in the whole of England and Wales (Covent Garden and Drury Lane), which were both located in London, were licensed for the performance of plays. Unlicensed places got around the prohibition on drama by offering musical programmes interspersed with scenes from a play or burletta – a musical rhyming drama that was a forerunner of the musical. All these performances had to be licensed by local magistrates. From the beginning of the 18th century, many of the magistrates turned a blind eye to the fact that plays, rather than just music, were being offered.

From 1768, provincial theatres began to receive patents that enabled them to put on plays, and companies of actors were openly established. Counties had a number of theatres around which a company would tour during the year, usually spending the winters in the most important town. CMB records of actors will be found in the registers of the towns on their particular circuit.

The coming of the railways in the mid-19th century weakened and then ended the circuit system. Many provincial theatres closed due to competition from the cinema in the 20th century. Records of theatres may have been deposited with a local record office or be in the Theatre Museum.

CIRCUSES, FAIRS AND SHOWMEN

In addition to these performers, there were all kinds of other travelling entertainers: individual people with performing animals, such as bears; those who sang and played musical instruments; jugglers and acrobats; and freak shows, where people with unusual physical attributes exhibited themselves.

Many toured with circuses or fairs. Since they were frequently in trouble with the authorities, due to drunkenness and fighting, references to them may be found in Quarter Sessions records and newspapers.

RESEARCHING ITINERANT ANCESTORS

Most travellers of one kind or another did follow regular routes, depending on events, such as fairs, and also on the seasons. Looking at parish and other records, such as newspapers, along these routes could help you to reconstruct your ancestors' lives.

Some parishes were reluctant to baptize the children of non-residents in case they tried to claim settlement or support under the Poor Laws. The parishes that did baptize them marked

An itinerant labourer rests between villages where he would look for casual work.

the entries with the word "traveller". The word "sojourner" in a register means someone who was there for a short time, and may encompass both itinerants and visitors who were staying with friends or breaking a journey at a local inn.

The trade magazines *Era* (1838–1939) and *World's Fair* (1904–present) may report the activities of fairground and showmen ancestors or suggest further avenues of research.

Appendices

The first part of this book contains the basic information needed to start constructing your family tree and finding out more about the people on it. The miscellaneous subjects gathered in this section complement the rest.

Pre-1800 research

All over Britain there is a variety of record offices, local history centres and libraries, which together hold an enormous amount of material. This information was accumulated (in some cases over centuries) without any clearly defined policies, which makes it difficult to know where exactly the material you need is actually held. The following is a rough guide to what you can expect to find in the different types of repository.

IDENTIFYING WHERE TO FIND YOUR INFORMATION

At this early stage in your research, this wide range of repositories might seem very confusing, but, as you work your way through the rest of this book, you will find that the location of each type of record will be given at the relevant point, so you will know where to go. Please note that most record offices and some libraries require users to have a reader's ticket, so find out before you go what proof of identity you need, as well as any other form of documentation, such as a letter from an official body.

The National Archives (TNA)

This important record centre holds all the records to do with national government. It produces a series of leaflets giving details of its holdings, which you can either get at TNA or copy from its website. It issues its own

The National Archives' building in Kew, Surrey, holds records related to national government matters.

ABOVE AND RIGHT The County Record Office for Lancashire is in Manchester. Its documents and maps relate to the county administration, including parish records.

ticket, and, in order to get one, you need some identification that shows your address. You are also given a tour to find out where all the records are and how they can be ordered, so allow half a day for this preliminary process.

County Record Offices (CRO)

The CROs have various records concerning the local government of a county, including parish registers.

In the 1970s, the counties in Great Britain were reorganized and renamed. In the process, one or two disappeared, others were amalgamated, and some towns came under the aegis of a different county. Despite this reorganization, however, the records of the old counties generally stayed where they were, since moving the accumulated documents of several hundred years was generally not a feasible option. Huntingdonshire, for example, was absorbed into Cambridgeshire, but there is still a record office in Huntingdon covering the ancient county. For records before the 1970s, you need to know where the place you are interested in was situated. The majority of CROs belong to the County Archives

Record Network (CARN), and any participating office will issue a ticket that you can use in all the others.

Diocesan Record Offices (DRO)

A diocese is the area under the jurisdiction of an archbishop or a bishop. Before the mid-19th century, the Church carried out many of the functions later taken over by local and

national government. The DROs hold records concerned with Church administration, particularly wills before 1858. Dioceses did not follow county boundaries, and so you will need to find out where the records you want are: they may have been kept in a separate archive, divided between CROs or deposited in one of the CROs in the diocese.

Staff in record offices will help you to locate material from their resources, but they are not able to do extensive research for you.

records concerned with local administration. They may have copies of census returns after 1841 for their particular area. You may also find copies of local newspapers here.

These centres have a policy of collecting material concerned with their area, so you should find all sorts of non-governmental records here: local businesses, photographs, personal diaries, etc. Most of these will be from the late 19th century onwards, with the majority dating from the 20th century. The centres rarely require a ticket, but it is wise to check in advance.

District Record Offices

Within individual counties there may be District Record Offices, which hold records to do with a fairly large area within the county or a particular town. These can usually be found in the CARN system.

City/town record offices

Individual cities and towns, usually those that originally had borough status, such as York and Colchester, may

have a separate archive, which can include some of the surrounding area. All record offices and most libraries hold maps and photographs. CROs should also have criminal records of one kind or another.

Local history centres

These have clearly defined local boundaries, usually several boroughs, and they hold books on local history, copies of parish registers and other

Local studies libraries

These are usually located in the main library of an individual borough. They hold books and documents related to the borough in which they are located. This may include copies of parish registers and other administrative documents, particularly local council records. There may also be copies of newspapers here. These records will usually date from 1888, when the Local Government Act set

ABOVE LEFT Microfilms/ microfiches of original records may be obtainable in a number of places so you can choose the nearest location.

LEFT The British Library, located at St Pancras in London, holds books, manuscripts and specialist collections useful to the family historian.

Visiting your chosen repositories

While you are looking through your files and notes, ideas about where you might look to find solutions to problems or to get further information will occur to you. Keep a sheet for each record office, history centre and library, and note down each potential avenue of research.

When you have accumulated a few record sheets, it will be time to visit the place in question. Here are a few rules to guide you when using these resources.

- Take pencils with you, since most record offices and libraries forbid the use of ink pens, which might permanently mark their books and papers. Many also forbid the use of erasers.
- Take a transparent plastic bag to hold your notebooks and record sheets, since the majority of repositories do not allow researchers to take bags into the search rooms.
- Take change for lockers (usually £1 coins) and also for photocopying, microfilm and/or microfiche machines.
- Telephone in advance to find out whether they hold the records you need and to get as much information about what is held.
- Find out how to get there and if there are any places nearby where you can get lunch. Quite a few are isolated, so if you don't want to waste precious time, take your own food.
- Plan on spending at least two days there. Since you will not be able to sort out which information is useful and needs more research and which is irrelevant to your work while you are actually copying it, you will need to spend some time sorting it all out. This process will give you ideas about what needs to be followed up, so that you can make a list of further work to do.
- When you arrive, spend a little time seeing what research has already been done. Are there name indices? You don't need to follow up references immediately, but you should take a note of what there is.
- While you are there, pick up all the information sheets you can about their holdings as well as any about other sources of information in the area, such as museums. It's worth having a file into which you can put all these sheets for future reference, since you will usually have to return to a record office several times.

up the borough councils. The libraries rarely require a ticket, but you should check about this in advance.

National libraries

These hold material related to their particular specialism, for example the British Library Newspaper Library at Colindale in north London, which has newspapers and magazines dating back to the mid-17th century.

To use the main branch of the British Library at Euston, which holds books and official publications, you will need a reader's ticket. It's quite easy to get one to use for just a day with some form of identification, but for longer periods of research you must also be able to prove that you cannot get the books you need elsewhere, such as your local library. If you want to look at just newspapers, you can get a separate ticket for the Colindale branch.

The British Library's Newspaper Library at Colindale in north London is microfilming its newspapers and magazines.

University libraries

In addition to academic books and material relating to the university itself, a university library may hold private papers that have been deposited there by individual families, particularly benefactors of the university. Most university libraries, like the British Library, will issue a temporary reader's ticket if necessary; others will ask you how long you think you may need for your research, and give you a pass for that period.

FURTHER HELP

Cole, Jean and Church, Rosemary
In and Around Record Repositories in Great Britain and Ireland
(Armstrong Boon Marriott Publishing)
Short Guides to Records (Series 1 Guides 1–24, Series 2 Guides 25–48) (The Historical Association)

Name changes and important dates

The county divisions in the British Isles have their roots in pre-Conquest times, but since then they have been changed to a degree. In 1888 and in 1974 changes were made and the boundaries reorganized.

ENGLISH COUNTY NAME CHANGES

A major reorganization of the English counties in 1974 means that some, but not all, were amalgamated or renamed. The ones which altered were as follows:

Cambridgeshire (enlarged to include Huntingdonshire)

Cumbria (previously the counties of Cumberland and Westmoreland)

Hereford & Worcester (previously the counties of Herefordshire and Worcestershire)

Humberside (created from parts of Yorkshire and Lincolnshire)

Leicestershire (enlarged to include Rutland)

Yorkshire was divided into North, West and South Yorkshire (previously North, East and West Ridings)

Six larger metropolitan counties were also created:

Greater Manchester
Merseyside
South Yorkshire
West Yorkshire
Tyne and Wear (including parts of Northumberland and Durham)
West Midlands
Greater London, which increased to absorb almost all of the old county of Middlesex as well as parts of Essex, Surrey, Kent and Hertfordshire, was also created.

SCOTLAND

The regions in Scotland, which resulted from changes made in 1973, are as follows:

Highland (Caithness-shire, Inner Hebrides, Morayshire [part], Nairn, Ross & Cromarty, Sutherland)

Grampian (Banffsire, Kincardineshire, Morayshire [part])

Tayside (Forfarsire, Perthshire [part])

Lothian (East Lothian, West Lothian, Nairn)

Borders (Berwickshire, Midlothian (part), Peebles-shire, Roxburghshire, Selkirkshire)

Central (Clackmannonshire, Fife, Kinross-shire, part of Perthshire, most of Stirlingshire, parts of West Lothian)

Strathclyde (Buteshire, Argyllshire [part], Ayrshire [part], Lanarkshire, Renfrewshire and Perthshire [part])

Dumfries & Galloway (Dumfriesshire, Kirkcudbrightshire, Wigtown)

IMPORTANT DATES

Because much of the information available to the family tree researcher is recorded by the Church, it is useful to be aware of the history of the established religious denominations in this country.

The history of Nonconformity

1570s Presbyterians and Independents founded.

1580 Separatists founded.

1604 Brownists founded.

1611 Anabaptists and Baptists founded. Anabaptists do not believe in baptism at all. Baptists, who believe that adults, not children, should be baptized, are further divided into General and Particular Baptists. The problems created for the family historian by people who do not baptize infants are obvious.

1624 The Religious Society of Friends, who became known as the Quakers, founded. They are unusual among early Nonconformists in keeping good records from the beginning.

1640 Independents and Congregationalists founded.

1649–1660 The Commonwealth Period. Seekers, Ranters, Fifth Monarchists, Muggletonians, etc. were tiny sects that never attracted a significant number of followers or established church buildings but lingered on after the Restoration (in the case of the Muggletonians to 1979).

1716 Unitarians split off from the Presbyterians.

1723 Moravian Church brought to England from Germany.

1730 Glasites founded by John Glas in Scotland. They did not believe in baptism. A follower, Robert Sandeman, came to London in 1760 and founded the Sandemanians. By 1870, they had died out in Britain but continued in America until 1890. (Registers were not surrendered in the 19th century.)

1740 Methodism founded.

1744 Hearers and Followers of the Apostles founded (disappeared before the end of the 18th century).

1753 Inghamites founded by Benjamin Ingham, formerly of the Moravian Church. United with the Scottish Daleite Society in 1814.

Welsh county name changes

Following an Act of 1972, the old Welsh counties were reorganized and renamed as follows:

Old name	New name (from 1972)
Brecknockshire	[Breconshire pref. spelling]
Montgomeryshire	no change
Radnorshire	Powys
Cardiganshire	no change
Carmarthenshire	no change
Pembrokeshire	Dyfed
Caernarvonshire	no change

Merionethshire	no change
Anglesey [plus part of Denbighshire]	Gwynedd
Denbighshire	no change
Flintshire [plus part of Merionethshire]	Clywd
Monmouthshire [plus part of Breconshire]	Gwent
Glamorgan	South Glamorgan West Glamorgan Mid-Glamorgan

1772 Ann Lee becomes leader of the Shakers, who went to America in 1774.

1779 The Countess of Huntingdon's Connexion split off from the Methodists.

1788 The New Church (Swedenborgians or New Jerusalemites) came to Britain.

1792 Universalists developed from the Unitarians.

1797 Methodist New Connexion founded.

1801 Primitive Methodists founded.

1806 Independent Methodists founded.

1815 Bible Christians split off from the Methodists.

1827 Plymouth Brethren founded. (They did not surrender their registers in the 19th century.)

1827 Catholic Apostolic Church (Irvingites) founded. They are not connected to the Roman Catholics but were ejected from the Scottish Presbyterian Church.

1836 Campbellites split off from Scottish Baptists.

1837 Church of Jesus Christ of Latter Day Saints (Mormons) first sent missionaries to Britain and encouraged converts to emigrate to the USA.

1857 United Methodist Free Churches founded. Those who decided against this union formed the Wesleyan Reform Union.

1865 Salvation Army founded.

1878 American Branch of the Salvation Army founded.

The history of British Catholicism

1661–5 A series of Acts were passed that were intended to enforce conformity to Anglicanism. Lists of Roman Catholics were often included in parish registers.

1661 The Corporation Act laid down that every elected official in local or national government had to take Holy Communion in a Church of England service. Those who did so were given a sacrament certificate, which was presented at Quarter Sessions for local government posts, or to one or other of the national courts, depending on the job involved. The former will now be in CROs and the latter in TNA.

1672 The Test Act widened the categories of the Corporation Act to include all officials, civil or military, who also had to take the oath of allegiance to the Crown and the oath of supremacy, which asserted the primacy of the Church of England. It was not until 1828 that a declaration was substituted for the sacrament certificate. This insistence on the Church of England meant that Nonconformists had difficulties taking the oath as well.

1676 Bishop Compton tried to discover how many Catholics there were in England. Only those over the age of 16 were recorded, mainly men. Surviving records are in the Diocesan Record Offices (DROs) in Canterbury, Winchester and Lichfield, with others in the Bodleian Library at Oxford University.

1696 The Solemn Association, an oath to support the (Protestant) succession, had to be taken by all office holders. Other groups of people were also encouraged to take it, and in some areas it seems that all men who had some status did so.

1702 The Security of Succession Act introduced an oath, which all officials had to take, denying the right of the exiled James II's son (Bonnie Prince Charlie) to succeed to the throne. As James and his son were both Roman Catholics, this created problems for some of their co-religionists.

1778 Catholics permitted to take the Oath of Allegiance, which was recorded on separate rolls from those used for Protestants.

1789 The Toleration of Catholics Act.

1829 The Catholic Emancipation Act.

Writing family history

At some stage, you need to consider writing up your findings in a way that other people can enjoy reading. This might be an article for a magazine, a booklet for your family or even a full-scale book. Family trees and their related notes will be fully understood only by genealogists, and they record only isolated events that happened to your ancestors, rather than giving a fuller idea of their lives. It is therefore much better to turn your work into a narrative. Remember that family history work never ends – there's always another discovery to be made, always a gap that might be filled – but don't put off writing it up "until it's finished". It never will be.

CORRELATING LIVES AND WIDER EVENTS

As you go along, you can keep notes that will help to prepare your complete family history, and work out a system of recording from the start. Use a loose-leaf or ring-backed binder filled with paper, and choose one branch of the family. For each opening, use the sheet on the left- or right-hand side for events in each ancestor's life and the opposite sheet for events in the world outside or their public lives.

Busy ancestors living in interesting times may need an entire sheet for everything that happened to them each year of their lives. Others may need just one sheet for the first ten years (which may be mainly taken up with the births of their siblings), half a sheet for each year of their apprenticeship or teenage years and then a sheet or half a sheet for the rest, depending on how much happened to them.

Photographs can tell a huge amount about the lives of people of the time.

RESEARCHING THE PERIOD

For those of us who are lucky enough to have ancestors who led action-packed lives there is little difficulty in producing a narrative. Most of our forebears will, however, have lived fairly humdrum existences, and this is where extra research into local and social history comes in. What was the place like where your forebears lived? What events – local, regional and national – would have affected their lives? Also, what would life at work have been like? Finding out all this information will help you to flesh out the bones of your family story.

Background information

Most places, however small, have had publications about their history written. Some are mainly architectural but others detail the main events that might have affected your ancestors.

You may have already looked through the parish records to find references to your ancestors, but it's worth going through them again to see what other events might have impinged on their lives. You may find epidemics of smallpox or measles in burial registers, or perhaps a mention of a neighbour dying of rabies. In the quarter sessions or manorial courts there may be complaints about the conditions of the roads. You may find that someone local kept a diary that has been deposited in a local record office or library or even published.

From the mid-19th century onwards much of the local history will come from newspapers. What were the big events in the town or village? When was gas or electric lighting introduced? What was happening in the cultural life of their town or village? Was there a theatre or, in the 20th century, a cinema, and, if so, what was being shown?

You will also find directories listing the inhabitants and tradespeople useful. They usually contain background information such as market day, fairs, the main industries in the area, schools, almshouses, etc. These may give clues as to who your ancestors socialized with if they were gentry, who their rivals were if they were tradespeople and where they were likely to have shopped or gone for a drink if they were working class.

You can illustrate your family history with old pictures, either photographs from record offices or postcards bought from shops or specialist fairs. If the family's home has not changed a great deal, you can take photographs yourself.

If your family lived in a village or town that hasn't changed much, it's a good idea to go there and get a sense of what it is like. What would they have seen as they walked along the High Street? Did they pass the churchyard or cemetery, and, if so, which of their ancestors were buried there? Was the pub in existence when they lived there?

Occupations

What was involved in the work that your ancestors did? You may find museums helpful here to see the type of tools and objects they would have used and what they would have produced with them. There are also many books about occupations in the past. If you have medical ancestors, for example, a history of medicine will tell you which drugs they were likely to have used, which treatments were in fashion when they were practising and which innovations came in during their working lives. For military and naval ancestors, you will find books that detail land and sea battles they were involved in.

In addition to what your ancestors did, you can find out what they would have been likely to earn. During the 19th century, social reformers collected information about the earnings of poorer people and how they were spent. Prices can be gleaned from newspaper advertisements and, in rural areas, from reports of how much agricultural produce was being sold for in the markets. When we read about old prices, we always marvel at how cheap things seem – only 50s (£2.50) for a Harris Tweed suit in 1912 – but this takes no account of how much people were earning. Try working out how long your ancestor had to work in order to afford something. In 1912, the average wage was

Family portraits should be used to illustrate your family narrative.

about £1 a week, so it would have cost two and a half week's wages to buy such a suit.

From all this, you can reconstruct a typical day for your ancestors. What time would they have got up? What would they have worn? What would they have eaten for breakfast? What route did they take to work?

WRITING UP YOUR RESEARCH

Once you've gathered enough material to start writing, you need to assemble everything into a narrative. This is news to your readers, so what you are essentially doing is reporting what happened, as a journalist does.

Journalists are taught that what they write should answer six fundamental questions: who, what, when, where, why and how. Bear this in mind as you write: who was involved, what happened to them, when did it happen, where did it happen, why and how? The last two usually require some speculation, because we rarely have concrete evidence about why an ancestor made a particular decision, though we can often guess. The most obvious example is moving from one place to another. This might be for economic reasons or for personal ones. If your ancestor moved away from his home town to his wife's, might that have been because her family needed support? Was her mother a widow, or did she die soon after, suggesting that she was ill? Were there employment opportunities where she came from?

All the research notes made in record offices need to be turned into stories, not only of events that happened but why they may have done so.

How something happened is likewise often a matter of speculation. On the subject of moving house, did the family go by coach, cart or walk? A guess can be made depending on a combination of distance, level of income and what was available. Directories usually give the times and routes of coaches and carriers, which you can incorporate into your narrative, for example, "In 1839, William and Elizabeth moved from Elstree to Shenley. They might have caught the coach that left from the Red Lion every evening at six o'clock, but he was a poor labourer and it was only a few miles. As young and healthy people, they probably chose to walk so that they could save the money to help furnish their new home."

You can also guess how your ancestors must have felt when some event befell them. We can all put ourselves into the shoes of a pregnant woman whose husband has just died leaving her to raise four children alone, but what if the death occurred during the Civil War with a battle being fought 16km (10 miles) away? Her worries about the future would have been doubled: she would have felt not only grief for her personal misfortune and anxiety for her future but also fear about what would happen to her and her children if the soldiers reached their town.

Be careful to distinguish between fact (what you can corroborate by references to documents) and speculation (what might have happened). Generally speaking, it is reasonable to speculate about the implications of a factual event, but to speculate from the speculation is a step too far. For example, how a name is spelled in a document might lead you to suspect that your ancestor was French. That is a possibility, but then to speculate that this supposedly French ancestor came from a village in Provence where you once had a holiday and met an innkeeper with the same name is not justifiable. Beware of writing, or saying, "he or she must have" to fill a gap in the facts. Either you can produce evidence or you must stick to "may have".

Writing style

Use active, not passive, verbs to describe something happening. Don't say "John was given a medal for good attendance at school", say "John won a medal for good attendance at school." It makes John sound a much more interesting person: he didn't just sit and wait to be given a medal, he went out and achieved something. A careful choice of verbs can give your writing a sense of activity and movement as well as bringing your ancestors to life.

Vary the length of your sentences and their structure. Avoid long lists of "Then... then... then..."

Many writers confuse writing in a convoluted and polysyllabic way with good style. "It was not long ere they knew a little stranger was on the way", is a facetious and unnecessarily elaborate way of saying, "Soon they were expecting a child."

Be sparing with exclamation marks! The reader finds it irritating to be constantly told what they should find important. You can make your point much better by your choice of words.

If you're not very confident about punctuation, there are a number of useful guides. Alternatively, you can get someone to proof-read your work. This has the further advantage of getting a second opinion on what you have written. You've been immersed in the research for so long that you will probably find it hard to realize what you need to explain to your readers. It may be clear in your mind, but will not be to them.

References and bibliography

As you write, put in references to where you found the information. This can be as footnotes at the bottom of

During the 20th century, the two World Wars affected every family in the land. Finding out where and when a photo was taken will show what part an ancestor played in military or naval campaigns.

the page or as endnotes at the end of each chapter or at the end of the book. Endnotes are less intrusive. Standard computer programs allow you to do this quite easily. The usual way of writing references from archives is to put the name of the archive first, then the document's reference number. Rather than endlessly writing out "The National Archives" or "Society of Genealogists", abbreviate them and put a list of the abbreviations at the beginning of the endnotes.

Books are referenced as author/ editor, title (publisher/place of publication, date), page number, e.g. Silverthorne, Elizabeth (ed.) *Deposition Book of Richard Wyatt, J.P. 1767–1776* (Surrey Record Society 1978) p.15.

It is useful for future researchers to know which records you have already searched. If you have the space, it is helpful to list what you have consulted, even where nothing was found. Whether you decide to do this or not, you should list the books you read for background information, such as local histories, accounts of the development of an occupation or the history of a religious denomination.

PUBLISHING

There are a number of ways of getting your family history into print. You may find that you have enough material to make a full-length book, especially if you are writing up different branches of your family and they had eventful lives. Unless, however, you have exceptional ancestors, who had some effect on the times in which they lived, you will not find a commercial company that will pay to publish it. There are publishers whom you pay to produce books, but self-publishing is not an enterprise to be undertaken lightly: there are a lot of unscrupulous and expensive companies in this field.

The younger members of a wedding group may still be alive, and will have their memories of the day and of other people in the photograph.

Computer programs

There are desktop publishing (DTP) packages that will help you produce very professional-looking results, incorporating illustrations, which can be scanned in on your computer. You can do this from a very early stage in your research, perhaps sending out a newsletter to interested parties from time to time.

The simplest option, if you simply want to give copies to your relations, is to print out from your computer enough copies on both sides of the paper and put them into a binder bought from a stationery shop. If you want more copies than can be reasonably achieved like this, your local print shop will be able to photocopy and bind the pages, either with a plastic ring-binding, wire spiral binding or perfect-bound, where the pages are sealed along the edge with hot glue. Some will do this from a disc.

Somewhere between the two extremes of professionally produced hardback book and photocopied sheets lie the booklets produced by specialist printing companies. They manufacture short runs of stapled booklets from a computer disc and are worth considering if you want to make more than 25 copies, which is usually their minimum number. You may be able to get your family to contribute to the costs.

By whatever means you publish your family history, please be sure to deposit copies with the Society of Genealogists as well as your County or Local Record Office. If you produce a hardback book, the British Library and the other copyright libraries in the United Kingdom will also need copies, and you should get an ISBN number allocated for it.

FURTHER HELP

Titford, John *Writing and Publishing Your Family History* (FFHS)

Pascoe, L.C. (ed.) *Encyclopaedia of Dates and Events* (Headway/Hodder & Stoughton)

Timeline

Kings and Queens are shown in bold type. As well as knowing who was on the throne during your ancestors' lifetimes, it's useful to know what was happening in their worlds. Some of the more important, or interesting, events and inventions are given here but it should be remembered that they rarely had an immediate influence on people's lives. Additionally, inventions are seldom the result of one person's efforts but build on and incorporate previous achievements.

1509 Henry VIII

1519 Cocoa beans brought from South America to Europe by Spanish explorers

1524 The use of hops in brewing beer introduced from Italy

1535 First Bible in English printed in Germany

1546 First book printed in Welsh

1547 Edward VI

1549 The Book of Common Prayer issued

1553 Jane (queen for nine days from proclamation to being deposed)

1553 Mary I

1555 Persecution of Protestants, described in John Foxe's *Book of Martyrs* (published 1563), begins

1558 Elizabeth I

1563 The 39 Articles, foundation of the Anglican faith, formulated (revised 1571)

1564 The lead pencil invented in England

1576 First theatre in England opened in London by Richard Burbage. William Shakespeare (1564–1616) was among those who wrote for his company

Queen Elizabeth I's Great Seal of Ireland.

1577 Francis Drake embarked on his round-the-world trip in the *Pelican* (renamed the *Golden Hind*). Returned 1581 bringing tobacco and potatoes

1590 First paper mill in England established at Dartford, Kent

1596 Water closets, designed by Sir John Harington, installed in the queen's palace. The idea didn't really catch on for the rest of the population until the 19th century

1603 James I (James VI of Scotland)

1605 The Gunpowder Plot to blow up Parliament discovered. Commemorated on 5th November every year since

1611 Authorized Version of the Bible published

1621 Slide rule invented by William Oughtred which, combined with Scotsman John Napier's logarithms, made mathematical calculation easier. Not superceded until the 20th century by electronic calculators

1625 Charles I

1628 William Harvey discovers the circulation of the blood

1649 Commonwealth period.

Oliver Cromwell Protector until 1658, succeeded by his son Richard Cromwell

1659 Habeas Corpus Amendment Act required prisoners to be brought before a judge within a specified time period

1660 Restoration of Charles II

1665 Epidemic of plague in London

1666 Great Fire of London

1685 James II

1688 William III and Mary II

1696 First insurance company in England founded

1698 Thomas Savery constructed first practical engine to harness steam power

1701 Jethro Tull invented the first horse-drawn drill to sow seeds

1702 Anne

1709 First piano built by the Italian Bartolomeo Cristofori

1709 Abraham Darby used coke to power blast furnaces, making the production of iron and steel more efficient, thus paving the way for the Industrial Revolution

1714 George I

1727 George II

1730 Viscount Townshend begins experiments on improving agricultural crops by using fertilization

1760 George III

1769 Paper patterns for dressmaking invented by the Frenchman F.A. de Garsault

1796 Edward Jenner given the credit for discovering that inoculation with cowpox protected against smallpox (although its benefits had been recognized and used by non-medical men for some time)

c.1800 Thomas Telford and John Macadam developed ways to improve the construction of roads

1803 New paper-making machine invented by Nicolas-Louis Robert of France allows paper to be produced ten times faster than the old handmade process

1805 Charles Stanhope, 3rd Earl Stanhope, develops method of stereotyping which allows printed material to be produced faster. Also improves the design of the printing press to increase efficiency

1814 Friedrich Konig harnesses steam power for printing

1820 George IV

1823 Charles Babbage devised a calculating machine that is the forerunner of computers

1825 Factory Act, first to regulate working conditions in factories

1826 Rev. Patrick Bell of Forfarshire produces a prototype of the first mechanical reaper

1830 William IV

1831 Cotton Mills Act introduces 12-hour working day for under 18s

1835 First photographic process to allow multiple copies invented by William Fox Talbot (although the principles of photography had been known since at least 1816)

1837 Victoria

1840 Rowland Hill introduces adhesive postage stamps in Britain

1843 Charles Goodyear of America invents vulcanization of rubber

1846 William Morton, the first person to use ether as an anaesthetic, extracted a tooth in Massachusetts, USA.

1859 Publication of Charles Darwin's *Origin of Species*, setting out his theories of evolution

1860 Cigarettes created by putting

T. Edison, inventor of the phonograph.

tobacco into paper tubes.

1865 Plastic invented by Alexander Parkes

1865 Joseph Lister recognized the importance of asepsis in medical treatment. Until now, although surgeons could perform invasive operations, patients frequently died of infections

1875 The first Public Health Act, which began the transfer of matters related to public health from national to local government

1876 Dr Charles Knowlton of America published *The Fruits of Philosophy*, the first book on contraception aimed at the general public, which caused great outrage. Although condoms were in use from at least the mid-17th century, they were mainly used to protect against venereal disease

1877 Thomas Edison invented the phonograph, forerunner of the gramophone

1886 First linotype machine, employing hot metal to produce lines of type rather than using individual, pre-produced letters, used to print the *New York Tribune*

1888 Radio waves discovered by the

German, Heinrich Hertz

1890s Sigmund Freud develops his theories of psychiatry in Germany

1895 The Lumiere brothers showed moving pictures in Paris

1895 Wilhelm Rontgen of Wurtzburg, Germany, discovered X-rays

1898 Pierre and Marie Curie discovered radium

1901 Edward VII

1901 The vacuum cleaner invented by Hubert Booth

1907 Introduction of probation for minor offences

1908 Creation of juvenile courts

1910 George V

1927 What is generally agreed to be the first talking picture, *The Jazz Singer*, made in America

1933 Gerhard Domagk of Germany discovers antibiotics

1936 Edward VIII (from January–December)

1936 George VI

1937 Work on modern computing begins in USA

1947 Mobile phone developed in America

1947 Disposable nappy invented by Marion Donovan in America

1950 Credit card invented by Ralph Schneider of America

1952 Elizabeth II

1953 The structure of DNA discovered in Cambridge, England

1954 American Jonas Salk created a safe polio vaccine

1965 Abolition of the death penalty for murder in Britain

1969 The first internet, made possible by previous work done simultaneously in Britain and America, set up by the American Department of Defence

1978 Louise Brown, the first baby to be produced by in vitro fertilization, born

Specialist museums and libraries

Museums and libraries can be a fruitful source of information for the family historian, either because they have information relating to an ancestor or because their holdings give information about his or her profession. The staff are usually very knowledgeable about people who have a particular interest in a subject or who are collecting biographical information.

MUSEUMS

Only the major museums have been mentioned throughout this book, but there are many other establishments, particularly local ones or those that recreate some aspect of the past, that might help family historians to understand more about their ancestors' lives.

The Rural History Centre

Until the mid-19th century, the majority of people lived in the countryside, and so most genealogists will have agricultural labourers among their ancestors. The Rural History Centre has a large collection of archives, photographs and objects where many organizations involved in agriculture have deposited their records. It contains material on Ireland as well as Britain, and has a museum. There are many other local museums that cover agriculture in their regions.

The Bank of England Museum

The Bank of England was founded by Royal Charter in 1694. Wills often mention money or stock held in the Bank of England, which you may be able to follow up in its archives. It also holds records relating to employees. It might also be worth investigating the archives of other old banks, such as Coutts or Hoares.

The National Portrait Gallery

In addition to its major collection of portraits and photographs of the famous, dating from medieval times to the present day, the National Portrait Gallery holds pictures of important Government officials.

LIBRARIES

Libraries may have more than books and documents in their collections, especially if they have been given family or estate papers, which might include portraits or photographs.

Copyright libraries

There are five copyright libraries to which a copy of each book published since 1911 in the British Isles must be sent. They also house historic collections of books. The libraries are:

Bodleian (Oxford)
British Library (London)
National Library of Scotland (Edinburgh)
National Library of Wales (Aberystwyth)
Trinity College (Dublin)

The British Library

The British Library holds a vast range of manuscripts and documents, including private papers deposited by families. It contains the Oriental and India Office Collection and the National Sound Archive. The Newspaper Library is a division based at Colindale in north-west London.

The Wellcome Institute for the History of Medicine Library

Although this is mainly an academic library covering medicine all over the world, the family historian may find forebears here, either because they wrote a book or article on some aspect of medicine or because they are mentioned in the papers of individuals or organizations held there. The library also has an extensive iconographic collection, although there are relatively few pictures of individual medical practitioners. A reader's ticket is necessary, but it can be issued there with proof of identity.

FURTHER HELP

Museumnet www.museums.co.uk is a website giving details of and links to museums all over the country.

Aslib, Staple Hall, Stone House Court, London ECD3 7PB www.aslib.co. uk This is the Association for Information Management. Its directory lists libraries, including those inside companies and other organizations.

Rural History Centre, University of Reading, Whiteknights, PO Box 229, Reading, Berkshire RG6 6AG

www.reading.ac.uk/Instits/im/index.html

Bank of England Museum, Threadneedle Street, London EC2R 8AH www.bankofengland.co.uk

National Portrait Gallery, St Martin's Place, London WC2H 0HE

Wellcome Institute for the History of Medicine Library, The Wellcome Building, 183 Euston Road, London NW1 2BE www.wellcome.ac.uk/library

Directories and ratebooks

Directories and ratebooks are particularly helpful to family historians researching people in cities (especially London) and towns because they help to locate an individual. County directories also provide information about those living in villages and rural areas. They were not official publications but were produced as commercial ventures by a number of different publishers.

DIRECTORIES

The first directories were produced for the City of London in the mid-17th century, and thereafter their numbers increased. The biggest growth was from the mid-19th century, when they included private residents, not just businesses. Not everyone living at an address is listed: only the main householder's name is given, and his or her tenants are not included. The best-known publishers were Kelly's Directories and Pigot & Co.

County directories

These were published from the mid-19th century. As well as Kelly's and Pigot & Co.'s publications, many local firms produced directories of their counties or areas. They have descriptions of the towns and villages in them, and list the gentry and tradesmen and women, giving the street in which they lived. The poor are not included. The information that the publishers gave about the towns and villages can also be useful in building up a picture of your ancestors' lives. Dates of fairs, for example, may be given, and the times that mail and other coaches left, with the route taken, are usually included.

A page taken from the 1893 edition of Kelly's Directory.

Trade directories

Trade associations have been producing yearbooks for their section of industry since the late 19th century. These list companies involved in a particular area of commerce and may also carry advertisements. They will also list the members of their associations.

Using directories

Directories are mainly of use to discover your ancestor's occupation. Using a directory with a map can help you to discover in which parish in which city or town your ancestor lived at a particular time, and this will help you to locate other records that may give further information.

RATEBOOKS

Rates were based on the value of a property. The parish and, later, local authorities decided how much money they needed to collect from each householder in order to provide their services, and set the rate accordingly as a proportion of the property's nominal value. This system lasted until the end of the 20th century. In the early period, separate rates were collected to pay for highway maintenance, supporting the poor, etc., but later a general rate to cover all services was collected. Surviving ratebooks will be found in CROs.

Using ratebooks

Combined with a map, ratebooks can make it possible to work out in which house your ancestor lived before the advent of house numbering. Numbers, when given, tend to follow the route taken by the person collecting the rates.

The amount collected will indicate the size of your ancestor's property and thus give an indication of his or her level of wealth.

The franchise (right to vote) was based on property: an ancestor who paid rates on a property valued above a certain level would be entitled to vote in local and national elections.

By checking ratebooks over a number of years, you can get an idea of when your ancestor either left a place or died, which will suggest further avenues of research.

FURTHER HELP

Facsimile editions of various directories have been published both as books and on CD-ROMs.

Addresses and Acknowledgements

Unless otherwise stated, all places are in the United Kingdom.

Army Personnel Centre, Disclosure 2, Mailpoint 515, Kentigern House, 65 Brown Street, Glasgow G2 8EX www.veteransagency.mod.uk

Bodleian Library, Broad Street, Oxford OX1 3BG www.bodley.ox. ac.uk

Borthwick Institute of Historical Research, University of York, St Anthony's Hall, Peasholme Green, York, YO1 2PW www.york.ac.uk/inst/bihr

British Library, 96 Euston Road, London NW1 2DB www.bl.uk

British Library Newspaper Library, Colindale Avenue, London NW9 5HE www.bl.uk/collections/newspapers

Church of Jesus Christ of Latter-day Saints, Family History Library, 35 North West Temple Street, Salt Lake City, Utah, 84150-3400 www.family-search.org

College of Arms, Queen Victoria Street, London EC4V 4BT www.college-of-arms.gov.uk

Family Record Centre, 1 Myddelton Street, London EC1R 1UW www.pro.gov.uk

Federation of Family History Societies, PO Box 8584, Shirley, Solihull B90 4JU www.fhs.org.uk

General Register Office for Scotland, New Register House, Edinburgh EH1 3YT www.open.gov.uk/gros/

General Register Office (Northern Ireland), Oxford House, 49–55 Chichester Street, Belfast BT1 4HL www.nics.gov.uk/nisra/gro/

General Register Office, Joyce House, 8–11 Lombard Street, Dublin 2, Republic of Ireland www.groireland.ie

Guildhall Library, Aldermanbury, London EC2P 2EJ www.ihrinfo.ac.uk/gh

House of Lords Record Office, London SW1A 0PW www.parliament.uk

Institute of Heraldic and Genealogical Studies, 79–82 Northgate, Canterbury CT1 1BA www.ihgs.ac.uk

Irish Manuscripts Commission, 73 Merrion Square, Dublin 2, Republic of Ireland www.irmss.i.e/

Ministry of Defence, CS(R)2, Bourne Avenue, Hayes, Middlesex UB3 1RF

National Archives of Ireland, Bishop Street, Dublin 8, Republic of Ireland www.nationalarchives.ie

National Archives of Scotland, HM General Register House, Edinburgh RH1 3YY www.nas.gov.uk

National Library of Wales, Aberystwyth, Ceredigion SY23 3BU www.llgc.org.uk

Oriental and India Office Collections, British Library, 96 Euston Road, London NW1 2DB www.bl.uk/ collections/oriental

Public Record Office for Northern Ireland, 66 Balmoral Avenue, Belfast BT9 6NY www.proni.nics. gov.uk

Scottish Association of Family History Societies, 51/3 Mortonhall Road, Edinburgh EH9 2HN www.safhs.org.uk

Scottish Genealogy Society, 15 Victoria Terrace, Edinburgh EH1 2JL www.scotsgenealogy.com/

Society of Genealogists, 14 Charterhouse Buildings, Goswell Road, London EC1M 7BA www.sog.org.uk

The National Archives, Kew, Richmond, Surrey TW9 4DU www.nationalarchives.gov.uk This office was formed from the amalgamation of the Public Record Office and the Historical Manuscripts Commission.

If you need a researcher to do work for you, the following professional associations can supply lists of their members.

Association of Genealogists and Record Agents, 29 Badgers Close, Horsham, West Sussex RH12 5RU www.agra.org.uk/

Association of Scottish Genealogists and Records Agents, PO Box 174, Edinburgh EH3 5QZ

Association of Professional Genealogists in Ireland, 30 Harlech Crescent, Clonskeagh, Dublin 4, Republic of Ireland http//indigo. ie/~apgiAll photographs other than those listed below are copyrighted to Anness Publishing Ltd.

Index